CAROL MILLER LIEBER

Partners in Learning

FROM CONFLICT TO COLLABORATION
IN SECONDARY CLASSROOMS

esr
EDUCATORS *for* SOCIAL RESPONSIBILITY

ESR wishes to thank the following foundations and donors for graciously supporting the development and production of this work: Surdna Foundation, Inc., Shinnyo-En Foundation, Lippincott Foundation, Sidney Stern Memorial Trust, and John C. Haas.

EDUCATORS *for* SOCIAL RESPONSIBILITY
23 Garden Street
Cambridge, MA 02138
617 . 492 . 1764
www.esrnational.org

Partners in Learning: by Carol Miller Lieber

Printed in the United States of America.
ISBN 0-942349-17-2
Cover and book design: Sharon LeBoeuf-Dubois, Elan

Inquiries regarding permission to reprint from Partners in Learning should be addressed to Permissions Editor, Educators for Social Responsibility, 23 Garden Street, Cambridge, MA 02138

ACKNOWLEDGMENTS

Partners in Learning represents a lifetime of work in education and fifteen years of developing and facilitating programs for Educators for Social Responsibility. In 1997, several ESR colleagues suggested that we needed a different kind of resource for classroom teachers in high school— a book that would integrate important principles of conflict resolution, prevention, and social and emotional learning into daily practice and classroom management. Five years, 200,000 air miles, a hundred schools, thousands of teachers and students, and many revisions later— the book is finally finished!

This effort would not have been possible without the support of many people. On a personal note I would like to thank my mother and late father who nurtured, and at times tolerated, a fiercely independent, curious, and idealistic kid who didn't lose her vision as a grown-up. Professionally, I would like to thank ESR's executive director, Larry Dieringer, who provides the organizational leadership and support so necessary for the development of new programs and publications.

Many colleagues have been true partners in helping to grow this book. In particular, I would like to thank:

- Rachel Poliner, who has been a tireless listener to the good stories and bad ones. For years, we have been each other's mentors, editors, and sounding boards as we debriefed our latest projects and traded our latest reflections on schools, kids, teachers, and learning.

- Sherrie Gammage, my friendship twin, who kept me honest and open to other perspectives throughout the writing process. Her unflagging commitment to school equity and her spirit of inquiry inspire me everyday.

- Jim Halligan, Mary James Edwards, Elly Greene, Lynn Simon, Michelle Harbin, Mike Kerosky, Wendy Constantine, Jane Harrison, Susan Allen, and Sam Diener who make the collaborative process of developing new work a rich and rewarding one. Their encouragement and feedback have made this a better book.

- Douglas Breunlin and Rocco Cimmarusti, whose contributions as researchers and practitioners have been invaluable to this project. Their empathy for young people and their systems thinking bring fresh insight to examining high school culture and how students experience schooling.

- Mitch Bogen, copy editor, and Sharon LeBoeuf-Dubois, graphic designer, who took the words and transformed them into a book.

I am most thankful and indebted to Jeff Perkins, my editor and friend, whose capacity to listen and question with a big heart and passionate intellect never wavered. Jeff remained clear eyed and focused when I was not, especially during the times of self-doubt and self-recrimination that any writer experiences. It has been a rare privilege to work with him. The vision of this book is as much Jeff's as it is mine.

Finally, I want to thank all of the teachers and students who talked with me about their successes and challenges, who offered practical suggestions about what works for them, and who shared their visions of the kinds of classrooms in which they want to live and learn. This book is dedicated to the spirit of hope and resilience within young people, especially those who have been left out and left behind by the adults around them. It is also dedicated to all the teachers who, every day, provide the inspiration, caring, and support to meet the needs of the students they really have—not the kids they wish they had and not the ones they used to have—but the students they have right now—all of them!

TABLE OF CONTENTS

INTRODUCTION

Do Today's High Schools Work for All of Today's Youth?

I wrote this guide from the point of view of a very grateful high school teacher. Although I have served as a principal, professor, curriculum writer, and consultant, my years in the classroom were probably the most memorable and meaningful. It was my good fortune to work in schools that valued all aspects of a young person's growth and development.

For fifteen years I worked in a small urban school for 7th through 12th graders. The school's 200 students were a diverse mix who, in another school, might have been labeled the bright and quirky, the "sort of smart," and the reluctant and resistant. During their six years with us, I watched them grow more competent and comfortable with the many selves they were trying on and wearing out during their adolescence.

A small school offered opportunities to work with the same students in different settings over many years. It wasn't unusual to teach a student in a 7th grade core class, meet her again in a cross-age elective, become that student's advisor in high school, and then work with her in an advanced level course. Other curricular structures also enabled us to know our students well. We combined core subjects into cross-disciplinary courses that reduced the number of students we taught by half. Long blocks of time provided students with the space to learn without feeling rushed and the opportunity to investigate the world outside and the world of texts with a rare intensity and purpose. Becoming partners in a learning community was aided by spending longer periods of time together.

As a faculty, we wanted to make sure every kid had significant educational experiences, both inside and outside the classroom, where they cared about what they learned and used their minds well in the process. Quarterly exploratory classes were a place where students and teachers could pursue individual interests and talents. Every year we expected every student to design and complete an independent learning project and engage in some form of volunteer service. As seniors, students took off-campus courses and participated in month long community internships. We stressed that there wasn't a right way to be a successful learner, although we did expect students to follow through to the finish. (I admit that "last minute Lucy" and "start over Sam" made me want to pull my hair out a few times.)

The payoff was witnessing the pride and satisfaction students felt when they met a standard of quality they hadn't thought they could achieve. We wanted students to know what it was like to do a job well. We also hoped they would learn enough about themselves to hold hopeful and realistic expectations about their future after graduation. Getting kids into the best schools was not our mission. Instead, we encouraged each student to develop a plan or enter a program that would be the best match for advancing their personal goals—whether it was a community college law enforcement program, a chef's apprenticeship, or a full scholarship to the Ivy League.

During my years in small schools, it was easy to forget what most high schools felt like. When I began consulting for Educators for Social Responsibility, I woke up from my reverie. Nearly every high school I visited housed over a thousand students in buildings where I kept getting lost!

As I assisted high school staffs in taking steps to build more peaceable classrooms and schools, the same questions kept lingering. I wondered exactly how students navigated their way through such huge institutions. Which and how many kids were really successful? Who and how many felt alone, bored, or defeated by the bigness and anonymity of these large institutions? I also wanted to know more about successful teachers who didn't work with the academic stars. What did they do to personalize learning for their students especially when scheduling, standards, and curricular constraints make it so difficult to know students well enough to know who they really are and how they learn?

How Do We Measure Success in High School?

When I began to investigate how high schools were doing, I discovered that on the surface, conventional American high schools look like they're doing a pretty good job. They offer a dizzying array of classes and activities that would seem to provide something for everyone. Test scores are going up and drop out rates are going down. Nationally, around two-thirds of high school graduates attend some form of post-secondary education. (Finnegan, 1999, p. 343)

Unfortunately, these statistics reflect the shiny side of the coin. On the flip side, large numbers never complete post-secondary training courses or enroll in a degree program. Less than half of all students who enter college actually receive degrees. So what's going on here?

Sobering data from "The Ambitious Generation," (Schneider and Stevenson, 1999, p. 5) reveals that over 70% of high school students say they want careers that require a degree or additional vocational or professional training. Yet, more than half lose their way before their goals are realized. I wondered if these were the same kids I saw just marking time through their last years of high school. What happened along the way to deflate the hopes and aspirations of so many?

"This school hurts my spirit," remarked one young women in a national survey of high school students, appropriately titled "Voices from the Inside." (Claremont Colleges, 1992) Other students have shared similar thoughts with me when I visit with them. The words of one academically successful junior can serve to sum up the most poignant comments I hear from a wide range of students. "In a lot of classes I am my grade point average. If my grade's in the 90s, I'm okay. If it's in the 70s, I'm not worth the time of day."

I'm no longer surprised when I hear a lot of young people describe high school as a cold-hearted and unfriendly place. According to nationally normed high school climate studies, nearly half of high school students feel neutral or negative about the curriculum, the learning climate in the classroom, and their relationships with teachers. (NASSP, 1995) These feelings are particularly true for students of color, students from lower income and less educated families, bi-lingual students, and kids who get in trouble—the very kids for whom high school should be a stepping stone to productive work experiences, and a meaningful adult life. (Nieto, 2000, pp. 38-45) Like society itself, high school reinforces a culture of "have's and have-not's," resulting in a widening gap between students who are academically successful, conform to school norms, and feel an attachment to school—and those who don't.

On the other hand, the experiences of many high achieving students, who appear to navigate effortlessly through school, aren't so great either. Relentless pressure to perform academically can leave lots of students anxious, overly competitive, fearful of intellectual risk-taking, obsessed with grades and test scores, and less than enthusiastic about learning for its own sake. School becomes a different kind of burden.

Moreover, high schools reward high achieving students with their own special universe of courses, clubs, activities, and honors that separate them from everyone else. Nearly every message from adults in the school setting tells them that they are the chosen, that their particular brand of achievement is more desirable and superior to every other kind of success and personal accomplishment.

Through their ethnographic study of California youth, researchers Phelan, Davidson, and Yu found white, middle class, high achieving students to be "particularly at risk for developing spurious ideas and stereotypes about others." (Phelan, Davidson, and Yu, 1998, p. 186) Their findings suggest that some successful students "are uninterested in knowing, interacting, or working with students who achieve at different levels, who are culturally or ethnically diverse, or who in other ways are perceived as "different." (Phelan, Davidson, and Yu, 1998, p. 186)

That high schools officially cultivate such a narrow definition of achievement and self-worth to the exclusion of a more multi-dimensional sense of personhood is not a winning formula for healthy growth and development. Students who can opt out from knowing and working with those who are different can acquire a smugness that downplays the importance of empathy in their relationships with others. Intellectually, the cost can become a diminished capacity to consider perspectives that challenge their own.

Furthermore, student homogeneity within a classroom may actually discourage teachers from helping high academic achievers develop the skills to communicate, collaborate, and negotiate with groups across the divides of race, culture, gender, and personality. In *Working with Emotional Intelligence*, Dan Goleman reminds us that "in the new workplace, with its emphasis on flexibility, teams, and a strong consumer orientation, this crucial set of emotional competencies is becoming increasingly essential for excellence in every job in every part of the world." (Goleman, 1998, p. 29) Given the future that these youth will inherit, we're shortchanging the very students that high school faculties would claim they serve best.

The "have-not's" of high school include another group we don't hear much about, the students I call the "invisible middle." They don't get in big trouble. They don't complain out loud. They don't attract a lot of attention. They cruise from class to class through the "shopping mall high school," (Powell, Farrar, and Cohen, 1985) dulled from just looking around and never buying anything that has personal value and meaning. It is both remarkable and understandable that the problems and realities of these kids are rarely discussed by administrators and faculty with any sense of urgency.

When staff are already overwhelmed by competing needs of kids at the top and bottom of the high school pecking order, who has time to be genuinely curious about students in the middle? How often do adults seek out these students, personally inviting them to talk about how they experience school? We know that for many young people, the quality of their relationships with teachers determines the quality of their engagement in the classroom. Whether a young person feels noticed or not influences her desire to do well. As a high school sophomore put it sadly, "My science teacher didn't even know my name until second semester, and by then I didn't care."

So how are most kids really doing in America's high schools? I would suggest not that well. Yet, according to the Public Agenda Foundation, although a majority of Americans express some dissatisfaction with the quality of public schooling in general, over three-quarters of parents are somewhat to completely satisfied with the education their children receive in their local schools. (Public Agenda Foundation, 2002) What's even more surprising are the high ratings that faculty generally give their own schools. School climate studies confirm that teachers' perceptions of the schools where they work are significantly more positive than those of their students. (NASSP, 1995)

So most high schools continue down a well-worn path where core academic content, learning structures, and classroom practices haven't changed a lot since the beginning of the last century.

In 1900, barely ten percent of young people attended high school and only six percent of all 14 to 17 year olds graduated. High schools prepared the elite for college and served as the final training ground for many women who moved on to teach younger children. With the introduction of compulsory education, child labor laws, and civil rights legislation, by the mid-twentieth century, the United States was well on its way to making K-12 education an opportunity for every child. (Renyi, 1993) By the year 2000, over 95% of all adolescents attended high school, achieving a graduation rate of over 85% of all young people.

Yet, most of today's high school students remain trapped in a century-old high school model where:
- The sequence and content of compartmentalized academic subjects remains the standard course of study, ignoring the interdependent systems and interdisciplinary knowledge bases that drive how we live and work in a post-modern world.

- University scholars, devoted to their academic disciplines and removed from the worlds of public schools and young people, continue to shape the development of academic standards and curriculum.

- The standard amount of instructional time for all types of learning experiences remains 45 to 60 minutes.

- The primary source of school knowledge remains the textbook, ignoring students' unlimited access to a technological, consumer, and media driven culture outside of school.

- The primary place of learning remains a classroom with four walls and a set of desks.

- The fields of adolescent development and behavioral and cognitive sciences remain at the periphery of how learning is conceptualized and organized for high school students.

- The primary task of high school educators continues to emphasize teaching an inflexible and prescribed curriculum rather than developing a flexible and responsive educational program that enables all students to learn and achieve.

The choice to stay this course is made with full knowledge that our world is dramatically different then the world in which that course was created. The percentage and diversity of adolescents attending high schools would have been unimaginable to even the most fore-sighted educators of the early twentieth century. Why is it so difficult to reimagine teaching and learning in ways that match the needs and realities of all of today's students?

The idea that adolescents come with differing sets of developmental needs runs counter to the prevailing view of teaching teenagers. That these needs influence how we reach, teach, and treat young people remains an elusive proposition rather than a guiding principle for most educators. American high schools have spent a hundred years institutionalizing a school culture where adolescents who are the exception are held up as the ideal norm. Consider the following portraits of two teens.

Juanita or Benita? Who's the Norm? Who's the Exception?

Juanita and her mom had already spent a day visiting Washington High School before she arrived as a freshman. This year she and her mom talked about her schedule, and Juanita decided on two electives. She loves to draw, so she will take that first semester, and then introductory drama, second semester, because she wants to try something new that might be a little challenging. She already knows she's going to college, like her older brother.

Juanita's favorite class is Honors English. Her teacher encourages students to freely express their ideas and opinions in class, but at the same time, students know they will need to defend their points of view. Juanita likes diving into the characters she reads about, imagining what she would do in their place. She has grown up around books. Everyone in the family reads. Juanita has gone to the library since she was three, so the printed word is familiar and comfort-able. She demonstrates an ease with intellectual tasks that require reflection and analysis.

Juanita doesn't like her math teacher very much. He's bossy and boring, so Juanita usually does her math homework first to get it over with. Her mom has talked to her a lot about dealing with setbacks and how to make the best of bad situations. So Juanita has decided to just grind it out and get the satisfaction of doing well in spite of the teacher.

Juanita uses a date book, just like her mom, to keep track of assignments, activities, and home stuff, so she can look ahead at the crunch weeks, and let her mom know when she's going to have to let other things slide to meet her responsibilities at school. When she was out sick for a week she called her buddies to get the scoop on what was happening at school and in class, so she wouldn't get that far behind. Even though her mom works late, the family schedules time at least twice a week when they all sit down for dinner and share what's going on in their lives.

Classes are tracked at school, so the students Juanita sees all day seem a lot like her. She has two best friends from school that she hangs out with—sometimes they study together, too. She also has a group of friends from church that she sees on weekends. They do stuff together as a whole group, not really dating—movies, spending time at each other houses, and they do service projects one Saturday each month in the community.

Juanita's teachers have these things to say about her: "Juanita is a self-starter. She has the determination and discipline to accomplish whatever she wants in life. She's even-tempered, well liked, and always comes prepared. Her curiosity sparks her desire to learn and her enthusiasm and active participation make her a joy to have in class."

Juanita is a terrific student and a terrific kid. Students like Juanita come to class with the drive, self-discipline, and internal motivation to take in whatever teachers dish out. It's true that they're a pleasure to teach. These kids are extremely goal-driven and show an amazing capacity to be ready and willing students seven classes a day, five days a week. They are also very "school smart," academically and socially. More importantly, they know how to set aside or manage personal needs and feelings with such skill that they can usually adjust or adapt to "get with the program." When they do experience setbacks, they can access resources and attitudes that will help them problem solve and make alternative choices and decisions.

The Juanitas of the world are more likely to live in families where education is valued above most other life endeavors, so guidance and conversation around schooling is a common occurrence. Juanita's family encourages her to plan, persevere, and explore a wider world, qualities that are equally rewarded at school. For Juanita, the kind of person she is supported to be at home mirrors who she's supposed to be in school.

Benita came in to register for classes the day before school started. She hadn't really thought much about her schedule and lets her counselor suggest classes for her. Although her mom expects her to be in school and stay in school, she gives Benita a friendly warning, "What you do is up to you. I'm counting on you to be responsible just like you are with your sisters." Benita takes great pride being the older sibling and contributing to taking care of things at home.

For Benita, a lot of school is boring and too quiet. It doesn't connect with who she is the rest of the time. She gets tired of sitting and listening and reading and writing notes. She likes to be active in class, and sometimes gets in trouble when she talks too much or is too loud. Being with her friends at lunch is the best thing about the day, which means she's usually tardy for the next class. One other thing that Benita loves to do is work in the afterschool program at the local elementary school. She and her best friend use some of the money they get paid to buy extra materials for projects they do with their afterschool kids. This is the second year she has been involved in this program.

Benita really likes her math teacher who makes her class do all kinds of crazy competitions. They work in math teams on big complicated problems that are hard, but really fun. Even though she doesn't always do her homework, she has worked hard enough to maintain her B. On the other hand, history class just feels like a big blur of stuff that's hard to remember, and it's really hard to take all those notes. A lot of times, Benita chooses to zone out or groan in the back of the class when frustration gets the best of her.

Benita doesn't like to read much, and the first novel for English class is about people from "olden days" that she can't relate to. She gets embarrassed when she's called on and doesn't know what to say. She hates being in the spotlight like that and responds by rolling her eyes and giving back a hard stare. She's put off her reading assignments for a week. Maybe she'll catch up on the weekend, but with a birthday party for her sister, a party she's going to with her boyfriend, and cleaning the house, maybe not.

Benita's teachers have a mixed impression of her, so comments about her seem to describe two different people. "Benita is very lively in class and drives her math group to really perform. Benita learned the hard way that being late has consequences. She frequently comes to class moody and hasn't taken any initiative to improve her English grade. She doesn't handle her frustration well, sometimes storming out or distracting others. Benita has proven to be a great lab partner in biology and we've worked out check-in's so she knows what to study and how to study for tests. Her commitment to improve her grade is impressive."

Benita's struggling to find her way. Social relationships are central to her life right now. At school she is discovering what she likes and what she's good at, learning lessons from the choices she makes, and finding out what will motivate her to meet a personal challenge and do well. When she gets support, when teachers notice the effort she's making, Benita responds positively and works to improve her skills. When she's expected to "just do it" and figure it out on her own, she gets surly and often gives up, not knowing where to begin or how to ask for what she needs.

Benita is also a great kid. Teachers who have taken the time to get to know Benita like her and recognize the assets that she brings as a student. For example, when her math teacher and her afterschool supervisor encourage her to use her "mother" skills to help a group get something done, Benita shines. On the other hand, the teachers who expect her to be like Juanita find her uncooperative and unmotivated.

Of course Juanita and Benita don't represent the full range of adolescent experience. Yet, Benita more accurately reflects the behaviors and sensibilities of the majority of American teenagers. The years from 14 to 18 are exactly the time when most young people are acquiring the skills and developing the maturity to navigate competently and responsibly through their worlds of peers, school, and community. If Juanita's level of skills, maturity, and family support are held up as the norm, kids like Benita, who fall short of this ideal, are more likely to be seen as problems and problem learners.

Who Are High Schools Designed to Teach?

High schools are designed best to serve kids like Juanita, even though her portrait characterizes only a small percentage of students. Juanita is the dream student most high school teachers covet, and consciously or unconsciously all other students are compared to her. Neither Juanita nor Benita are problem kids. The problem lies in our perceptions of these two students. High school culture pretends that Juanita is the norm, even though she's the student who comes to high school fully equipped. Her developmental needs are met and supported to such an extent that her motivation to learn far outstrips her need for emotional and academic support from teachers. Juanita is the student whom high school educators are trained and prepared to teach. What a surprise it is (often mixed with frustration and resentment) when most adolescents are more like Benita. By idealizing the exceptional student, schools leaders, parents, and the public continue to support the myth that good high school teaching is mostly about presenting subject matter to students with enough passion and panache to engage students in learning it.

I wanted to hear more how teachers described their students and characterized their world. I was curious to know how their understanding of adolescents, culture, and development informed their practice in the classroom. So I began setting aside time in workshops and staff development dialogues for teachers to discuss what they thought about the kids they taught. I noticed how the tension and discomfort spiked whenever adult groups struggled to construct an honest portrait of who high school kids really are. It was as if knowing more about kids might interfere too much with the ways of schooling.

These conversations left me confused. For all but a handful of teachers, knowledge about adolescent development and the learning sciences seem to have little impact on their day-to-day teaching or relationships with students. For many teachers, the inner life of adolescents and the world outside school are viewed as the proper domains of guidance counselors and support staff. "That's their job, not ours," teachers would say. To put this belief in perspective, imagine an early childhood educator insisting that she could teach a young child without knowing how cognitive development, socialization, and emotions influence the way a child learns.

If we hope to help all of our students become successful during their high school years and afterwards, we will need to understand the complexity and range of normal adolescent behavior and teach with that understanding in mind. The assumption that students' thinking, feelings, and behavior function independently of each other continues to drive the organizational culture of most high schools, where the myth of the divided self goes unchallenged. Relentless departmentalization sanctions specialized roles of adults in high schools—the content expert in the classroom, the child expert in the guidance center, and the discipline expert in the dean's office. When these roles and artificial boundaries are allowed to harden, we get in trouble. Everyone loses when high schools condone a fragmented approach to working with young people.

Improving Achievement by Linking Principles of Prevention and Instructional Reforms
Traditionally, when adolescents perform poorly, get into trouble, and engage in risky behaviors, the burden of blame is on students and parents. In place of this "blame game," schools might consider addressing, one by one, the barriers many students face that get in the way of learning, achievement, and healthy development. Barriers that place students at risk academically and behaviorally include internal biological and psychological factors and external factors within the family, among peers, and in the larger community. Unfortunately, schools rarely acknowledge the institutional policies and structures and staff attitudes and biases that may place already vulnerable students at even greater risk. (See Barriers to Healthy Development and Learning, pp. 10-11)

Pioneers in prevention and resiliency research (Catalano and Hawkins, 1992; Henderson, Benard, and Sharp-Light, 2000) concur that positive attachment to school and academic achievement and positive adult and peer relationships nurture healthy adolescent development and seem to offer the greatest protection against most risky behaviors. The practices and strategies presented throughout this book reflect important principles of prevention and resiliency. They include efforts to:

- Increase pro-social bonding among peers and develop more positive, personalized relationships between adults and adolescents

- Set clear, consistent boundaries for young people

- Set and communicate high expectations that promote positive social norms and a culture of excellence

- Provide high caring and high support so that adolescents can thrive emotionally and succeed academically

- Cultivate within youth a positive sense of identity and hope in the future

- Model, teach, and practice life skills that promote respect and responsibility and effective communication, problem solving, and decision making skills

- Provide opportunities for meaningful participation through student-centered learning and leadership that encourages voice and choice in the classroom, the school, and the community.

These principles already drive school-based prevention programs, although they hold little sway over teaching and learning in the broader school environment. Instead, much of conventional school reform focuses on major overhauls of school governance, scheduling, and school size; reconfiguration of student-faculty groupings and teaching-learning time; and changes in curriculum and instruction.

Barriers to Healthy Development and Learning
Outside the High School

Based on a review of over 30 years of research, Hawkins and Catalano (1992) identify common risk factors that reliably predict such problems as youth delinquency, violence, substance abuse, teen pregnancy, and school dropout. These factors also are associated with such mental health concerns as school adjustment problems, relationship difficulties, physical and sexual abuse, neglect, and severe emotional disturbance. Such factors are not excuses for anyone not doing their best; they are, however, rather obvious impediments, and ones to which no good parent would willingly submit his or her child. The majority of factors identified by Hawkins and Catalano are external barriers to healthy development and learning.

Internal Factors (biological and psychological)	**External Factors***
Differences: (e.g., being further along toward one end or the other of a normal developmental curve; not fitting local "norms" in terms of looks and behavior, etc.)	**Community:** • Availability of drugs • Availability of firearms • Community laws and norms favorable toward drug use, firearms, and crime • Media portrayals of violence • Transitions and mobility • Low neighborhood attachment and community disorganization • Extreme economic deprivation
Vulnerabilities: (e.g., minor health/vision/ hearing problems and other deficiencies or deficits that result in school absences and other needs for special accommodations; being the focus of racial, ethnic, or gender bias; economical disadvantage; youngster and/or parent lacks interest in schooling, is alienated, or rebellious; early manifestation of severe and pervasive problems/antisocial behavior)	**Family:** • Family history of the problem behavior • Family management problems • Family conflict • Favorable parental attitudes and involvement in the problem behavior
Disabilities: (e.g., true learning, behavior, and emotional disorders)	**School:** • Academic failure beginning in late elementary school **Peer:** • Friends who engage in the problem behavior • Favorable attitudes toward the problem behavior

*Other external factors include exposure to crisis events in the community, home, and school; lack of availability and access to good school readiness programs; lack of home involvement in schooling; lack of peer support, positive role models, and mentoring; lack of access and availability of good recreational opportunities; lack of access and availability to good community housing, health and social services, transportation, law enforcement, sanitation.

Source: Center for Mental Health in Schools at UCLA. (2001). Enhancing Classroom Approaches for Addressing Barriers to Learning: Classroom-Focused Enabling.

Barriers to Healthy Development and Learning
Inside the High School

What we rarely examine are the factors inside the high school that may, however unintentionally, create further barriers, intensifying the difficulties our most vulnerable students face. Because high school is such a significant and enduring experience in an adolescent's life (teens spend more time involved in school-related activities than any other activity) barriers inside the school may diminish chances for healthy development and successful learning as much as barriers outside the school.

Structural and Policy Factors	Staff Realities and Attitudes

• Lack of availability and access to good student support programs—too few counselors, social workers, and on-going partnerships with community agencies that support students and their families
• Sparsity of high quality schools
• Schools are not necessarily welcoming to students and families who don't conform to dominant norms
• Schools are too large with too many students per class
• Lack of positive, on-going relationships between students and staff that endure over several years
• Few opportunities for small groups of students and faculty to build relationships with each other
• Too many learning periods in a day that are too short (50 minutes or less) for completion, closure, reflection, and intense learning experiences
• Punitive disciplinary systems without instructional components that can support students in changing their behaviors
• Curriculum that is deadening, fragmented, culturally inappropriate, and disconnected from students' lives and future goals
• School bias that favors courses, activities, and rewards that reflect the preference of dominant culture students who come to school with the fewest barriers
• Punitive grading systems that favor those who are already successful and disadvantage students who come to school with more barriers
• High stakes testing and exit exams as the critical measure of a student's success
• Classroom practice that doesn't meet developmental needs of diverse learners
	• Lack of significant numbers of school personnel whose personal experiences have more parallels with students who experience multiple barriers
	• Bias that favors students who come to high school ready to meet the traditional demands of course work
	• Bias that favors traditional over non-traditional learners
	• Bias that stresses teacher-centered over student-centered learning
	• Bias that blames students for life circumstances that are not within their control
	• Bias that diminishes the importance of developmental concerns as students get older
	• Little awareness of developmental connections between intellectual, social, and emotional development
	• Little training to reach, teach, and support students with commonplace learning, behavior, and emotional problems —this includes:
	  • Teaching that accounts for differences in learner interests, strengths, weaknesses, and initial limitations
	  • Approaches that overcome avoidance motivation
	  • Structure that provides personalized support and guidance
	  • Instruction designed to enhance and expand intrinsic motivation for learning and problem solving
	• Little awareness of prevention and resiliency research and the field of youth development
	• Most educators do not see their work as political; so reducing the inequality of opportunities among students may not a big priority

One of the most distressing aspects of reform in big high schools is how little impact these efforts have had on underserved, underachieving students. (Sarason, 1990) Most reform initiatives appear to provide the greatest benefits to students who are already at least moderately successful and feel at least neutral about the school climate. Critics contend that uneven results occur in part when instructional reforms don't adequately address issues of adolescent mental health, prevention, and youth development. (Adelman and Taylor, 2001)

When prevention and school reform initiatives evolve separately within the same school, it can feel like a tug of war for principals, parents, and students. Counselors, social workers, health educators, and prevention and youth specialists are on one side of the line pitted against department chairs, faculty, and instructional specialists on the other, each group contesting for time, programs, and resources that will help them meet separately conceived agendas. One group is entrusted to take care of kids' physical, social, and emotional needs while the other group serves as students' intellectual guardians. If we fail to appreciate how students' academic success is intricately linked to efforts that support healthy development, we are unlikely to change the outcomes of the students we want to help the most.

The alternative to this fragmentation of good intentions is to integrate prevention and instructional reform initiatives into one coherent vision of school change. In this configuration, all efforts to reduce barriers to learning and to nurture healthy development and achievement are viewed as interdependent. (See Integrating Prevention and School Reform Initiatives into One Vision of School Change, p. 13)

A more holistic approach to continuous school improvement can also produce greater cohesion and collegiality among the staff. At its best, a common vision holds the possibility that all adults will develop a shared understanding of adolescents and a common commitment to support students' intellectual, social, emotional, and ethical growth. Prevention research strongly suggests that programs to improve school culture and increase student learning are more effective when all of the adults who work with a particular group of young people share consistent expectations, beliefs, language, and practices.

Improving the quality of relationships among and between adults and young people stands at the center of successful prevention and instructional reform. These efforts converge in the classroom when we take Thomas Sergiovanne's advice and place equal value on two qualities of effective teaching: "You need to know students well to teach them well" and "You need to be passionate about what you teach if students are to value what is taught." (Sergiovanni, 1994, p. 27)

Most high school faculty have to live with constraints of too little time to work with too many kids. Yet, even in this less than desirable reality, teachers notice a positive difference when they integrate principles of prevention into their classroom practice. One teacher leader summed up her experience this way: "The better I got to know my students and placed their needs at the center of my teaching, the more academic improvement I saw from even my most reluctant students."

Integrating Prevention and School Reform Initiatives into One Vision of School Change

Changing the structures, practices, and content of **teaching and learning** to facilitate healthy development and improved student achievement

Clarifying school mission and changing management structures, policies, and practices to improve school climate and facilitate improved student achievement

Reducing and eliminating barriers to healthy development, learning, and achievement

- Changes in classroom practice that meet social, emotional, and cultural needs of diverse learners; promote resiliency, increase readiness and motivation to learn; and encourage pro-social attachment and belonging among peers and adults
- A safer, more respectful and inclusive school climate that promotes greater attachment to school
- A seamless system of school-wide discipline and student support that reflects a problem solving orientation and encourages personal responsibility and constructive behavioral changes
- Home involvement in schooling
- Primary prevention that includes health and wellness education, public health and safety programs, recreation and enrichment programs, conflict resolution, drug and alcohol education
- Systems of early intervention that provide early identification and support and treatment for students and families
- Outreach and coordination with community partners, agencies, and volunteers
- Systems of care that include crisis and emergency assistance and treatment of severe and chronic problems

Adapted from the work of Howard Adelman and Linda Taylor

Becoming Partners in the Classroom

Over thirty years ago, I walked into my first classroom, facing 30 students who projected a gamut of emotions ranging from intense anticipation to total disinterest. I immediately felt both the excitement and the anxiety that most young teachers experience. The excitement of teaching motivated me to become very good at teacherly tasks. I prepared lessons, projects, and tests with Olympian dedication hoping to create a stimulating place to learn.

Yet, the performance jitters that came with my inexperience were never far away. It didn't take kids very long to figure out what made me uneasy. My daily measure for success was whether class went smoothly without incident or disruption. When it didn't—and students relished placing their personal footprints all over my best laid plans—I became stiff, strident, or disconnected. My road to rethinking what I was doing in the classroom began with Marvin, a charming and squirrelly fourteen year old, who always had the courage to say out loud what a lot of other kids were thinking.

One day Marvin stuck around after a particularly disappointing world history class, where I had inhabited the glories of 5th century Greece while my students were still residing in the present. He looked at me, cracking a smile that revealed, "I'm going to give you some inside information, so use it." Marvin proceeded to give me my comeuppance. "Ms. Lieber," he explained, "just because you get excited about this stuff doesn't mean we do. We're just kids, so teach us that way."

Teaching "after Marvin" changed for me. I took the risk to pay more attention to who I was teaching than what I was teaching. This didn't mean I stopped teaching *The Iliad* or Shakespeare or Hawthorne or Wright. It did mean that I framed what we were reading in my students' language, in their cultural experiences, in their adolescent dramas. As I learned more about my students and what mattered to them, I relaxed and discovered that what happened between the spaces of instruction was often more important than the formal lesson. More and more, how my students learned and what triggered their interest influenced how I taught. They loved listening to good stories; they liked moving around and consulting with each other on projects; they hated answering the questions at the end of a chapter the same way every time; they were very willing to try on roles as writers and historians when their questions were at the center of research and investigation.

As I developed more personal relationships with students, I got more interested in their world and they became more tolerant of mine. They especially liked thinking they were pulling a fast one by maneuvering discussion away from the topic; this, of course, became the game. Could I find the needle in their haystack and use it to sew up my summary points? It became a challenge to find the right pop icon, movie, or current controversy to serve as a catalyst for making connections to historical and fictional figures of the past. Sometimes what I served up hit the mark for most kids, but not always. I had to get over the perfection thing. The only perfect class I was every going to experience was in my dreams.

The Goal of this Guide

Good teaching not only supports the intellectual development of adolescents—it nourishes their spirits and touches their hearts. Through her work with high school reform initiatives at the Academy of Educational Development, Connie Warren has interviewed hundreds of young people who tell her they want a new set of three R's in high school: relevance, relationships, and rigor.

They want teachers who care about them; they want course work that connects to their lives and the world they live in; and they want to be academically challenged and held accountable for meeting those challenges. This guide is an opportunity to showcase proven classroom practices that enable teachers and students to become partners in a community of learners that feels real.

The goal of this guide is to explore how changes in classroom teaching and organizational and disciplinary practices can set the stage for establishing classrooms where students feel important and learning feels important. All of the ideas and activities in this guide help integrate four crucial aspects of teaching and learning into day-to-day classroom life. They are:

1. **Personalizing relationships and learning in the classroom**
   - How do we develop positive connections among and between students and staff?
   - How do we support student-centered learning that is personally meaningful?

2. **Co-creating a caring, respectful, and responsible learning community**
   - How do we establish clear norms, boundaries, procedures, and consequences?
   - How do we build a cohesive community of learners?

3. **Meeting developmental needs of diverse learners**
   - How do we set high expectations for all students and provide high caring and high support so that all students can meet our expectations?
   - How do we affirm diversity in the classroom and normalize the vast range of differences among adolescents?
   - How do we integrate multiple ways of knowing and learning in the classroom in order to meet a variety of students' learning needs, interests, and preferences?

4. **Integrating life skills into daily classroom practice**
   - How do we help students develop greater personal self-awareness and self expression and help them learn and practice self-management skills that increase their readiness and capacity to learn?
   - How do we help students develop and practice effective interpersonal communication and problem solving skills?
   - How do we help students develop and practice effective cooperation, group participation, and leadership skills?

The book combines concrete strategies and activities you can use in your classroom with essays, stories, and discussion points in each chapter. I've broken these themes into ten practices that can be integrated into your classroom routines, rituals, and daily practice. (See the list of Ten Practices below) Chapter One introduces two key practices that help personalize relationships and learning in the classroom. Chapter Two introduces two key practices that help create a caring, respectful, and responsible community of learners. Chapter Three introduces three key practices that help you meet the developmental needs of diverse learners. Chapter Four offers a step-by-step guide for starting the school year that highlights preparations before school begins, the first day of class, and the first month of school. Chapter Five presents a guided discipline approach to classroom management and organization that balances consequences and support and encourages problem solving and self-correction. Chapter Six illustrates what a Partners in Learning classroom looks, sounds, and feels like and offers ideas for implementing classroom changes by yourself and in collaboration with your colleagues.

Ten Classroom Practices That Help Teachers:

Personalize learning and the learning environment

 Develop personal connections among and between students and teachers

 Emphasize student-centered learning that is personally meaningful

Co-create a caring, respectful, and responsible learning community

 Establish clear norms, boundaries, procedures, and consequences

 Build a cohesive community of learners

Meet developmental and cultural needs of changing adolescents

HH Set high academic and behavioral expectations and provide high caring and high support to meet them

 Affirm diversity in your classroom

⌘ Integrate multiple ways of knowing and learning

Model and integrate the practice and teaching of Life Skills

 | Self-awareness, self-expression, and self-management skills

 | Interpersonal communication and problem solving skills

 | Cooperation, group participation, and leadership skills

A Note On Integrating Life Skills Into Daily Classroom Practice

The following life skills reflect the social and emotional competencies outlined by Dan Goleman in his groundbreaking book, *Emotional Intelligence*. Educational and business leaders now acknowledge that the degree to which people manage themselves and relate to others effectively influences how well or how poorly they perform the tasks in front of them. There is common agreement that the learning and practice of social and emotional competencies (or life skills as they are called in this book) enhance students' personal and interpersonal efficacy, thus enhancing internal motivation and their capacity to learn as individuals and within a group. (Adelman and Taylor, 2001) Life skills include the abilities to manage oneself effectively, make responsible decisions, establish positive social relationships, handle interpersonal problems and conflict productively, and strengthen group participation and leadership skills. These competencies are all part of the maturing process and influence all human activity and decision making.

According to CASEL, The Collaborative for Academic, Social, and Emotional Learning, "the aim of social and emotional learning (SEL) programs is to foster the development of students who are knowledgeable, responsible, and caring, thereby contributing to their academic success, healthy growth and development, ability to maintain positive relationships, and motivation to contribute to their communities." (Payton, Wardlaw, Graczyk, Bloodworth, Tampsett, Weissberg, May, 2000, p. 180)

CASEL recommends several guidelines for integrating emotional, cognitive, and behavioral learning throughout all aspects of classroom learning. (Zins, Elias, Weissberg, Greenberg, Haynes, Frey, Kessler, Schwab-Stone, and Shriver, 2000)

• Engage students as active partners in creating a classroom atmosphere in which caring, responsibility, trust, and commitment to learning can thrive. Research indicates that encouraging student involvement in classroom decision making strengthens their attachment to school and their interest in learning.

• Integrate social and emotional learning programs into the regular curriculum and life of the classroom and school. Social and emotional learning skills can readily be connected to other thinking skills such as analytical thinking, prediction, synthesis, analogy, and metaphor.

- Use a variety of teaching methods to actively promote multiple domains of intelligence. Howard Gardner's work has made it clear that the various domains of intelligence are interrelated. Activities that call on a variety of intelligences, such as cooperative learning, artistic expression, group discussion, and self reflection allow for the strengths and weaknesses of a range of children.

- Teach by example – a powerful instructional technique for emotional and social learning.

- Weave a consistent conceptual thread supporting social and emotional learning throughout the entire school curriculum, rather than introducing a series of fragmented activities focusing on isolated issues.

The term "life skills" is used here instead of SEL for several reasons. Social and emotional competencies are often referred to as life skills in the field of youth development. This is also the term used to identify social and emotional competencies in many local, state, and national standards documents. In addition, labeling these competencies as life skills makes sense to adolescents, given high school's emphasis on helping students make successful life transitions to work, college, and other post-secondary learning experiences.

Students who demonstrate these competencies in school are more likely to be academically successful and perform better as independent learners and group participants. Equally important, success in adulthood is influenced by the opportunities students have to practice life skills during their high school years. An individual's mastery of these skills will influence the quality of her/his relationships for a lifetime – as a worker, a life partner, a parent, a friend, and a citizen. It's normal for every adolescent to "strive toward feeling competent, self-determining, and connected with others." (Adelman and Taylor, 2001, p. 24) Strive is the key word here. Life skills are the tools that help students mature into young adulthood. Here are some of the ways in which life skills can help young people:

- You need them to be a successful student
- You need them to get a job and keep a job
- You need them to be a responsible citizen
- You need them to be a friend & keep a friend
- You need them to be a good life partner
- You need them to be a good parent
- You need them to have fun with other people
- You need them when life deals you a bad hand

Although there are many curriculum-based programs that help students learn life skills through direct instruction, most high school teachers find it very difficult to teach a series of sequential lessons within their academic courses. This guide places the emphasis on teacher modeling, direct instruction through guided discipline and conferencing, and student practice of life skills during regular classroom instruction and assessment. Each practice lists the life skill connection that is being taught through the series of activitites, strategies, and routines.

Young people do learn more from what we do than what we say. "According to both social learning theorists and cognitive scientists, it is through modeling—not direct teaching—that most human learning occurs." (Benard and Marshall, 1997, 5(1)) How and when adults model life skills in their interactions with students will in large part determine whether students actually use these skills in the classroom. For example, teaching students to negotiate and problem solve in their own lives rings hollow if we don't invite students to negotiate and problem solve with us in the classroom. Furthermore, adolescents are more likely to internalize the value of these skills when they practice them in an authentic context. Youth leadership, peer education, and peer mediation programs provide compelling evidence that adolescents' social and emotional competencies improve when these skills are embedded in activities that students find personally meaningful.

Life skills are clustered into three specific categories:

 1. Self-awareness, self-expression, and self-management skills;

 2. Interpersonal communication and problem solving skills; and

 3. Cooperation, group participation, and leadership skills.

The following is a list of skills associated with each category. The check list provides a quick summary of skills and can be used to prioritize skills that you want to emphasize in your classroom. The check list can also serve as a self-assessment tool where students can identify:
• Skills they use competently and routinely without thinking about it
• Skills they want to improve and use more often
• Skills they are not using currently that they want to learn and practice

As you support students' development and practice of life skills, two other points come to mind. Prevention research suggests that developing a specific skill competency requires six to eight hits—in other words, a one time experience will not produce a change in behavior. Consequently, teachers need to consider how they incorporate opportunities for exposure to and instruction of a new skill, practice in multiple settings and different contexts, coaching and feedback, and demonstrations of mastery.

All of the major strategies and activities in Chapters One, Two, and Three serve "double duty." They provide concrete examples of key classroom practices and indicate how each of these examples provides an opportunity to practice specific life skills. (See the Life Skills Connection below each strategy box.) For example, in Chapter Two, "Teach Win-Win Basics" and "Create Opportunities for Negotiated Learning" are linked to Life Skill 24: Use WIN-WIN problem solving to negotiate satisfactory resolutions to conflicts that meet important goals and interests of people involved.

Life Skills Check List
Cluster #1: Self-awareness, self-expression, and self-management skills

1. Recognize and name your own feelings

2. Express feelings appropriately and assess the intensity of your feelings accurately
    (on a MAD scale of 1 to 10, I feel...)

3. Understand the cause of your feelings and the connection between your feelings
    and your behavior

4. Manage your anger and upset feelings (know your cues, triggers, and reducers)

5. Know what you do that bothers others and accept responsibility when you mess up

6. Self-reflect on your behavior; be able to learn from it, self-correct, redirect,
    and change when you need to

7. Make responsible choices for yourself by analyzing situations accurately
    and predicting consequences of different behaviors

8. Deal with stress and frustration effectively

9. Exercise self-discipline and impulse control

10. Say, "NO" and follow through on your decisions not to engage in unwanted,
    unsafe, unethical, or unlawful behavior

11. Seek help when you need it

12. Focus and pay attention

13. Set big and little goals and make plans

14. Prioritize and "chunk" tasks, predict task completion time, and manage time effectively

15. Activate hope, optimism, and positive motivation

16. Work for high personal performance and cultivate your strengths and positive qualities

17. Assess your skills, competencies, effort, and quality of work accurately

Cluster #2: Interpersonal communication and problem solving skills

18. Exercise assertiveness; communicate your thoughts, feelings, and needs effectively to others

19. Listen actively to demonstrate to others that they have been understood

20. Give and receive feedback and encouragement

21. "Read" and name others' emotions and non-verbal cues

22. Empathize; understand and accept another person's feelings, perspectives, point of view

23. Analyze the sources and dimensions of conflict and utilize different styles to manage conflict

24. Use WIN-WIN problem solving to negotiate satisfactory resolutions to conflicts that meet important goals and interests of people involved

25. Develop, manage, and maintain healthy peer relationships

26. Develop, manage, and maintain healthy relationships with adults

Cluster #3: Cooperation, group participation, and leadership skills

27. Cooperate, share, and work toward high performance within a group to achieve group goals

28. Respect everyone's right to learn, to speak and be heard

29. Encourage and appreciate the contribution of others

30. Engage in conscious acts of respect, caring, helpfulness, kindness, courtesy, and consideration

31. Recognize and appreciate similarities and differences in others

32. Counter prejudice, harassment, privilege, and exclusion by becoming a good ally and acting on your ethical convictions

33. Exercise effective leadership skills within a group

34. "Read" dynamics in a group; assess group skills accurately; identify problems; generate, evaluate, and implement informed solutions that meet the needs of the group

35. Use a variety of strategies to make decisions democratically

Challenges to Changing Classroom Practice

We tend to teach the way we were taught and teach the way we learn. Our personal experience of schooling shapes what we do in the classroom. If we succeeded and felt affirmed, noticed, and rewarded in a tracked high school where faculty taught a traditional curriculum using a teacher-centered approach, what's not to like? The majority of us who teach high school excelled in a system that works so poorly for so many others. It takes courage, distance, and an open heart to re-examine and critique prevailing practices in the very place that inspired many of us to become teachers.

What we are learning about adolescents and how to teach more of them more effectively is counter intuitive to the norms and assumptions that drive secondary education in the US. The myths that we sometimes carry around about adolescents and learning are so embedded in high school culture that letting them go is tantamount to culture shock. Although high school educators might not verbalize these assumptions, we act on these "unexamined shared mental models or 'theories-in-use'" (Senge, 2000, p. 35) as if they were true. Current research and thinking in the behavioral and learning sciences do much to explode many deeply held assumptions about kids and learning in high school. It is worth exploring some of these assumptions with the purpose of thinking about how we arrived at these assumptions and why we hold onto them.

Assumption #1: My job is to teach you, not motivate you. Your job is to learn it.

In a society where traditional authority is increasingly ineffective at home, at school, and at work, motivating students in ways that invite their cooperation, good will, and interest in learning is probably the most important and challenging role of high school teachers. For adolescents, motivation—the "natural capacity to direct energy in pursuit of a goal"—is both extrinsic and intrinsic. (Wlodkowski and Ginsberg, 1995, p. 22) Parents' and teachers' affection, respect, and support are powerful extrinsic motivators for teens. In addition, students' motivation to learn will also depend on whether they perceive learning tasks as achievable and important. Think of motivation as a combination of two things: a student's expected outcome (Am I more likely to fail or succeed at accomplishing this goal? Will I derive a sense of satisfaction when the goal is completed?) and the degree to which a student values the goal and the process of accomplishing it. (Adelman and Taylor, 2001, pp. 66-69) One of challenges of teaching diverse learners is designing student work that considers students' prior knowledge and developmental needs and captures students' personal interests.

Assumption #2: A lot of kids are smart and some kids are dumb. I don't believe that all kids can really learn what I teach or pass my class.

The emphasis on ability and final performance reinforce the deficit model of learning—"one of my primary jobs is to show you what you don't know and can't do." This "ability orientation" to learning favors kids who come to school already "school smart" and devalues the role that effort plays in the learning process. The result of this assumption is that many students, early on in their high school careers, see themselves as 'not smart', give up, and shut down. However, we know that when effort and the process of learning are valued and supported, more kids learn more. (Silverman and Casazza, 2000)

And this warning comes from *Your Adolescent*, a guide for parents and teachers from the American Academy of Child and Adolescent Psychiatry. Adolescents who believe that intelligence is fixed tend to see achievement in terms of ability—"I'm smart in this class or dumb in this class and there's nothing I can do to change that." Kids with these beliefs tend to avoid tasks that may appear difficult so they're not perceived as dumb; they also tend to see errors as failure. On the other hand, kids who see effort as making a difference are more likely to recognize errors and other academic difficulties as being part of the process of learning; they are less afraid of taking risks, and more likely to persist and persevere to gain mastery. (Pruitt, 2000, p. 130-131)

Assumption #3: Taking time in class to establish a community of learners and teach students how to work together effectively are off-task behaviors that take away valuable learning time.

Building a sense of community and developing students' participation skills are both on-task learning activities that result in more effectively managed classrooms and help students practice skills vital for the social construction of knowledge and high performance in the work place. (SCANS Report, Jobs for the Future, High Schools for the Millennium)

Assumption #4: Learning is an intellectual activity.

Research in the field of cognitive science tells us a much different story, revealing the interdependence between knowing and doing, mind and body. High school curricula reflect a decidedly Western intellectual orientation that prizes verbal/linguistic and logical/ mathematical gifts above all other kinds of intelligences. (Gardner, 2000). Yet, even verbal and mathematical aspects of intelligence are given short shrift in schools when they are presented as abstract exercises of the mind, without concrete experiences or a social/emotional context. For most people, not just students in school, understanding and insight go deeper and last longer when multiple intelligences and a variety of senses are part of a learning experience.

Assumptions #5: Academic courses are the place where students experience rigor and serious work. Elective and vocational courses are the cotton candy of the curriculum.

This assumption carries with it some ironic twists. A recent University of Chicago study of thousands of adolescents (Csikszentmihalyi and Schneider, 2000), confirmed once again that students' favorite courses in high school are electives—but there doesn't seem to be much curiosity about why this might be the case. If one does agree that learning involves intellectual, physical, social and emotional dimensions, consider what goes on in most elective and vocational classes as compared to traditional academic courses:

- Students make choices about the projects they will work on and how they will go about doing it.

- Kids get to spend lots of time working on something intensely and usually have additional time to revise, reassess, and correct. They may even experience failure in their first attempt and have the opportunity to begin again using lessons learned.

- Students get to experience the satisfaction of personal mastery and competence, often using sophisticated tools and techniques.

- Whether a student is designing a house using CAD (computer assisted drafting), rehearsing a dramatic monologue, preparing a meal for eight people, throwing a pot, practicing with the drill team, or proofing the blue lines for the next newspaper—in all of these endeavors students are expressing themselves in some way that has personal meaning for them.

- Electives involve authentic assessment of some sort—whether it's a product, project, performance, or portfolio of work.

- Students are learning by doing and solving problems.

- Students practice of a range of critical and creative thinking skills. These skills as described in Bloom's Taxonomy and Art Costa's list of intellectual behaviors are a natural, logical occurrence in electives and vocational courses.

No wonder lots of kids excel more, remember more, and like what they're doing more in elective and vocational classes. These courses tend to involve a rhythm, sequence, and integration of tasks that nurtures high quality and results in learning that sticks. High schools would do well to consider how to make 'academic' courses look and feel more like electives and vocational courses. Even better would be to eliminate the false dichotomy between 'academic' and 'other' kinds of course work altogether.

Think about the prevailing norms of teaching and learning in your own school. Do any of the assumptions described here feel familiar? Are there other obstacles to changing classroom practice that you would add to the list?

An Invitation to Change Your Practice, Not Your Passions
This book is an invitation to change your practice, not your passions. It is not about giving up high standards, watering down your curriculum, or shortchanging students' intellectual development. Rather, it's about the big and small things you can do and say to help more kids love what you love. All of the information, discussion points, and practices in this guide share a common purpose: to increase the level of motivation, effort, skillfulness, and achievement that students demonstrate in your classroom.

As you read further, I hope you will be thinking about how you can strengthen your own skills as a teacher, mentor, coach, and facilitator. For many of you this guide provides a way to make good practices you already do more intentional. Some ideas may offer new twists on familiar strategies and activities. Others may look and sound very different from your usual routines. And some suggestions in this guide may serve as a reminder of things you have wanted to do, which you are now ready to try out. It's helpful to note that it can feel awkward to try on a different way of doing things—this is a normal and necessary stage of mastery— practice will help these strategies become useful tools in your teaching toolbox.

I hope that reading this guide will, at times, feel like a conversation. Talk back to the text. Argue with the ideas presented here. Bring a spirit of open inquiry to what you read. How does your own experience as a learner and a teacher connect with the stories and experiences shared in this book. Notice your reactions to various topics and issues discussed in the book —what grabs your attention and what misses the mark?

Powerful learning and personal insight emerge from struggling with new ideas and new ways of thinking that may feel downright wrong-headed the first time we hear them. The fancy term for this is cognitive dissonance. I expect that some of the things presented in this guide may contradict what you may have always believed about students and learning, teaching and discipline.

Writing this book felt a little risky—you might choose to toss it out the first time your eyebrows furrow, your face tightens up, and your mind says, "Wait a minute. I'm not sure about that." Instead, I invite you to invite in the discomfort. Ask yourself, "What is it that's making me feel confused, uneasy, or resistant to this idea?" Or "How might students benefit from this approach or practice?" Or "How would I feel if I were a student in this situation?" Testing out and grappling with new information and ideas is what learning is all about. Real change is organic—it happens slowly. So take your time reading, picking and choosing pieces of the book that you find most appealing or provocative.

Like the students you teach, each of you brings a different set of perceptions, knowledge, and experiences to your reading of this guide. I don't presume that everything in this guide will be equally useful to everyone who reads it. My hope is that you take from this guide what makes sense for you and use what you think will help your students learn and grow.

CHAPTER I

Personalize Relationships and Learning in the Classroom

Personalizing relationships and learning involves classroom practices that strengthen personal connections among students and teachers and create meaningful links between students' lives and what they are learning. The efforts you make to get to know each student personally mark the difference between relationships that feel caring and supportive and those that feel coercive and distant. Knowing each other well is the first step toward developing mutual respect and trust and forms the foundation of a classroom where students feel welcomed, seen, and heard in a positive manner.

Research indicates that for adolescent learners, especially those who are less successful or feel more alienated, personalizing the learning environment, by creating classrooms where everyone feels safe and supported and by emphasizing learning tasks that have personal meaning and value, contributes to greater motivation, increased attachment to learning, and improved achievement. (Adelman and Taylor, 2001) Personalizing learning is different from and should not be confused with individualized learning and instruction, where teachers map out a different educational plan for every student. Personalization refers to the need to "meet learners where they are in terms of their capabilities, interests, attitudes, and other intrinsic motivational considerations." (Adelman and Taylor, 2001, p. 19) Teachers who establish personalized classrooms offer more choices and options for what students learn and how they learn it. Student-centered learning that encourages more goal setting, planning, and self reflection can also help students develop more accurate assessments of who they are as learners.

This chapter describes what a personalized environment looks like and introduces two key practices that help teachers personalize their classrooms:

 Practice #1: Develop personal connections among and between students and teachers

 Practice #2: Emphasize student-centered learning that is personally meaningful

The section for each practice includes sample activities, strategies, and routines that illustrate the key practice.

What Does a Personalized Learning Environment Look and Feel Like?

What does school feel like when caring relationships and efforts to personalize learning are valued throughout the school? Joe, a hypothetical sophomore, might describe it as follows:

I like this school because it's easy to make friends and there aren't that many cliques. I can be with my buddies on the track team, but I can also hang out with my partner in chemistry. My English teacher makes sure that we all get a chance to work with each other in class, so I'm less scared of being around people who aren't just like me. It's been fun learning more about other kids who came from different neighborhoods than mine. I guess I was surprised that we had more in common than I thought.

My classes are okay. My teachers know me as a person and help me to do my best. My Chem teacher really likes my jokes. And my History and English teachers don't think I'm stupid just because it takes me a long time to read something. When I'm having a hard time, I know I can talk to them and work out how to get back on track. If I mess up, I know it's not going to be held against me for the rest of my life—my grade doesn't just depend on a few big tests."

Classes aren't nearly as boring as I'd thought they'd be because we get to make lots of choices about how we do assignments and about how we're going to work together to learn stuff. Teachers don't just lecture at us the whole time—they want to know what we have to say and listen to our suggestions about how to make class better. Even reading isn't so bad anymore because I've gotten to read stuff that I can relate to and we get to talk about our own opinions.

What I like best is my Math class, because my teacher told us in the beginning of the year if we make an effort everyone will pass. Nobody is allowed to just sit in the back. He's helped us to really be a team so we make sure nobody's left behind. Not everyone gets A's, especially not me, but all of us have learned some things really well. After being here for a year, I'm more willing to put in the time to get good grades, because my teachers really notice when I make the effort. I know they're on my side.

I think my teachers are pretty fair—they won't let certain behaviors slide, but they also get that we all don't learn the same way and sometimes we need different kinds of help. For instance, my Social Studies teacher meets with some of us at lunch once a week so we can go over the readings that are hard for me to understand. I'm not so afraid to talk in class now because I've already talked about it beforehand.

I feel safe here at school. I pretty much know I'm not going to get picked on because the school slams down really hard on kids who fight or bully or make fun of other people. Teachers are really good about stopping put-downs and nasty remarks. I notice that a lot. And kids in sports and clubs really make an effort to support the school campaign around respect and diversity. Sometimes, it gets old hearing this stuff over and over, but it does get the point across that everyone has the right to be respected for who they are.

In advisory, I've gotten to know more about myself and how I handle my frustrations and relationships with other people. I know I can bring up almost any issue in my advisory and we can talk about it openly and honestly. I like it when my advisor checks in with me just to see how I'm doing. If I had a really big problem there are lots of people around who can help me. One of my friends just lost a parent and he's been really depressed and gets angry over nothing. He exploded in class one day, but instead of getting suspended, he talked to a counselor and joined a group with other students who have had somebody in their family die. That's been a really good thing.

Many more students would succeed in high school if their experiences were similar to Joe's. Personalizing the high school is about students feeling respected as people and being supported and encouraged to achieve regardless of their academic track. Joe wants to learn because teachers know him well and communicate that they're on his side. Joe has a sense that adults are looking out for him. He feels he can be his own person here because his school makes an intentional effort to promote a friendly atmosphere and a culture of caring.

PRACTICE 1

Develop Positive Connections Among and Between Students and Staff

For adolescents, we know that a sense of belonging is crucial to their sense of well-being. We also know that feeling connected in a classroom can improve motivation and academic performance. Connected teaching encourages students to care about what they are learning and care about each other. Integrating activities and strategies that encourage students to learn more about each other and work with each other will let your students know that relationships matter as much as subject matter.

Sample Activities, Strategies, and Routines:

	Meet and Greet Students
	The "meet and greet" that teachers do before class seems to be a critical benchmark for lots of students. They tell me how much it means when teachers hang out by the door saying 'Hello' and greeting them by name. Furthermore, kids say that teachers who "meet and greet" are the ones who also care about them personally, and this personal interest motivates them to do better in class. It's easy to assume that this is a common practice; yet, my informal polling with students indicates that this is the exception and not the rule. "Meet and greet" doesn't need to happen every day—two or three times a week is fine—and varying what you do keeps students guessing about what's going to happen in your class that day.
Life Skill Connection	**30. Engage in conscious acts of respect, caring, helpfulness, kindness, courtesy, and consideration**
Sample Activities, Strategies, and Routines	• 12 Ways to Meet and Greet

12 Ways to Meet and Greet

1. In the beginning of the year when you are trying to match names to faces, ask each student to say her or his name as she or he walks into class so that you can hear it and repeat it.

2. Shake hands and say students' names as they walk in the door.

3. Say "hello" to students in lots of different languages. If you have students who speak other languages ask them to write and pronounce "hello" in that language so you can make different "hello's" part of your greeting repertoire.

4. Give everyone a review question as they enter the room. Ask students to record their responses and remind them to discuss their responses with at least one other person to check for agreement. You might use this strategy as a way to begin review for a test or exam.

5. If you are reviewing concepts, sequential steps, or terms, pass out cards to each student as they come in. For example, one student's term matches another student's example, one student's concept matches another student's illustration, or one student has a step that forms a sequence with three other students. This is a way to get kids into small groups or a way to help students focus on the agenda for the day.

6. Cut up a set of about 40 two-inch squares and write the numbers from 1 to 10 on different squares. As students enter the room say "hello" and ask them to pick a number from 1 to 10 from your basket that indicates how they're feeling right now—10 (I'm ready, focused, feeling good) to 1 (I'm tired, grumpy, and would rather be any place else). When everyone is seated ask students to hold up their numbers to get a read where people are. Based on where they are on the scale, you might want to do a quiet energizer that helps everyone to focus.

7. Post a sign on your door that asks, "Are you ready? Name one thing you're ready and willing to do in class today." Ask students to share their "one thing" as you greet them at the door. Or post a sign that asks, "What's one personal goal you're bringing with you to class today?"

8. Once a quarter give each student a personal written greeting that mentions something you appreciate about their presence in your class. Alternate weeks for different classes so you create a cycle (1st period~Oct.____, 2nd Period~Oct.____, 4th period~Nov.____, 5th period~Nov.____, and 7th period~Nov.____) that you can repeat every quarter. One way to make this less daunting is to put a list of 30 or 40 appreciation responses on your computer. You can write in the students' names, print out your messages, and cut them into strips. For example:

Dear Cho, I know that talking in class is not your favorite thing, so I have really appreciated your participation in small group work.

Dear Alicia, I've noticed that you've been on time for the last two weeks. I really appreciate the effort you've made to do this.

Dear Manuel, Thanks for participating in the discussions we've been having. Your questions have challenged all of us to be really clear about what we mean.

Dear Mia, I have really appreciated your efforts to pick up and organize stuff at the end of class. It makes it so much easier to do projects when people are ready to pitch in. Thanks.

Dear Greg, I know this is not an easy class for you, so everyday you're here shows that you're willing to stick with it and keep trying. I appreciate your tenacity.

9. Make a sign that says, "Do not pass until you answer a question." Then ask a question to each student walking in. If you use content questions, ask a variety of questions that students can answer easily. You can also do a wacky version of this by asking everyone silly or personal questions that everyone can answer. For example, "What color are your shoes?" or "When did you get up this morning?" When students look at you as if you've lost it, you might say something like, "Just checking to see if everyone is alert and ready."

10. Pass out interesting quotations that students can write about in their journals, linking something about themselves to the quotation. If you type them up on cards and copy them, students can pick one at random.

11. As students come in, ask them to share something that they've learned in the last week in any class they're taking.

12. Use your computer to create a "Thought for the Day". Use a label template to repeat the same thought on the page 20 times. Print out several copies on card stock, cut them apart, and pass them out to students.

Gather Data and Key Information
So You Can Find Out Who Your Students Are

It is unlikely that you will be in a situation where you can personally interview each student in the beginning of the year. So gathering data and key information about your students the first day and the first few weeks can help you develop a more complete picture of each student. This kind of information comes in handy for several reasons:

- It helps you make connections between individual students and what is being learned in your curriculum.
- It provides a starting point for personal conversations.
- It gives you a "heads-up" about issues that might affect a student's progress and learning.
- It provides a bridge for parental/guardian contacts.

Keep the data and information you collect in a special folder for each class, so it's easy to review and retrieve it.

Life Skill Connection	**16. Work for high personal performance and cultivate your strengths and positive qualities**
Sample Activities, Strategies, and Routines	**• First Day Student Profile** **• Personal Inventory** **• I Feel Survey**

First Day Student Profile

On the first day, you don't want to put students in a position of disclosing all sorts of personal stuff about themselves. You do want to collect information that will give you the basics that you would like to know about each student from the beginning. The following handout provides you with a sample student profile.

HANDOUT I

First Day Student Profile

Last Name: _____

First Name: _____

Middle Name: _____

Birth date: _____

Three words that best describe me are _____, _____, and _____.
I was born in ❑ United States or ❑ _____
My first language is ❑ English or ❑ _____

Home Address:

Street _____ Apartment _____

City/Town _____ Zip Code _____

How long have you lived at your current address? _____ years or _____ months
How long have you lived in this community/town/city? _____ years or _____ months
Home Phone Number (_____)_____ Email Address_____

Family Information:

Full name of parent/guardian   Full name of parent/guardian

_____   _____

Place of work _____   Place of work _____

Occupation _____   Occupation _____

Born in ❑ US or ❑ _____   Born in ❑ US or ❑ _____

First Language:
❑ English ❑ Other_____

First Language:
❑ English ❑ Other_____

Names and ages of brothers and sisters:

Name _____ Age_____   Name _____ Age_____

Name _____ Age_____   Name _____ Age_____

Name _____ Age_____   Name _____ Age_____

Educational Information:
This is my ❏ first ❏ second ❏ third ❏ fourth year at this school.

The last school I attended was _____

Are there any health issues that might affect your attendance, on-time arrival to class, or class participation?
❏ No or ❏ Yes _____

During the school year, I work at _____ about _____ hours per week.

After high school graduation, I am currently planning to:
❏ Get a full time job
❏ Work part-time and go to college part-time
❏ Attend college full-time
❏ Attend technical school
❏ Get an apprenticeship

Course Schedule: (to be filled out later in the week)

Class Period	Name of Course	Class Period	Name of Course
1st		5th	
2nd		6th	
3rd		7th	
4th		8th	

Personal Inventory

Develop a personal inventory to find out more about your students including what they care about, what interests them, and what they are concerned about. Students often assume that most teachers only care about their academic performance. Surveys or questionnaires can be a first step in making personal connections with each student. While you are developing this survey, think about what might be fun, interesting, and helpful to know about students that you think they would be willing to share. Depending on your students, before they fill out the inventory, you might want to humor them by acknowledging that sex is a possible response to many of the questions. You could say something like, "Since I already know that, I'd prefer that you not get that personal. So stretch your thinking a bit." Here are some starters:

1. Something I think about all the time is
2. Something I do outside of school that is very important in my life is
3. One thing I can teach others to do is
4. Three things I love to do with my friends are
5. Favorite music group / TV show / movie / website / athlete / radio station
6. Something I like/enjoy doing that would surprise people is
7. Something I worry about is
8. Two people I really admire and respect are
9. The most boring thing in my life is
10. The most exciting thing in my life right now is
11. I make my family proud when I
12. One thing my family expects of me is to
13. One thing that makes my family special/different/fun is
14. Three jobs I expect to have sometime are
15. The job I want most in my life is
16. Three things I will need to do to get this job are
17. Things I participate in at school: sports/community service/clubs/special groups/other
18. What do you like most about being a student? What is your "best thing" as a student?
19. What do you like least about being a student? What is your "worst thing" as a student?
20. As your teacher, what should I know about you that will help you learn and do your best in this class?

I Feel Survey

If you use any of these questions for journaling you might want to give students the Feelings Vocabulary words (page 285) to help broaden their personal repertoire of feeling words.
• When I enter a new group, I usually feel... because...
• When I meet new people, I usually feel... because...
• When I enter a new space, I usually feel... because...
• When I'm in a sports crowd, I usually feel... because...
• When a stranger speaks to me, I usually feel... because...
• When a teacher calls on me, I usually feel... because...
• When I stand up in front of a large group, I usually feel... because...
• When I'm with my friends, I usually feel... because...
• When I'm involved in a conflict with someone, I usually feel... because...
• When I'm alone, I usually feel... because...

Learn Students' Names as Quickly as Possible

 If people don't know each other's names, it's hard to call a group a community. Learning and remembering everyone's name is a sign of respect. Taking time to discover who we are in a group always pays off. The more we know about each other, the more comfortable we feel working together.

Life Skill Connection

30. Engage in conscious acts of respect, caring, helpfulness, kindness, courtesy, and consideration

Sample Activities, Strategies, and Routines

• Seven Ways to Quickly Learn Student Names

Seven Ways to Quickly Learn Student Names

If you've got four to six classes of students, learning students' names is no easy task. Yet, like "meet and greet," this is one of those practices that makes a tremendous difference to students. Too often, students tell me about teachers who still don't know their names by the end of first semester. How you learn names may depend on your room set-up and the memory devices that work for you. The following suggestions come from teachers who have learned everyone's name within two weeks. It's also important to give yourself permission to get names wrong the first few times. Simply apologize when it happens and correct yourself.

1. At the start of the school year, have students say their first names every time they speak.

2. Have students create triangular name plates out of 8 1/2" x 11" card stock. Ask students to fold the sheet into three strips. Then ask them to write their first names in large letters on the middle strip. Then fold the sheet into a triangle that will stand on its own in front of the table or desk where each student is sitting. Have a box for each set of name plates and ask students to pick them up and return them to the box each period.

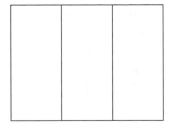 

3. When students are writing, reading quietly, or working in pairs or small groups, spend this time saying each person's name silently three times as your eye roams from one end of the room to the other. Keep the same order of saying names a couple of times, and then try to connect names with faces randomly in no particular pattern.

4. Link a word that begins with the same letter as the student's first name to each student—any word that describes something positive about that student.

5. Tell students they can't enter your classroom until you say their names correctly. Give students bonus points if you can't remember.

6. Take a "head shot" picture of each student. Ask volunteers from each of your classes to create a photo collage, either assembling them in a framed space on a bulletin board or gluing photos and names on a large cardboard "pizza round" to hang from the ceiling.

7. Do a name game or introduction game:

    • **Silent Names A to Z:** Line up silently by First or Last Name alphabetically and then have students say their names.

    • **Name Toss:** On a 5"x 8" note card, ask everyone to write one word that begins with the first letter of their first name that reflects something about them (e.g., Carol=creative). In a circle ask everyone to say their name, the word, and the connection they have to the word. Place the cards in the center of the circle. Using a timer, ask for three volunteers to see how long it will take them to return the correct card to the person who wrote it. Do this a number of times to see if successive groups can beat the previous time.

    • **Name Game with Motion:** Have the group form a circle. Ask students to say their names and make a gesture that goes with their name. After each person says his or her name and makes a gesture, everyone in the group repeats the name and the gesture. Model the activity first, then go around the circle.

    • **Group Juggling:** Get eight to ten soft fabric balls that are three to five inches in diameter. Ask students to form a circle. If you have more than 15 people, you might want to split the group in half and have one facilitator for each group. Say to the group, "We're going to establish a pattern of tossing and catching the balls. I will say a student's name and then toss the ball underhand to her. That student will then say another student's name and toss the ball to him. You need to remember who tossed the ball to you and who you tossed the ball to. You will always catch the ball from the same person and always throw to the same person. We will do this a couple of times using one ball to get the pattern." After you've practiced with one ball, tell students that you are going to steadily add more balls and remind students to say the name of the person to whom they are tossing their balls. The goal is to see how many balls the group can juggle. Stop the activity and start over when too many balls are dropped.

When your selected activity is over, take a few minutes to discuss the activity. What did you like about the activity? What didn't you like? What kinds of skills did you need to be successful? Was there anything we could have done as a group to be more successful? What made this activity challenging? Can you make any connections between being successful at this activity and being successful in class?

Create Opportunities for Students To Get To Know Each Other and Work With Each Other

 Take five to ten minutes several times during the first two weeks to engage students in activities that help them get to know each other. These activities also provide ways to practice active listening, expressing feelings, and cooperation.

Life Skill Connection	**25. Develop, manage, and maintain healthy peer relationships**

Sample Activities, Strategies, and Routines	• **What Do We Have in Common?** • **Find Someone Who** • **Finding Out About Who We Are** • **"You Like, I Like ..."** • **Mix it up when students work together**

What Do We Have in Common?

Give each student a sheet that has three columns and a place for three students' names. Then ask students to pair up with someone they don't know well or use grouping cards to place people in pairs. Give each pair two minutes to write down all the similarities they can think of (physical characteristics, family stuff, things they both do, possessions they both own, etc.). Then ask students to pair up two more times repeating the process. At the end of the activity, ask: "What surprised you about what you discovered you had in common with someone else?" "How many similarities did you find the first time?" "The last time?" "Did it get easier for anyone?" "Why?" Point out that when we are having a disagreement or having trouble working together, it's especially important to remember what we have in common.

Find Someone Who

Create a bingo sheet using the information you collected from the *Personal Inventory Survey* (page 36) so that each box asks for something students need to find out about each person in the class that only matches that one person. For example, "Find someone whose birthday is on _____; find someone who was born in _____; find someone who knows how to _____; find someone who has visited _____; find someone who speaks _____; find someone who has _____."

Finding Out About Who We Are

Create an interview sheet with the following questions. Have students find a partner and choose a question that interests both of them. Have them interview each other and jot down their partner's name and something they want to remember that their partner said. Give them a few minutes and then have them find a new partner. You could end this activity by asking students what they learned about each other.

- Describe your family. What is something funny, weird, unusual, or special about one person in your family?
- What's one place you would like to visit in your lifetime? Why do you want to go there?
- What's your favorite TV show and why do you like to watch this show?
- If you had to eat the same meal everyday for a month, what would it be?
- What's one thing you would like to change about your neighborhood that would make it a better place to live?
- What worries you the most about the world you live in today?
- Name one thing you could teach someone else how to make or how to do?
- What's your favorite holiday of the year? What makes this holiday your favorite?
- What's one thing that you would like to change about your school that would make it a better place for you?

"You Like, I Like..."

This is a terrific activity that meets two goals: you get to hear everyone's names repeatedly and you find out something interesting about each person. Call out a question that invites students to name something they like or like to do. Going around the circle, each person must repeat the names of the five previous students and what they like. For example, if the question is, "What are your two favorite things to wear?" and the first person who speaks says, "I like to wear jeans and hoop earrings," the next person would say, "Marisa likes to wear jeans and hoop earrings, and I like to wear patched overalls and leather jackets." Continue around the circle until everyone has had a turn to speak.

Mix It Up When Students Work Together

If one of your expectations is that every student works with every other student by the end of the first quarter, here are some suggestions for making this happen.

- When students are engaged in pair activities have them partner with students to their right, left, back, and front.

- If your first activity involves partners, give every student someone's name as they walk in the door and invite students to find a place in the room to stand and discuss the question with their partner.

- Use any of the random grouping strategies (page 197).

- Whenever students are working with someone new, ask them to say their names and ask them to each respond to a light hearted "Question of the Day."

- When you've got a few minutes at the close of the period or need to shift the energy, invite students to name five students and one thing they know about each of them.

Make Connections Through 10 Second "Hits"

Imagine for a minute that every student is a web site, generating "hits" everyday. Some students get deluged with positive social and academic hits all day long from peers and adults. Others may get more negative than positive hits, but a hit is a hit nonetheless—someone is paying attention. Now think about some of your students who belong to the "invisible middle"—these are the kids who might go through a whole day with no hits at all from peers or adults. Everyone wants to feel noticed, important, and respected. When teachers take the time to direct specific comments to individual students, kids feel that someone cares about them personally.

| *Life Skill Connection* | **26. Develop, manage, and maintain healthy relationships with adults.** |

| *Sample Activities, Strategies, and Routines* | **• Some Sample 10 Second "Hits"** |

Some Sample 10 Second "Hits"

These "10 second hits" help build rapport and strengthen the connections between students and teachers. For some kids, these "10 second hits" can make all the difference in motivation to learn and succeed in your classroom. Before class, during class, or after class, make comments to individual students that let them know that you notice who they are:

- Say something about their appearance—a new hairdo, a cool T shirt, unusual earrings, a different color finger nail polish, a jacket you like, etc.

- Ask or comment about things that kids are doing outside of your class—sports events, extra curricular activities, other events and projects that students participate in, inside and outside of school.

- Give students positive feedback about something they've done well in class recently.

- Check in with kids who look tired, upset, worried, or rambunctious by reflecting to them what you see. The suggested responses below give you a way to acknowledge and learn more about what you see, and give students a way to name what they're feeling and get ready to refocus for class. For example:

  - *"You look kind of tired; it's been a long day, huh?"*

  - *"Wow, you look like you've got energy to spare. We can sure use your energy in the activity we're doing today."*

  - *"So _____, you look like this has not been your best day, need a minute to get it together?"*

- When you are summarizing a discussion or linking ideas, mention students' names and comments they made earlier that contributed to a better understanding of the topic.

Create Opportunities When You Only Listen

 Sometimes teachers are first-rate talkers and second-rate listeners. It's easy for us to interrupt, over-explain, finish a student's ideas, give advice, correct someone too quickly, or make sure we have the last word, especially if it's clever or funny. It takes a conscious effort to only listen without responding. This simple gesture surprises students when we do it.

Life Skill Connection	**19. Listen actively to demonstrate to others that they have been understood**
Sample Activities, Strategies, and Routines	**• Listening to Students**

Listening to Students

Here are a few ways to try it out:

1. Check yourself during discussions. When you really want to listen to what students have to say, use a timer, set it for five or ten minutes, and invite students to respond to an open-ended question that might generate lots of different viewpoints.

2. When you have made a choice to conference with students one-on-one (especially when you've discovered that there's a concern or a problem), use your favorite opener to invite someone to talk. For example, "So what's going on?" or "How's it going?" or "You don't seem your usual self. Anything going on that's getting in the way?" Then stop. Don't fill the space with conversation. Sit with the silence and listen.

3. Here are some questions you might ask students when you take time out to only listen. Let them know that you'll set the timer for five to ten minutes and invite students to speak to any these questions. Remind students that this is an opportunity to hear different perspectives—it is not the time to begin a debate, but to really listen to each person's take on the question.

- What do you like best about going to school here?

- What do you like least about going to school here?

- On a scale of 1 to 10 how respectful do you see the staff being to students? How about students being respectful to staff? students to students? staff to staff? Say a little about the number you chose.

- On a scale of 1 to 10 how safe do you think students feel here at school? What kinds of things make a school feel safe for students? What kinds of things make school feel unsafe to students?

- Are there some groups of students here who seem to get more attention, more resources, more privileges than other groups? Why do you think that is?

- Are there some groups of students you think feel left out at school? Who gets less attention? Who gets targeted or harassed more? Who can't seem to find a place where they belong? Why do you think that is?

- If you could make changes in scheduling or the curriculum what would you recommend? How would these changes benefit students?

- Are there any ways that you feel some students are treated unfairly?

- When you talk to your friends, what do they complain about the most? What worries them the most about going to this school?

Make Time for Meaningful Closure Activities at the End of the Course

In high school, the concepts of closure and celebration are part of big events like graduation and awards assemblies, but not usually daily classroom life. We get so caught up in the testing and grading cycle that it takes incredible discipline to invite students to stop and reflect on their classroom experience. Develop rituals that give you an opportunity to acknowledge what the class has accomplished and give students a chance to reflect on what they've learned, appreciated, and experienced throughout the course.

Life Skill Connection	**29. Encourage and appreciate the contribution of others**
Sample Activities, Strategies, and Routines	• **Closing Rituals** • **Invite Students to Write Letters to Students Who Will Be Taking This Course Next Year**

Closing Rituals

1. Give every student someone's name in the class—their task is to write an appreciation note to that person that might include something you appreciated about this person as a classmate; something you got to know about this person that you found interesting; something this person did in class that you thought was cool, funny, smart, impressive, or unexpected; something you'll remember about this person from the year. Collect the cards and pass them out on the last day.

2. Create a memories bulletin board where students can write their responses to any of these sentence starters:

   • One thing I won't forget about this class is...
   • At the end of this class, I'm more aware of...
   • At the end of this class, I'm no longer nervous about...
   • For me, the best thing about this class was...
   • The funniest thing that happened in this class was...
   • Before this class I thought that... Now, I think...
   • This class got me thinking more about...
   • The biggest challenge for me in this class was...
   • One thing I would change about this course is...
   • I surprised myself this year by...
   • The one thing I never want to do again is...
   • Goodbye _____. Hello _____.

3. At the close of the course, ask each student to share a response to one of the sentence starters above.

4. If students keep a journal, ask them to write about any of the sentence starters above or any of the questions suggested in the letter writing activity below, or incorporate a reflection essay into your final exam experience. Students turn in their essay on the day they take their exam.

5. For each class you teach, share a few memorable stories that stand out for you.

6. Review the "big goals" and expectations you set for the year. Discuss whether and how successfully the class met them.

7. Create a congratulations banner or poster that acknowledges what students have accomplished during the year.

Invite Students to Write Letters to Students Who Will Be Taking This Course Next Year

Here are some ideas for what students might include in their letters:

1. What's the one piece of advice that you would give a student who is taking this course next year?

2. What are two things you liked best about class and two things you disliked.

3. What did you find to be most challenging about the course?

4. What did you find to be kind of fun?

5. What did you find to be the most interesting and least interesting things that you studied or learned how to do?

6. What was the biggest surprise for you during the year?

7. If students want to "learn the ropes" to be successful in class, what should they know?

8. What's something they will need to learn how to do well during the year?

PRACTICE 2

Emphasize Student Centered Learning That is Personally Meaningful

One of the major shifts in secondary classroom practice is the move away from teacher-directed to more student-centered instruction—matching what and how you teach to who your students are and how they learn. Every major report on rethinking high schools recommends the development of courses and academic programs that create a seamless web between the academic and the practical, the formal learning in schools and the informal learning in the world outside, teachers' passions, and students' interests and personal experiences. Student-centered learning also places more emphasis on "learning how to learn" skills that involve personal goal-setting, reflection, and assessment. This guide doesn't pretend to be a primer for developing meaningful and rigorous learning experiences. However, this section offers some beginning steps that support a student-centered learning orientation.

Sample activities, strategies, and routines:

Offer Choices from Day One

One of the ironies of adolescence is how little choice students experience in the classroom. My colleagues and I have often observed that kindergartners have more choices of what to do in a day than a sophomore might have in a week's worth of classes. The power of choice confers ownership and makes almost any task feel more do-able and more satisfying.

Providing more choices is a Win-Win solution for teachers and students. First, choices convey that there isn't just one way to meet a goal or complete a task, thus acknowledging that every class exhibits a wide range of learning preferences, styles, and motivators. Second, choices encourage self-efficacy and self-expression. Students get to say to themselves, "I chose to do it this way and here's why." Third, providing more opportunities for choice comes with the expectation of being more personally responsible and accountable. And finally, offering academic and behavioral choices invites cooperation, reduces student resistance to learning, and minimizes adversarial relationships between students and teachers.

Life Skill Connection | **16. Work for high personal performance and cultivate your strengths and positive qualities**

• Examples of Everyday Choices and Options

Examples of Everyday Choices and Options

1. Develop a list of options for how students can demonstrate what they know and what they've learned that includes non-traditional assessments like the seven P's:
    - Participation
    - Projects
    - Performances
    - Presentations
    - Products
    - Portfolios
    - and Problem Posing and Analysis

    Then let students choose several assessments to do for a particular unit of study.

2. Give five homework options a week. Students choose three they want to complete.

3. Give some assignments at the beginning of the week that are due at the beginning of the next week. For those who complete their assignments by Friday there is no weekend homework. Others have the weekend to finish.

4. Give students one free homework pass each quarter.

5. Choose different ways that you and students present information on a particular topic. During the year, ensure that each student has an opportunity to teach something to the class.

6. Create 120 point tests in which students need to complete items that total 100 points, including some required items.

7. If students keep a portfolio of their work, ask students to choose pieces that they polish and correct until the results are a "perfect" paper. These will then be included in a folder sent home to parents at grading period. Or choose a set of papers that reflect a continuum of progress during a semester to discuss in an assessment conference or to send home to parents at the grading period.

8. Create at least one opportunity every quarter or semester where students engage in some form of independent learning where they choose what they want to learn more about or what they want to learn how to do.

9. When you offer a menu of choices for assignments leave room for students who want to develop their own ideas as long as they meet the assignment criteria.

10. Give students the option of creating one 3″x5″ study card that they can use while taking a test. You would be surprised how creative students are in organizing information on one little card. By creating the card they have gone a long way toward learning the content.

11. Give students several options for how they want to be tested on specific content.

12. Review and grade tests in class (have special pens or colored pencils so students aren't tempted to rewrite original answers rather than correcting or adding new information). Encourage students to make notes and ask questions. Then offer opportunities for students to take the test again.

13. Invite students to create questions and problems for tests and performance demonstrations.

14. Have students choose "study buddies" who help each other review and study before a test.

Make Personal Goal-Setting and Reflection Regular Practices

 These "learning to learn" skills increase students' self-awareness and self-efficacy. Try integrating these practices into gatherings, closings, journal writing, and debriefing after an activity has been completed.

Life Skill Connection	13. **Make big and little goals and make plans** 17. **Assess your skills, competencies, effort, and quality of work accurately**
Sample Activities, Strategies, and Routines	• **Personal Pathways** • **Thinking About Personal Goal Setting and Planning** • **Reflection Sentence Stems** • **See, Feel, Think, Do** • **General Debriefing Questions for Experiential Learning Activities** • **Two Glows and a Grow**

Personal Pathways

The following activity was developed by Rachel Poliner. It works well at the beginning of the school year as a way for students to reflect on their past and set goals for the current year.

HANDOUT 2

Personal Pathway

Personal Pathway for _____

Think about your life experiences, people who are important to you, and goals. Fill in the areas along your path with drawings or writing representing where you have been, people and events along the way, and where you might be headed.

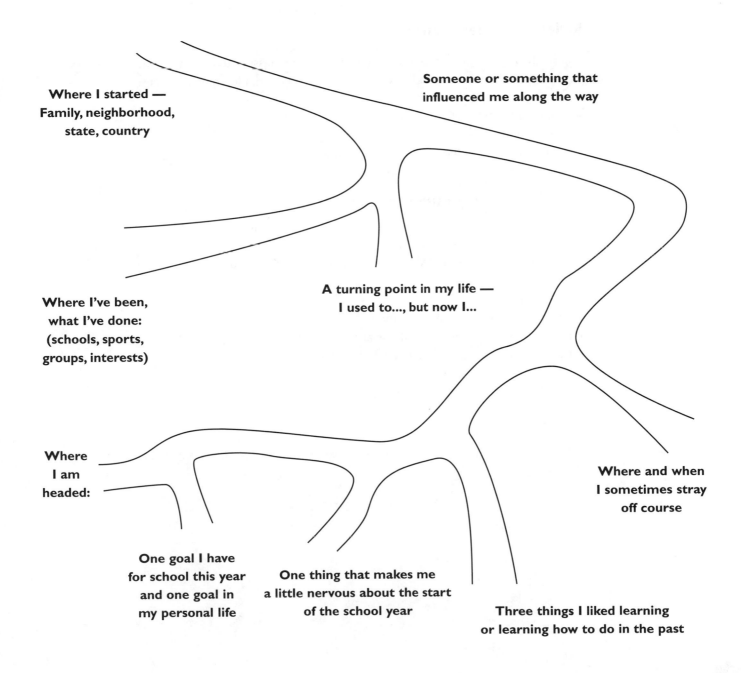

Where I started —
Family, neighborhood,
state, country

Someone or something that
influenced me along the way

Where I've been,
what I've done:
(schools, sports,
groups, interests)

A turning point in my life —
I used to..., but now I...

Where
I am
headed:

Where and when
I sometimes stray
off course

One goal I have
for school this year
and one goal in
my personal life

One thing that makes me
a little nervous about the start
of the school year

Three things I liked learning
or learning how to do in the past

Thinking About Personal Goal Setting and Planning

Is their goal specific enough so that students can answer the following?
• What exactly are you proposing to do?
• What steps will it take to accomplish your goal?
• How long will it take to complete each step?
• How will you know when you are half way there?
• What will you need to accomplish your goal?
• How can others help you work on your goal?

Reflection Sentence Stems

You might want to post these sentence stems in your classroom and invite students to choose one to write about or respond to verbally when you debrief learning activities.
• As I began this activity, I felt...
• At the end of this activity, I felt...
• One thing that surprised me was...
• As we worked together, I kept thinking about...
• Now I'm more aware of how important it is to...
• I liked this activity because...
• I would have changed this activity by...
• One thing that was fun, challenging, or eye-opening was...
• After participating in the activity I realized...
• In thinking about our classroom, it would be great if we could...
• I found it really difficult to...
• I found it easy to...
• This helped me to learn more about...
• I can take what I learned from this and apply it to...
• I want to remember this experience the next time I...

See, Feel, Think, Do

Use the following questions to help your students reflect on their experience after an activity.

- **See:** What did you observe? What did you notice about what you were doing and what others were doing?
- **Feel:** What feelings did you experience during this activity? In the beginning? In the end? What were your reactions? Did your feelings change?
- **Think:** (the so-what question) How did this work for you? What insights did you gain about yourself, or others? What did you learn about _____? Given your insights from this exercise, what are the implications for _____? Why does this matter?
- **Do:** (the now-what question) Now that you are aware, what will you differently? How can you use these insights and information? What might you want to change? What actions might you want to take?

General Debriefing Questions for Experiential Learning Activities

At the close of an activity, a project, or a learning unit, use reflection questions to debrief what students have experienced.

- What tools, skills, and attitudes helped you to be successful? Helped you complete the task? Helped you meet or achieve the goal?
- How did this activity work for you? What made this experience (interesting, hard, frustrating, comfortable, uncomfortable, strange, different, surprising, challenging)?
- Was there anything you didn't like or would have changed?
- What's one thing you want to remember from today?
- What's one thing you can take from today and apply it in your life?

Two Glows and a Grow

Use the following handout to have students reflect on their day.

HANDOUT 3

Two Glows and a Grow

Something you did today
that felt productive
and satisfying for you

One way you felt you put forth
your best effort as a learner

Something you experienced today
that was a growing edge for you –
a skill or competency you want
to continue to strengthen and improve

Use Self-Assessment Tools Throughout the Course

On any given month try not to overuse one assessment tool. Incorporate a mix of what you assess (specific activities, the week, a unit, mastery of a learning standard, quarterly progress, the end of the year) and how students are assessed (verbally in whole group sharing, pairs, or in a quick conference with you; journaling; or entrance and exit slips.) Below are a number of tools to use at different times during the year.

Sample Activities, Strategies, and Routines

- **Assessment Questions for Throughout the Year**
- **Making the Grade**

Assessment Questions for Throughout the Year

There are several ways that you can use these assessment questions with students:
- Choose some of these questions for a written assessment.
- Give students the whole series of questions and invite students to select a few that they choose to answer.
- Select some questions for discussion in small and large groups (you might want to tape record responses) and select some questions for written reflection.

Assessing the Day's Class or a Specific Learning Activity
- What worked best for you today?
- Any new insights or ideas?
- Are there any questions or issues you want to make sure get addressed tomorrow?
- Any other comments or suggestions?

A Weekly Assessment
Take time every week in your classes to do a quick informal assessment using any of these suggestions:
- Something important that you learned.
- Something that you want to remember.
- Something you learned that you want to know more about.
- Something you learned about yourself as a learner that surprised you or made you think about yourself differently.

Looking Ahead Questions for Before a Test, Performance, or Demonstration
- What topics do you feel confident about?
- What topics are you unsure about?
- How are you going to clear up the concepts that you have yet to master?

Looking Back Questions for After a Test, Performance, or Demonstration
- What strategies did you use to prepare for the test?
- Which strategies were the most helpful in preparing for the test?
- Did you do as well as you felt you should have based on your preparation?
- Why did you get the grade you did?

- What will you do next time?
- If your friend were taking this test tomorrow, how would you tell him or her to prepare?

Assessing a Learning Unit

Pick one unit of study and post a list of every activity and task that has been part of that unit. Ask students to review the list and respond to these questions:

- What three activities helped you most to understand _____. Why?
- What two activities helped you most to demonstrate what you learned? Why?
- What activity would you have left out of the unit or added to this unit? Why?
- What activity did you like best? Why?
- What activity did you like least? Why?

At the End of the Quarter, Semester, or Course

Give students the whole series of questions and select a few that you want all students to answer. Invite students to select a few additional questions that they would like to answer.

- What are three things you want to remember most from this course?
- What are two of the most important things you've learned in this course?
- What's a skill you've learned and used that you're sure you will use again?
- Give one example of how you know yourself better as a learner at the end of this course.
- Think of specific situations in this course (inside or outside the classroom) that show how you managed yourself successfully in the following ways:

  - An experience when I felt really self-disciplined (I did what I needed to do without being nagged or getting it together at the last minute.)
  - An experience when I overcame my frustration, upsetness, or anger successfully
  - An experience when I felt self-motivated
  - An experience when I did whatever it took to complete a project/assignment successfully

- Describe one thing you've learned about yourself that surprised you.
- What questions do you have at the end of the course that you'd like to think more about?
- In what ways was this course taught differently than other courses? Describe two or three activities you liked the best and two or three activities you liked the least. Why?
- What two or three issues and/or activities do you wish all students in your school could experience? Why would you recommend these issues or activities?
- In thinking back on this course, what images and experiences stand out the most for you? Why?
- Did this course make it easier for you to get to know other students? Explain.
- Did you feel safe enough in this course to take the risks of being open and honest and sharing your stories with others? Why or why not?
- If you were to summarize what this course was about to another student, what would you say? Use two or three sentences.
- Do you think this course will change the rest of your time in high school? How? What might you be more aware of or do differently because you took this course?
- What's one attitude or skill you hope students will take from this class when they leave?

Making the Grade

You might also ask students to predict their grades several times a quarter—naming what grade they would give themselves and identifying one or two reasons why they feel this grade is an accurate reflection of their effort in class. You might also invite students to predict what it would take to improve their grade over the next few weeks.

Invite Students' Worlds into the Classroom

Acting like a kid ("Let me show you how cool I am" or "You'll like me as a teacher because I'm just like you") turns students off. On the other hand, letting students know that you're curious about their world, that you're paying attention to their reality gets you lots of points. Connected teaching is all about how you meet students where they are (acknowledging what they are thinking and feeling here and now) and how you link their lived experiences to what they are doing and learning in the classroom.

Life Skill Connection

22. Empathize; understand and accept another person's feelings, perspectives, point of view

31. Recognize and appreciate similarities and differences in others

Sample Activities, Strategies, and Routines

• **Connecting to Students' Worlds**

Connecting to Students' Worlds

• Use examples, metaphors, and analogies from their world to make learning real. One of the best pieces of advice I ever got about teaching was to collect examples, metaphors, and analogies from students' everyday experiences that I could use to reinforce and illustrate what we were learning in the classroom. Think about how young people spend their time outside of school, what kinds of big ideas or issues grab their attention, or what they know a lot about—then begin making connections:

  • When you're teaching a particular skill, in what ways might it connect to the skills one needs to play a particular sport, drive a car, work on a food service line, play in a band, complete a job or college application?

  • Link the everyday conflicts students experience with friends, parents, siblings, supervisors, police, customers, or teammates to conflicts they encounter in literature and social studies classes.

  • Adolescents gravitate toward any conversation about money and power, sex and violence. Use their perceptions and experiences around these big ideas as a connector to key concepts in politics, economics, biology, chemistry, etc.

- Ask students to do a five minute brainstorm around this question: What's going on in your world right now that's cool/uncool, fascinating, unfair, outrageous, or worrisome? Once you've got a list, keep your eyes and ears peeled for examples from their world that can help explain and illustrate your world in the classroom.

- Use learning strategies that get students talking to each other. Make time in any curriculum unit for students in pairs and threes to share...

  - What they know about a particular topic

  - Their opinions and perceptions of an issue being discussed

  - The thinking processes they use to solve problems

  - How they might respond given a particular situation—what they think would be a good or bad decision, and why

- Acknowledge where your students are and then get started. When they are anticipating a big school event or rite of passage that's happening the same day or week, take a few minutes to acknowledge it by saying, "I have a hunch (some, most) of you are thinking about _____." Invite them to share a few comments about what's going on, what they're thinking or feeling about this, or why they're dreading or looking forward to this event. If it's SAT's, report card day, college acceptance letter day, or the like, reassure your students, using your own brand of humor, that no one will die, that they will get through this, and that you will see them all the next day. Then say, "So here we are in _____. What's one thing you can do that will help you focus for the next _____ minutes?" Get a couple of comments and close with your version of "Okay, let's do it."

- Check out what young people are reading, viewing, and listening to. One way to check into their world is to ask them occasionally what's going on out there. Sometimes when you have a minute or two of a class period remaining before end time, ask your students one of these questions or bring in something to share that piqued your curiosity.

  - "So it's the weekend. Got any suggestions for a video I should rent?"

  - "I'm actually going home today right after school's out. If I wanted to take a look, is there anything good to watch on TV?"

  - "In the last week, I've heard people say _____ a bunch of times. What does that mean to you and your friends?"

  - Hold up the school newspaper or local paper and share an article that has a youth connection. Ask students what they think about the topic or issue.

- Sometimes when there's a new fad, fashion, or music group that grabs kids' attention and leaves you scratching your head, just ask kids. "I noticed/heard/saw _____. What's that all about?" A lot of kids are more than happy to tell you something they know that you don't.

- "If I had two hours this week just to hang out, what three websites should I check out? What TV shows should I check out? What radio station should I listen to?

- Create a Teen Trading Bin. Place a box somewhere in your classroom where kids can drop in magazines, paperback books, computer games, tapes, etc. that they don't want anymore and are willing to trade for something else. As long as they've put something in the box, they can take something out.

Link the Real World to Project-Based Learning in Your Course

Consider making project-based learning an important feature of every semester's work. Independent or small group projects meet a number of learning goals, including the following:

- Students have the opportunity to make many choices within a framework of clear expectations and project criteria.
- Projects offer the opportunity to link academic class work to real world problems and investigations.
- Projects enable students to experience a full range of learning tasks, from development of an idea to the final presentation or product.
- Projects enable students to capitalize on their personal interests and learning strengths while developing new skills.
- Teachers have the opportunity to provide more personalized guidance, coaching, and support to individual students.
- Goal-setting, reflection, assessment, and revision are embedded in the project process from start to finish.

Life Skill Connection	**16. Work for high personal performance and cultivate your strengths and positive qualities**
Sample Activities, Strategies, and Routines	**• Linking the Classroom to the Real World**

Linking the Classroom to the Real World

Invite people who practice your discipline in the world outside of school to listen, discuss, and assess your students' work around a specific problem or project that places students in role of writer, historian, scientist, mathematician, artist, media consultant, investigator, chronicler, etc. Ask practitioners to be part of a discussion about ways students can expand and complicate their thinking about their work.

When presenting a project or problem that you expect every student to complete, work along with students completing your own project or solving your own problem during the same timeline.

The Six A's of Instructional Design for Project-Based Learning

Project-based learning is at the heart of *Schooling for the Real World*, a wonderful how-to guide to student-centered real world learning in schools and classrooms. Adria Steinberg has developed a framework called "The Six A's of Instructional Design" as a guide for creating rigorous and relevant projects across the disciplines. Use them to connect your projects to life outside of school walls.

Authenticity
- Where in the "real world" might an adult tackle the problem or question addressed by the project?
- How do you know the problem or question has meaning to the students?
- Who might be an appropriate audience for students' work?

Academic Rigor
- What is the central problem or question addressed by the project?
- What knowledge area and central concepts will it address?
- What habits of mind will students develop (for example, concern for evidence, viewpoint, and cause and effect; precision of language and thought; persistence)?
- What learning standards are you addressing through this project (for example, those of the district or state)?

Applied Learning
- What will the students do to apply the knowledge they are learning to a complex problem? (Are they designing a product, improving a system, organizing an event?)
- Which of the competencies expected in high-performance work organizations (for example, teamwork, appropriate use of technology, ability to communicate ideas, and ability to collect, organize, and analyze information) does the project provide opportunities to develop?
- Which self-management skills (for example, developing a work plan, prioritizing pieces of the work, meeting deadlines, identifying and allocating resources) does the project require students to use?

Active Exploration

- What field-based activities does the project require students to conduct (for example, interviewing experts, participating in a work site exploration)?
- Which methods and sources of information are students expected to use in their investigations (for example, interviewing and observing, gathering and reviewing information, collecting data, model-building, using online services)?

Adult Connections

- Do students have access to at least one outside adult with expertise and experience relevant to their project who can ask questions, provide feedback, and offer advice?
- Does the project offer students the opportunity to observe and work alongside adults during at least one visit to a work site with relevance to the project?
- Does at least one adult from outside the classroom help students develop a sense of the real world standards for this type of work?

Assessment Practices

- What are the criteria for measuring desired student outcomes (for example, disciplinary knowledge, habits of mind, and applied learning goals)?
- Are students involved in reviewing or helping to establish the project criteria?
- Which methods of structured self-assessment are students expected to use (for example, journals, peer conferences, teacher or mentor conferences, rubrics, periodic review of progress vis-a-vis the work plan)?
- Do students receive timely feedback on their works-in-progress from teachers, mentors, and peers?
- What work requirements are students expected to complete during the life of the project (for example, proposals, work plans, reflection papers, mini-presentations, models, illustrations)?
- Do students prepare a culminating exhibition or presentation at the completion of the project that demonstrates their ability to apply the knowledge they have gained?

The Six A's of Instructional Design for Project-Based Learning

Authenticity
Academic Rigor
Applied Learning
Active Exploration
Adult Connections
Assessment Practices

Source: *Schooling for the Real World* by Adria Steinberg and Kathleen Cushman, Copyright 1999 Jossey Bass. This material is used by permission of John Wiley & Sons, Inc.

CHAPTER 2

Co-Create a Caring, Respectful, and Responsible Learning Community

Creating a caring, respectful, and responsible community of learners is the starting point for creating a positive and effective learning environment and reducing adversarial relationships. Creating community helps build cohesiveness, a common purpose, interdependence, and support within the group. As students feel more connected to the group, they are more likely to invest in becoming responsible and productive group members. Conscious efforts to build a community of learners invite students to practice negotiated decision making, exercise voice and choice, and strengthen their participation and leadership skills.

This chapter explores important elements that help create community and introduces two key practices that help teachers and students establish and maintain a caring, respectful, and responsible learning community:

 Practice #3: Establish clear norms, boundaries, procedures, and consequences

 Practice #4: Build a cohesive community of learners

The section for each practice includes sample activities, strategies, and routines that illustrate the key practice.

What Creates a Sense of Community?

The soul of a classroom is the psychological sense of community created among and between the students and the teacher. Howard Adelman and Linda Taylor describe community in this way:

"People can be together without feeling connected or feeling they belong or feeling responsible for a collective vision or mission. In school and in class, a psychological sense of community exists when a critical mass of stakeholders are committed to each other and to the setting's goals and values and exert effort toward the goals and maintaining relationships with each other. Such an effort must ensure effective mechanisms are in place to provide support, promote self-efficacy, and foster positive working relationships.

A perception of community is shaped by daily experiences and probably is best engendered when a person feels welcomed, supported, nurtured, respected, liked, and connected in reciprocal relationships with others, who is contributing to the collective identify, destiny, and vision." (Adelman and Taylor, 2001, p. 25)

A number of factors challenge the rationale for creating community in high school classrooms, making it difficult to achieve. There are the obvious pressures of content coverage and testing. If we spend time building community, that's less time spent on the topic. Short class periods that are long on direct skill instruction may provide few opportunities for students to function as a community or work as a team. High school students are conditioned to view the classroom as a vehicle for demonstrating individual mastery, not a container for holding a vision that's shaped by the collective performance of the whole group.

What may be the greatest barrier, however, is the dynamic of a classroom—there's one teacher and up to thirty kids, many of whom may have no interest in creating community at all. Thus, the initial inspiration and responsibility for establishing a sense of community lies in the hands of one person—the teacher. Students' experience of community or non-community will hinge on their teachers' beliefs. Teachers who believe that building community can result in increased student motivation and learning, will make it happen. If they don't see the connection, they won't.

Thomas Sergiovanni, who has written extensively on school culture and school leadership sees building community (in and outside the classroom) at the heart of school improvement. He suggests that, first and foremost, a community must have a sense of vision and purpose. (Sergiovanni, 1994, pp. 71-95)

Vision, Purpose, and Intentionality

Do we give students compelling reasons for why we're doing what we're doing that make sense to them, not just us or the local school board or department chair? How do we construct a vision of we, not just I? How can we go about developing a sense of shared goals that all of us value? How do we plan ahead, set the stage, seed the ground so students will do what we'd like them to do? If students come without the skills and attitudes we expected, what can we do to help them strengthen their academic and social competencies? What kinds of meaningful opportunities do we provide for students to feel positive about themselves as individual learners and as members of a group?

Three other conditions support the development of a genuine community.

Trust

It's all about the relationships we create with students and that students create among themselves. Trust emerges when relationships are supported and maintained through dependability, predictability, genuineness, honesty, competence, integrity, consistency, and personalization. A sense of trust deepens when we feel safe and know that if the boundaries of safety are broken, violations won't be ignored. What can kids count on from us time after time after time? What can kids count on from each other day in and day out?

Respect

Respect begins by developing an appreciation for each other's uniqueness and what we each bring to the classroom. It's nurtured by cultural sensitivity (The classroom will be a place where I will be conscious of positively welcoming, noticing, and learning about the diversity of my students and teach to their differences.) A respectful classroom is a place where students aren't embarrassed, insulted, belittled, or humiliated. A climate of mutual respect is supported through the courtesy of asking, inviting, requesting, and by listening before judgment or punishment. Teachers model respectfulness by focusing on the issues—not attacking the person. They are mindful of using a tone of voice and words that communicate that each person has dignity and each student has something important to contribute.

Optimism

Optimism begins by holding a positive image of human beings as able and capable. We convey our optimism by valuing an individual's efforts, not just his or her ability. We hold high hopes in life for every student. From smiles to immediate feedback to personal conferencing, we let students know that we are confident in their capacities to learn, grow, and change. We believe that students can succeed and don't downplay small successes. (The lesson wasn't perfect, the students weren't perfect, and still it was successful!) In fact, we encourage students to see mistakes, missteps, and setbacks as opportunities to imagine different choices and possibilities. Above all, we do everything we can to let young people know they have the power within them to choose the kind of human beings they want to be in a future of their making.

Consider out-of-classroom experiences that offer a compelling sense of community and require exemplary practice of effective teamwork—a basketball team, a drama production, or a school newspaper. In each of these arenas, high performance or quality production are dependent on each individual's skills and the collective efforts and skills of the whole group. No coach or sponsor would diminish the role that inspiration, motivation, and attitude play in helping kids to think like a team. Nor would they neglect to teach and assess the specific skills that help a group behave like a team.

PRACTICE 3

Establish Clear Norms, Boundaries, Procedures, and Consequences

Developmentally, adolescents need and want clear norms, boundaries, procedures, and consequences. They also want to help develop the guidelines that shape their lives in the classroom. When students have opportunities to discuss classroom management issues they get a clearer picture of the "why's" behind classroom norms that promote a positive and productive learning environment. They need to know when they have crossed the line with you and others, and they need to know how they can self-correct to get back on track.

Sample activities, strategies, and routines:

Clarify Classroom Boundaries

Effective discipline begins with the boundaries and limits you set in the classroom. Rachel Kessler, a colleague who has spent a lifetime exploring what makes a classroom a genuine learning community, has this to say about discipline. "We as teachers must take primary responsibility for creating an environment that is safe. Effective discipline includes clarity of purpose, a positive image of what discipline means, inner strength to be able to risk being disliked, and an understanding of and willingness to use one's whole person in an expression of personal power." Students need to know what you stand for as a teacher and as a human being. Think about how you choose to use your power and authority to create a safe environment where everyone can learn, where everyone feels safe, and where everyone belongs.

Most issues about how students work and learn together in your class can be negotiated. However, every teacher has some no's and bottom lines that are non-negotiable; these are the issues where you're willing to exercise your authority consistently and fairly with no exceptions. Boundaries and bottom lines are good for everyone. Students learn what your values are through what is absolutely not okay. They also learn important life lessons when they violate boundaries and bottom lines. A useful guideline is "fewer are better." For more on boundaries, procedures, and consequences see page 279 in Chapter 5.

Life Skill Connection

7. **Make responsible choices for yourself by analyzing situations accurately and predicting consequences of different behaviors.**

• **Clarify What's Negotiable and Non-Negotiable in the Curriculum**

Clarify What's Negotiable and Non-Negotiable in the Curriculum

As you discuss course expectations and course requirements, students need to know what's negotiable and what's not. There may not be many options and choices about what students need to learn; however, there may be many options and choices for how students can meet a course requirement, complete an assignment, or demonstrate what they have learned. Make a list of five or six boundaries that are non-negotiable. On the "What's Negotiable?" list, begin with two or three suggestions and as a group brainstorm possible ideas for what can be negotiated within the course content and what procedures and policies might be negotiable around homework, tests, and in-class tasks, etc. Here is a sample:

What's Non-Negotiable?	What Could Be Negotiable?
Everyone must demonstrate proficiency in...	Students can choose from several options for how to demonstrate their proficiency in meeting some standards.
Everyone will read four required books during the year.	
Students who fail a test must retake the test until they pass it.	The class can negotiate and come to agreement on two books to read as a whole group.
Everyone will be required to take a final exam.	On major exams there will be optional sections and questions that students can choose from to complete the required number of points for an exam.

Create a Vision of Your Classroom Community

What makes a classroom a safe space to be? What kinds of work is a challenge for different students? As the teacher, what do you hope that every student will learn and experience? When you create a vision together, you engage everyone's imagination in the art of the possible. The result is a road map to help you make it happen. Students are often surprised and pleased to know that their ideas and suggestions are taken seriously. As you develop frameworks for learning together, implement a couple of student suggestions right away in the first week or so. It's your actions that will let students know you're paying attention to their ideas and feelings.

Life Skill Connection

18. Exercise assertiveness; communicate your thoughts, feelings, and needs effectively to others

- **Four Ways to Gather Data**
- **Questions for Creating a Classroom Vision**
- **How Can You Use This Student Data?**

Four Ways to Gather Data

Creating a classroom vision is an opportunity to discover what students have to say about classroom life. It's also a chance to get a sense of who they are as learners and what they look for in a teacher. Using any of the questions that follow this section, try one of these strategies for generating students' ideas:

1. Post several questions, set the timer for 10-15 minutes, and take time to only listen when students are sharing their ideas—no interrupting, summarizing, or sermonizing. This is harder to do then it sounds, but students will appreciate it when you give them uninterrupted air time.

2. Type up a set of your favorite questions to give to students. Invite students to choose three or four questions to write about in their journals.

3. Hand out blank note cards and invite pairs of students to respond to several questions from your list. Have students share their responses out loud, but also collect their response cards so that you can collate all of their data.

4. Post questions on separate pieces of chart paper around the room and invite small groups to write down their ideas for each question using a "rotation station" learning strategy.

Questions for Creating a Classroom Vision

Personal Perspectives:
- What things can I do as a student to be successful in this class?
- What can the teacher do to support my success in class?
- What kinds of support from teachers help me to do my best, especially when I'm struggling?
- What makes a classroom a safe space where I can be honest and open, where I can say what's on my mind?
- What kinds of learning tasks, activities, and homework are easiest for me to do?
- What kinds of learning tasks, activities, and homework are hardest for me to do?
- What do kids do and say that annoys me the most? What happens in class that makes me mad?
- What hopes do I bring with me to this class?
- In what ways do I like to be challenged?

- Are there any hesitations that I have about this class that might get in the way of my success? (I don't know whether... ; I'm unsure about... ; I don't like spending a lot of time... ; I think the biggest potential problem for me will be...)
- When I'm having difficulty or get stuck, what can a teacher do to help me get back on track?

Classroom Perspectives:
- What are three ways that teachers can show respect toward students?
- What are three ways that students can show respect toward students?
- What are three ways that students can show respect toward each other?
- What are the most important qualities of a good teacher?
- What are the most important qualities of a good student?
- What can you do to support other students to do their best in class?
- What makes learning fun in class?
- What things do you hope a teacher will never say or do?
- What things do you hope students will never say or do?
- What kinds of pressures and obstacles do some students face that make it tough to be a successful student?

How Can You Use This Student Data?

1. These conversations and the information generated can become the foundation for making group agreements (page 70).

2. Summarize and post suggestions that emerge from student pairs and rotation stations. Use this summary as a way to stay on track and assess how things are going in class.

3. You can summarize key points from students' personal journal responses to illustrate how no one strategy or activity works equally well for all students. This information gives you a way to let students know that you will be introducing lots of different strategies and learning activities, knowing that each person will like and learn more from some experiences more than others.

4. You might put students' personal journal responses to these vision questions in their assessment folders. This information can be useful as you work with each student and can be especially helpful when students are experiencing difficulties.

Talk About the Issue of Respect

Everyone needs to talk about respect as a foundation for building positive relationships in the classroom. Versions of "You disrespected me" are the most common sources of conflict between and among students and teachers. Respect is a global word that can mean something different to each person in the room. It is very helpful for you and students to identify specific, observable behaviors that individuals perceive as being respectful and disrespectful. It is also helpful to explore why people are disrespectful so that the group can counter experiences of disrespect with behaviors that encourage everyone to be more respectful of each other.

One more thing, the "Golden Rule" is not enough in diverse learning communities where students come from many different family experiences and cultural and religious traditions. Yes, it's important to consider treating others as we would like to be treated; but it's just as important to treat others as they tell you they would like to be treated.

Life Skill Connection	**30. Engage in conscious acts of respect, caring, helpfulness, kindness, courtesy, and consideration**
Sample Activities, Strategies, and Routines	• **Whom Do You Respect?** • **On Self-Respect** • **Learning Carousel on Respect**

Whom Do You Respect?

Ask students to write down (very quickly) three to five names of people (living or dead, young or old, personal acquaintances or people in the larger world) whom they respect a lot, and to identify two or three characteristics/qualities that all the people on their personal lists have in common. Ask students to close their writing by explaining why they associate these qualities of character with people whom they respect.

Invite students to share what they wrote. You might want to record these qualities on newsprint and follow-up with a few questions that deepen the dialogue:

• Is the way you show respect toward some individuals or groups different from the way you show respect to other individuals and groups?

• Is respect different from admiration, appreciation, and popularity? How so? Can you respect people and not like them? Why or why not? If you disagree with someone can you still show respect toward them?

• Is everyone entitled to be treated respectfully regardless of what they do? Are there people you are automatically respectful toward? Does everyone have to earn your respect regardless of age, position, and status? Or does everyone start out getting your respect, but earn the privilege of keeping your respect?

On Self-Respect

In groups of two or three, make a list of five Do's and five Don't's that are indicators of self-respect.

SELF-RESPECT	
The DO's of self-respect	**The DON'T's of self-respect**
Examples: I do keep my word and my promises. I do take care of myself physically.	Examples: I don't let people walk all over me. I don't take chances that put me in a dangerous situation.

Learning Carousel on Respect

Implement a "learning carousel" where each question is posted on newsprint and every group of four students has two to three minutes to add their responses to each question as they move as a group from one question to the next. These framing questions offer some critical entry points for a dialogue around respect.

Student to Student RESPECT	
What do **students do and say** that shows respect and disrespect toward other students?	
Disrespectful Behaviors	**Respectful Behaviors**

Teacher to Student RESPECT	
What do **teachers do and say** that shows respect and disrespect toward students?	
Disrespectful Behaviors	**Respectful Behaviors**

Student to Teacher RESPECT	
What do **students do and say** that shows respect and disrespect toward teachers?	
Disrespectful Behaviors	**Respectful Behaviors**

What are some ways students can disagree with a teacher and show respect at the same time?	**What are some ways teachers can disagree with students and show respect at the same time?**

Think about why people are disrespectful. What have people experienced that may lead to disrespectful behaviors toward others?	**What kinds of experiences help people become more respectful?**

Make Group Guidelines and Agreements

Shifting the emphasis from "my rules that you follow" to "guidelines we agree to implement together" communicates mutual responsibility for establishing a positive classroom climate where everyone is a stakeholder. When we invoke tons of rules in the classroom, we may unintentionally pit the rule breakers against the rule keepers. Furthermore, rules tend to keep the focus on negative behaviors—catching kids doing the wrong thing becomes the goal.

In contrast, agreements that describe desirable behaviors that are observable, concrete, and positive invite everyone to recognize and encourage the regular use of these behaviors. In addition, group guidelines become a natural assessment and reflection tool. Teachers and students can engage in an on-going process of reviewing how well agreements are kept and discussing how to modify agreements so they are more effective.

Group guidelines can make any learning process more meaningful. When students know how to approach a learning task and know what skills and behaviors will help them complete the task, more kids will be more successful. In addition to developing general classroom agreements, students can help develop specific guidelines for: making an effective oral presentation; working effectively in teams; discussing controversial issues when students may bring strong feelings and disparate opinions to the dialogue.

At both levels, students engage in authentic practice of conflict resolution skills: defining the problem; sharing perspectives and listening to all points of view; exploring what's negotiable and what's not; identifying mutual interests; brainstorming possible solutions; and reaching a mutually satisfactory agreement. Students can use this process later for class meetings and negotiating other classroom issues.

Life Skill Connection	**34. "Read" dynamics in a group; assess group skills accurately; identify problems; generate, evaluate, and implement informed solutions that meet the needs of the group**
Sample Activities, Strategies, and Routines	**• Suggested Instructions for Making Group Agreements**

Suggested Instructions for Making Group Agreements

1. Say, "The first thing we're going to do today is make some agreements that we can live with as a whole group. I'd like you to help brainstorm some guidelines that reflect how you think we should work together, talk to each other, and treat each other."

2. Say, "Here are a couple of examples of the kinds of agreements we can make." Choose two or three examples from the list below to write on the newsprint.

    ### Sample List of Group Agreements
    1. Let people finish what they have to say before someone else speaks.
    2. Share the talk space. Give everyone a chance to speak.
    3. Take care of your own needs. If you have a question, ask it. If you need to say something, say it.
    4. Start on time.
    5. It's okay to make mistakes and self-correct.
    6. Use "I" Statements. Speak from your own experience.
    7. Respect yourself and others.
    8. Listen carefully.
    9. Be honest and open.

> **Agreements**
>
> • Agreements work hand-in-hand with consequences and interventions you apply when students violate classroom boundaries or fail to follow procedures you have taught. (See pages 257, Chapter 5: Thinking about Discipline in a Partners in Learning Classroom)

10. Be a willing participant.
11. Help each other out.
12. Check things out before you make assumptions.
13. Have fun!
14. Confidentiality.
15. Don't make fun of what other people say or do.

3. Say, "What agreements would you like to add to the list that will make our time together productive and positive?" Another way to say this is, "What kinds of agreements can we make as a group that will make this class work for you, that will help you be your best?" Brainstorm for about 10 minutes and write down all suggestions on the chart paper.

4. Use any of these questions to review the list: "Now look at the list. Are there any final suggestions? Any suggestions you'd rather leave out? Any that can be combined? Any words or phrases that you're unclear about? Any objections or concerns about any of the suggestions? Any words that you would like to replace?"

Key Points to Remember:

- Respect is a word that illustrates the problems with "global language,"—i.e., language that is abstract and often means different things to different people. It is essential that students name very concrete behaviors that show (through words or actions) how to treat someone with respect. Here are two ways you can encourage students to clarify what they mean when someone says, "We need to respect other people."

  - *"What could someone do or say that would show you that you're being treated respectfully?"*

  - *"If I had a movie camera here in the classroom, what behaviors would I film that show you treating each other with respect?"*

- If this is challenging to students, you might begin by generating specific behaviors that show disrespect and then identify what you would like someone to say or do instead.

- Take the time to work through the wording of agreements until everyone is fairly comfortable with the list. This process lets your students know that it's okay to discuss areas of difference and that it's valuable to reassess and modify "first thinking."

5. Check the list for "positive framing." This is the time to transform any statements that are negatively framed into statements that are positive and pro-active. For example, in the sample agreements list above, #1 has been changed from "Don't interrupt," to "Let people finish what they have to say before someone else speaks."

Agreements

- Agreements in the classroom can't replace school-wide rules that are universally enforced (i.e. If there is a school-wide rule that no food or drink is allowed in classrooms, you can't make an agreement that supercedes the school rule.)

6. Use a consensus process to reach agreement. Explain that, consensus decision making means that everyone participates and has a say before reaching agreement on a decision that everyone can support. Remind students, "You have been using this process already. Now we've reached the final stage of consensus. Each of you needs to decide if you can live with and support this list of agreements for our class. It's important to remember that this list is not forever. We can revisit, discuss, and change these agreements if the group feels the need to do so. So I will ask two last questions."

- *"Are there any objections to the agreements as they stand right now? If you still have a strong concern or objection, it's important to bring it up now, and we can address it before we move on."*

- If there are no other objections at this time, move to the final question. *"Are these agreements good enough for right now so that you can support them and use them during our time together? I will ask each of you to say, 'Yes' or 'No.'"*

7. When everyone has said, "Yes," including you, you may want to suggest that everyone initial the group agreements that you have made.

8. Ask for a volunteer who is willing to rewrite the group agreements in large, clear print so that you can post them in the classroom.

Take a few minutes at the end of every week to revisit your agreements. Here are some questions you might ask:

- What have you noticed that indicates that we are keeping most of our agreements?

- Have you noticed anything that indicates that we are not keeping some of our agreements?

- Which ones are hardest for the group as a whole to keep? What can we do to help everyone get better at keeping this agreement?

- Is there anything at this time that you want to add, delete, or change?

- Would anyone like to share how these agreements have made this class a different experience for you?

> **Agreements**
>
> • The practice of making classroom agreements is carried out on two levels: general guidelines for how students work together, learn together, and treat each other and more specific guidelines for how to engage in a specific learning experience. General group guidelines involve all students in envisioning the kind of classroom in which students feel safe, respected, cared for, and motivated to learn.

will keep the work group has done "alive"

PRACTICE 4

Build a Cohesive Community of Learners

When Is a Group Not a Community of Learners?

Two school visits in the last year brought the issues of community and group identity to my attention, front and center. I was working with a charter school that structured their academic program so that no teacher had more than fifteen students per class. I observed a math class of twelve students for several class periods during the same week. I walked into the room thinking, "What a great opportunity to build a supportive environment for kids who have struggled with math in the past. Kids can get lots of individual attention and the group's small enough to get them juiced up to tackle problems together and experience the support that everyone can "get it" and the satisfaction that everyone "got it"."

What I saw did not match my hopes. The same routine happened during every visit. The teacher posted the math assignment for the day, gave clear "how-to" instructions using a model problem, and proceeded to check in with students who wanted help for the rest of the period. About half the group managed to focus on their assignments most of the time, while the other half found more interesting things to do. Nothing seriously awful happened while I was in there; in fact, nothing much happened at all. The teacher paid no attention to the group as a group, and consequently couldn't use the power of the group to ignite the classroom and make things come alive. From course to course, I observed the same phenomenon—students at their seats slogging through lessons alone, except for the teacher's one-to-one interactions with individuals. This picture paints the extreme version of absence of community and missed opportunity.

In fact, another set of observations raised more interesting and subtle questions about the differences between teaching individuals and teaching to the group. The first thing I notice in Ms. Johnson's art class are the instructions for solving a design problem, written as a giant invitation to her students. They have a number of options for how to go about this project; this is a class where kids have a lot of latitude to pursue what interests them and express themselves creatively. Most students focus immediately, get their materials, and begin to work. It's clear that everyone knows the routine and knows that Ms. Johnson will check in with each of them personally during the period. She begins a series of animated one-to-one conversations, asking questions, making observations, and providing encouragement as she moves around the room. This undivided attention goes a long way toward building positive relationships between the teacher and each student.

As students work independently, one notices an impressive degree of self-discipline and motivation. Ms. Johnson has worked hard to create an atmosphere of focused energy and purpose, pushing each student to think beyond the obvious and experiment with different solutions so they can get the most out of the course and the most out of themselves. But 40 minutes later, when Ms. Johnson wants the whole group to gather in a circle and discuss their work, they fall apart before they even begin. Some students are still working at their tables while others are scraping chairs across the floor mumbling, "Why do we have to do this?" When they begin the discussion, few kids are listening to each other or showing much interest in what's going on. The group doesn't yet have a sense of itself as a learning community; nor are students using the skills they need to function effectively as a group.

Ms. Johnson figures that if students work well individually in her class, they'll get it together as a group. It's a surprise to her when they don't. Her students' sense of self-direction and individual accomplishment is a direct result of the guided instruction, clarity of purpose, and personal feedback that she has provided. By contrast, Ms. Johnson has never given much thought to developing a vision of a community of artists in the classroom or thought much about the kind of deliberate instruction, practice, and coaching that would help her students get good at being a group.

Ms. Johnson's lack of attention around community goals and group skills isn't all that unusual in secondary classrooms. It's easy to assume that high school kids know why and how a classroom of 25 students is different from a space occupied by 25 students in separate cubicles, each working on their own. As teachers, we often hold out the wish that a group will just get better on its own—that over time students will come to know each better, care about each other more, and gradually become more skillful at working together as a whole group. Yet, everything we know about working well as a team or mastering any skill contradicts a laissez faire approach to establishing a sense of community and developing effective group skills in the classroom.

What Are the Benefits of Creating a Learning Community That Supports the Development of a High Functioning Group?

We expect students to respect each other, listen to each other, cooperate with each other, learn from each other, and support each other's efforts. But what do we actually do or say that gives them a clear message that working effectively as a whole group or in small groups really matters? When it comes to working in a group, it's perfectly reasonable for students to want a reasonable answer to their favorite questions: "Why should I?" or "What's in it for me?" or "Why are we doing this?" or the all purpose question honed by years of schooling, "Are we getting a grade for this?"

Our response to kids falls short. From a student's point of view, what's not graded may not have a lot of value. If we assess students only on their performance as individuals, why should they care about the quality of their skills or their contributions as members of a group? Second, even if we do change how we assess student performance, it would be nice to offer students a rationale more compelling than, "You're getting a grade for how you perform as a group."

It's impossible to support students' development of effective group skills if we don't have good reasons for helping students become a group. Here are a dozen reasons that make the case for establishing a more intentional community of learners:

- Students experience a sense of belonging and satisfaction from developing a common vision and making a collective effort to achieve group goals or solve problems successfully. When the bottom line is "sink or swim together" students have a genuine stake in supporting each others' successes.

- Students take greater responsibility for establishing and maintaining positive norms for classroom behavior resulting in fewer disruptions and discipline problems and greater cooperation and collaborative work habits.

- Students get to know each other better. The better they know each other, the more likely they are to work together successfully, acknowledge each other's strengths, and accept each other's limitations.

- A friendly, relaxed atmosphere is a result of a group seeing itself as a group, making it easier for everyone to learn. A state of relaxed alertness promotes high performance; if we're worried about being ridiculed or humiliated, we are less able to focus and concentrate on the learning task at hand.

- Adolescents engage in a social construction of their reality. They learn from interacting with each other, and how they interact with each other will either enhance or diminish the learning experience.

- Teachers and students who become partners in establishing a learning community are less likely to be adversarial and are more likely to maintain positive relationships when kids are experiencing difficulties.

- Students are recognized for their use of effective group skills—skills that might go unrecognized if they only function as individual learners.

- Students experience opportunities where their efforts are appreciated by their peers

- In a group, students practice civic participation skills for living and working in a pluralistic, democratic society—the arts of negotiation, compromise, and consensus; listening to other points of view; and exercising public voice and choice through responsible decision making.

- Students can develop skills to counter and reduce bias, prejudice, and stereotyping within and across groups.

- Navigating and negotiating successfully within a group fosters skills and attitudes that promote effective relationships with family, friends, colleagues, and co-workers.

- Participating in effective group experiences helps students transition from high school to work and post-secondary education, where knowing how to function well in different groups increases opportunity, choices, and options for being successful; in contrast, poor intergroup skills diminish one's life chances for success.

For Students to Use Group Skills Regularly and Effectively, They Need to Learn Them and Practice Them

Learning and mastering any skill, academic or otherwise, requires a sequence of steps that always proceeds along these lines:

- Give me a reason to learn this

  Which is to say that when we're not very clear about why being a skillful group member is important, we're all the less likely to engage students in the rest of the steps, which result in more habitual and competent use of effective group skills.

- Show me how to do it; model it for me
- Let me practice
- Give me feedback on how I'm doing
- Let me practice some more so I can get really good at this and assess how I'm doing on my own
- Let me lead by encouraging and supporting others to use this skill

Sample activities, strategies, and routines:

Introduce Gatherings

Gathering activities set the stage for learning by inviting everyone to participate in a brief common experience. Gatherings usually take about ten minutes. They are a quick and fun strategy to share personal information and perspectives. Through expressing one's own thoughts and hearing from their peers, students strengthen a sense of what I call "group-ness"—a feeling that we are all important and we all have something important to say. Gatherings are a great way to open Monday class and welcome in the new week.

Because gatherings elicit a lot of personal information, teachers get a fuller picture of who their kids are. The informal data gleaned from gatherings can provide direction for future interactions and instructional approaches with individual students.

In any of the activities described, allow students the "right to pass" if they are not comfortable responding to a particular question.

Life Skill Connection	**1. Recognize and name your own feelings** **18. Exercise assertiveness; communicate your thoughts, feelings, and needs to others** **28. Respect everyone's right to learn, to speak, and be heard**
Sample Activities, Strategies, and Routines	• **Opening Go-Rounds and Connection Time** • **Conversation Circles** • **Strong Feelings Pair/Share** • **Feelings Connection** • **"I Like My Neighbors Who..."** • **Pick a Color that Reflects _____?** • **Whip**

Opening Go-Rounds and Connection Time

Opening Go-Rounds give every student a chance to respond to a statement or question. Ask students to sit in an arrangement where they can all see each other. Introduce the Go-Round topic in the form of a statement or question. Students then take turns responding, going around the room. A person always has the right to pass when it's his or her turn to speak. After most students have spoken, you can go back to those who passed to see if they want to say something now.

If you don't feel you have enough time for everyone to speak during one class period, introduce variations of Connection Time where some, but not all, students will get the opportunity to speak.

• Set the timer for five to seven minutes and invite anyone who wants to share to speak to the statement or question; or

• Invite half the group to speak on one day and the other half to speak on the next day; or

• Invite students to speak to the statement or question on the basis of a specific category: everyone who's wearing glasses; everyone who ate breakfast this morning; everyone who's wearing black; girls only or boys only; anyone whose last name end in F through P, etc.; or

• Limit responses to the first 10 students who volunteer.

However you choose to mix it up, be sure that everyone gets a chance to speak at some point during the week.

Topics should be ones that all students can comment on without feeling embarrassed or defensive. Go-Rounds and Connection Time can be purely personal or they can connect to a subject topic, or classroom, school, or community issues. Here are a few examples of each:

Personal

- What's something new and good in your life right now?

- Five years from now, I'd like to hear people say this about me: _____ is a _____.

- What's a wish or hope you have for a friend or someone in your family?

- Yesterday I felt _____, today I feel _____.

- One thing I hated that now I like is _____.

- "What is something you have that you would fight for—even risk your life for—if someone tried to take it away from you? Why is this important to you?" (This can be a material possession or something intangible, like a good reputation.)

Community, School, or Classroom Related

- Share a recent story from the news about someone who made a life-altering choice, and ask students: What would you have done in this situation?

- What is one school-wide rule that you would change that you would think would make school a better place for everyone?

- What's something you would like to learn about or learn how to do that's currently not offered here at school?

- What's something you hope we do again in class; we never do again in class; we might do in class before the course is over?

- If you were a reporter for CNN right now, what story would you want to investigate?

Subject Matter Related

- **Literature:** So far this year, who is the character you've read about with whom you identify the most?

- **Math:** What math skill do you think you'll use the most when you graduate from high school? If you were a geometric figure, what figure would you most like to be? Why?

- **Science:** What chemical element would you most like to be? Why? If you were a scientist, what problem would you most like to explore and solve?

- **Social Studies:** What century would you most like to live in if you were not growing up in the twenty first century?

Conversation Circles

Divide students into two equal size groups. Ask one group to form a circle facing outward. Then ask the other group to form a second circle around that one, facing inward. Each person in the inner circle should be facing a partner in the outer circle. Tell students that they will each have about 45 seconds to share with their partners their responses to a question you will pose. All pairs of partners will speak simultaneously. Identify whether the inside partners or the outside partners will speak first. After the first partner has had a chance to share, signal that the other partner should begin speaking. When both partners have answered the question, ask students to move one, two, or three spaces to the right and pose another question to the group. Have students change partners for each new question.

Sample opening questions:

1. Talk about the neighborhood in which you grew up as a kid. Where was it? What did it look like? What was something you liked about growing up there?

2. What is the best present you've ever received? Why was it special?

3. What do you think makes life hard for kids growing up right now?

4. What do you think are the qualities of a good friend?

5. What's something special that's been passed down in your family (a story, an object, an event or tradition)?

6. Who is the most interesting adult outside your family that you've ever known? Why do you find this person interesting?

7. What is one thing your parents do or say that you don't ever want to do or say?

8. If you become a parent, what is one thing you'd want to teach your children?

9. What troubles you most about the world we live in today?

10. If you could change one thing about your neighborhood or town, what would it be?

Strong Feelings Pair/Share

Invite students to pair up and describe a strong feeling they have experienced in the last week and some reasons for that feeling.

Feelings Connection

This activity helps students link their feelings and behaviors. Ask students to form a circle. Choose a feeling word for the activity such as angry, peaceful, upset, happy, or scared. Begin by completing the sentence, "I feel [feeling word] when..." Use a soft ball or special object to pass to a student who would like to go next and complete the sentence. Ask that student to toss the ball or pass the object to another student. The second student repeats what the first student said, shares their statement and then tosses the object to another student. You can also use, "When I feel... because... it helps me to..."

"I Like My Neighbors Who..."

This activity is a variation on Musical Chairs. Have students arrange their chairs in a circle and sit down. Stand in the center of the circle and complete the sentence "I like my neighbors. I especially like my neighbors who..." (insert any descriptor that some students will also identify with i.e. who like basketball, who are wearing jewelry, who love to sleep late, etc.) All students who identify with the descriptor you've stated should stand up, leave their chairs, and try to move into another empty chair. At the same time you will try to find an empty chair to sit in. Whoever is left standing will complete the sentence, "I like my neighbors. I especially like my neighbors who..." and continue the game.

Pick a Color that Reflects _____?

Cut up a large quantity of 4" x 4" construction paper squares in a wide variety of colors. Be sure to include colors that are light and dark, intense and muted. Ask each student to choose a color or group of colors that reflects:

- how I'm feeling today.
- how I'm feeling about my progress/current project/upcoming exam in this class.
- my perception of conflict (or any other concept you want students to think about).
- the effort I'm putting into this class right now.
- my feelings about the coming week/the weekend.
- my thoughts/feelings about _____.

Either in the large group or in smaller groups of five or six, have students share the colors they chose and why they chose them. (If you split up into smaller groups, come back together at the end and ask a few volunteers to share which colors they chose and why.)

Whip

A whip is a positive, incomplete statement that is completed in turn by each person in a circle. It goes quickly with each person answering in a short phrase. Some possible whips are:

1. Something I'm good at that ends with "-ing"
2. I hate to spend time...
3. If you could trade places for one week with anyone currently living, who would it be?
4. If you could invite two people to have dinner with you and your best friend, who would you choose?
5. One word that describes how I feel today is...

Introduce Closings

Closing activities provide a way to wrap up the time the group has spent together and send off the group at the end of class or the end of the week. Like gatherings, closings create opportunities for every student to be heard. While gatherings focus mostly on sharing personal data, closings provide an excellent vehicle for students to give feedback on what they have experienced in class, communicate what they have learned, and assess their progress and personal development. The quick "read" you get from the group can help shape what you do the next day or guide changes you make to your instructional plan.

Life Skill Connection

18. Exercise assertiveness; communicate your thoughts, feelings, and needs to others

28. Respect everyone's right to learn, to speak, and be heard

Sample Activities, Strategies, and Routines

- **Closing Go-Rounds**
- **Connections**
- **Encouragement Cards**
- **Goodbye/Hello**
- **Checking It Out**

Closing Go-Rounds

Personal

- What's your favorite music to listen to when you want to relax?

- When you feel discouraged, what do you say to yourself to keep going?

- If you could drop two things from your life right now to ease the pressure, what would they be?

- What's the best thing that happened to you this week?

- What's one thing you're looking forward to this weekend?

- What's one thing you could do this weekend that would make someone in your family happy?

Classroom and Subject Related
- In five words or less, what's the most important thing you learned today about yourself, about the group, and about the topic?

- What's a banner headline of five words or less that would best summarize what we did/learned/discussed in class?

- When you have a lot of homework, what strategies do you use to re-focus and get it all done?

- As you think about tackling the homework problems tonight, what's the one thing you want to remember while you're working?

- As you continue reading tonight, what piece of advice would you give (name of character) in the book, _____.

- What's something you've accomplished this week that you're proud of?

For more reflection questions, see page 50.

Connections

If students have just seen a powerful film or listened to a moving story or speech, you might say: "Let's take five minutes for connections. After watching/listening to_____, what thoughts or feelings do you have right now? Anyone can speak who wants to. The only guideline is to speak about your personal reactions from your perspective, rather than responding to someone else's comments or opinions."

Encouragement Cards

Distribute index cards. Ask students to write anonymously one sentence expressing words of encouragement they might offer to other students in the class. Collect the cards and invite different students to read some of the cards at the end of class period.

Goodbye/Hello

Ask students what old habit they would like to say goodbye to and what new habit they would like to try on. Go around with each student completing the blanks in the statement, "Goodbye..., hello..."

Checking It Out

- Review learning goals (what students are learning and how students go about learning it) you set for class, and ask students to offer evidence that, as individuals or the whole group, they met or did not meet the goals for the day.

- If class did not meet your usual performance expectations, invite individual students to share one thing each person can do to make class run more smoothly tomorrow.

- Get a "group read" regarding students' readiness to move on by asking: "Using 1, 5, or 10 fingers indicate where you stand right now."

  - How prepared do you feel to _____?

  - How complete is your understanding of _____?

  - One more review of _____ would be helpful before _____.

Getting a quick read of the group can help you decide whether to proceed with the whole group, divide into different task groups, or pair students up to work together.

Introduce Teambuilding Activities

Whether they take 15 minutes or an extended time period, teambuilding activities help students strengthen the skills of cooperation, communication, leadership, strategic thinking, and problem-solving. A key objective of effective teambuilding activities is that no one wins unless everyone wins.

However much fun these challenges are to do, it is the debriefing and reflection questions afterwards that make these activities important learning experiences. The Recommended Resources at the end of this guide include many teambuilding activity resources.

Life Skill Connection	**27. Cooperate, share, and work toward high performance within a group to achieve group goals**
	33. Exercise effective leadership skills within a group
Sample Activities, Strategies, and Routines	• **"Chocolate River": A Group Challenge**

"Chocolate River": A Group Challenge

1. Explain to students that they are going to participate in a group challenge and then discuss it afterwards.

2. Set two ropes parallel to each other about 25 ft. apart. Divide the group in half, with each group on opposite sides of the ropes like this:

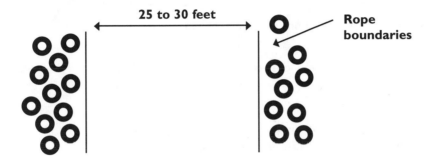

25 to 30 feet

Rope boundaries

3. Give each group cardboard or carpet squares about 12" x 12" in size using this ratio:
   20 students on each side = about 10 squares for each group
   15 students on each side = about 7 or 8 squares for each group
   10 students on each side = about 5 or 6 squares for each group

   Explain to the group, "The space between the ropes is a chocolate river. The problem is that it's boiling hot, so that falling in it would be a disaster. Your goal here is get everyone across the river, from one side to the other. The squares you have are marshmallows; they will float on top of the river, so if you use them to step on, you can get across safely. However, there is a problem. If you fall off a marshmallow or touch the river at any point, you have to go back and start over. And there's one more thing. I'm a monster in the river and I love marshmallows. If I see a marshmallow in the river that no one is standing on, I will snatch it up and eat it. You will have about five minutes to strategize with your group and then you will have about 15 minutes or so to solve the problem."

You might want to suggest three guidelines for this kind of physically active experience: PLAY HARD, PLAY FAIR, PLAY SAFE. Discuss with the group how they think each of these guidelines applies to this particular team challenge.

Let students know that you'll answer three questions before they begin. If anyone asks whether they can talk to the other group, you can say that each group can identify one person to negotiate with the other side. It's likely that both groups will figure out that if they share their resources and work together it will be much easier to get everyone across. Give the group about five minutes to strategize and then give them about 15 minutes to solve the problem.

Note: During the activity, if the groups are having a lot of difficulty listening to each other, or working cooperatively, stop, and ask everyone to freeze. Take three comments from the group, saying: "I'm open to hearing three observations from the group that help describe what's not working." Then say, "I'll take three suggestions from the group of strategies that you think will help you achieve the goal of getting everyone across Chocolate River."

4. Use any of these questions for post-activity discussion:

    • What happened? How did you feel about doing this activity? What did you like or not like?

    • How did your group decide what strategy to use? Was everyone listened to or included in the decision? How do you know?

    • What did you observe about how your group worked together? What did your teammates do or say that helped your team be successful? Is there anything you could have done that would have helped your group to be more effective as a team?

    • How would you describe the role you played? How did it feel to be a leader or a follower? What would you personally do differently next time if you were involved in a similar activity?

    • What learning can you take from this experience that you can apply to our work as a group in the classroom everyday?

5. Close the activity by saying: "We're not born with the skills to work together effectively in a group. We learn these skills by watching other people and practicing them ourselves."

Assessing Cooperation, Group Participation, and Leadership Skills

To work together effectively in groups, whether they be study groups, classrooms, groups of friends, or sports teams, people in the group need to exercise positive leadership, communication, and conflict resolution skills. We need to analyze the barriers to working together well and learn techniques to surmount them. This section includes a variety of tools and strategies for assessing cooperation, group participation, and leadership skills.

Life Skill Connection	**17. Assess your skills, competencies, effort, and quality of work accurately**
Sample Activities, Strategies, and Routines	• **Develop a Participation Assessment Log** • **Assess Positive Group Skills and Behaviors That Get in the Way**

Develop a Participation Assessment Log

Taking cues from agreements, procedures, and expectations that you have already established develop a list of specific behaviors and attitudes that indicate active participation in class. This list might include:

- Raises thoughtful questions that help the class gain a deeper understanding of an issue or topic of discussion.

- Takes a leadership role in carrying out an activity.

- Gives helpful feedback about class activities and experiences.

- Participates in debriefing discussions after an activity is completed.

- Takes on various roles and responsibilities in small-group learning activities.

- Shares personal perspectives with others in small and larger groups.

- Participates in role-plays and demonstrations.

- Helps to set up activities, distribute materials, and clean up.

- Gives words of encouragement to other students.

- Helps create a good humored climate that invites laughter and enjoyment.

- Shows appreciation for other students' contributions.

- Participates in problem solving when issues and concerns arise that affect the group and the class.

- Volunteers when help is needed.

- Shares responsibility within a group.

- Encourages all students within the group to participate.

- Takes a risk to try things that are new and challenging.

- Shows friendliness toward other class members.

- Provides positive energy when the group needs it.

- Takes turns recording and documenting small group work.

- Works effectively with different students.

- Listens to others without interrupting.

- Makes transitions from one activity to another easily.

- Respects other people's personal space and comfort zones.

- Stops and comes to closure when time is up.

- Speaks openly and honestly to make others aware of a problem or concern.

- Disagrees with others in ways that are respectful.

- Acknowledges and accepts other students' ideas.

The participation assessment log sheet can be used for teacher, student, and small group assessment. Make enough copies so you have a copy for each student and each student has a copy to keep in their portfolio.

Teachers can use the participation log sheets to:
- document students' participation grades, checking the behaviors you notice and jotting down observations that give you a snapshot of each student's skills.

- give students personal feedback on their participation skills throughout the course.

- set goals and check in with students to assess how they are meeting chosen goals.

Students can use participation log sheets to:
- assess the strengths that they already bring to class.

- identify skills they find challenging.

- set their own goals for skills they want to improve and use more regularly.

- reflect back on ways that their participation in class has changed and how those changes have affected how they think and feel about the class and their peers.

- write about one way that they have participated in class that has made a positive difference, something they have done or said that has helped make the class a better learning community for everyone.

- assess skills small groups have used effectively in cooperative learning activities.

- identify specific skills that individual students have used in large group activities.

Assess Positive Group Skills and Behaviors That Get in the Way

You can use the following as an assessment for students to identify their behaviors in a group. Before groups start working together, ask each student to fill out the first column on both sides of this sheet, asking themselves how often they engage in each skill set on the front side and each set of behaviors on the back side. Circling 1 means they never use it, 2 means hardly ever, 3 means sometimes, 4 means often, and 5 means they use that approach constantly. After they have completed the survey, have students think about at least one positive skill set they want to use more today. After the groups has finished its other work, ask students to fill out the second column on both sides of this sheet. Before groups disband ask group members to identify one skill set they used well and how their skills helped the group accomplish its task.

HANDOUT I

Assess Positive Group Skills and Behaviors That Get in the Way

Positive Leadership, Communication, and Conflict Resolution Skills	Until now, I've used this skill Never • Constantly	In this group, I used this skill Never • Constantly
Initiating/problem-solving: proposing ideas, experimenting, sharing feelings and observations, assertively and gently confronting disruptive behavior	1 2 3 4 5	1 2 3 4 5
Organizing/coordinating: keeping the group on track, focusing on goals, suggesting timelines, proposing fair divisions of labor	1 2 3 4 5	1 2 3 4 5
Seeking: identifying information and resources, researching, reading, asking related questions	1 2 3 4 5	1 2 3 4 5
Encouraging: encouraging everyone's participation, praising efforts and valuable contributions	1 2 3 4 5	1 2 3 4 5
Harmonizing: checking on feelings, helping find common ground, suggesting ways to work better together	1 2 3 4 5	1 2 3 4 5
Clarifying/summarizing: clearing up confusion, checking to see if you understood somebody, pulling together different ideas, suggesting conclusions	1 2 3 4 5	1 2 3 4 5

Behaviors that Get in the Way of Effective Group Functioning	Until now, I've used this approach Never • Constantly	In this group, I used this approach Never • Constantly
Dominating: telling people what to do, insulting or making fun of people and their ideas, doing too much of the talking, excluding other group members from participating, hogging the spotlight, claiming too much of the credit	1 2 3 4 5	1 2 3 4 5
Withholding: not participating, not speaking up, holding back ideas, not doing a fair share of the work	1 2 3 4 5	1 2 3 4 5
Distracting: talking about other topics, fidgeting to get attention, telling unrelated jokes	1 2 3 4 5	1 2 3 4 5
Blocking: disagreeing without listening, proclaiming the "right" and only way to do things, stubbornly refusing to budge on minor issues	1 2 3 4 5	1 2 3 4 5
Doom and Glooming: predicting that the group will fail no matter what, focusing on how bad the project is, discouraging people from trying	1 2 3 4 5	1 2 3 4 5

Group process questions for individual reflection, journaling, and/or group discussion

- Which of the positive skills do you find come easiest for you? Which do you find the most difficult or uncomfortable? How could you strengthen these abilities?

- What positive skills did you see other group members using? Please tell them you noticed.

- When you found yourself doing things which get in the way of effective group functioning, what were you feeling? How could you express those feelings in more positive ways? When you're feeling this, what could you do to help yourself? What might you want other members of your group to say or do that might help you, and the group, get back on track? How might you ask for this kind of help?

Group Feedback

Ask each group to record their responses to any of these questions:

1. Name one way each person in your group participated and/or contributed?

2. Name three specific positive behaviors you noticed that helped you meet your goal and complete the task.

3. What situations, actions, or statements made it more difficult for the group to work together effectively and how did the group handle these challenges?

4. How could you have worked together to be more effective? What positive leadership, communication and conflict resolution skills could you practice to improve the way you work together in the future?

Developed by Rachel Poliner and Sam Diener.

Form Home Groups

You may want to consider forming home groups in your classes. Home groups are usually composed of four students and last throughout the year. They provide a structure and safe place for students to support and work with each other during "the long haul." Wait a few weeks to do this, so that you know a little bit about how different students learn and students know a little bit about each other. Home groups are helpful when students need to discuss problems that arise in class and provide a structured forum for dealing with school-wide issues or community concerns that affect your students.

Life Skill Connection	**25. Develop, manage, and maintain healthy peer relationships**
Sample Activities, Strategies, and Routines	• **Ways to Use Home Groups** • **Options for Forming Home Groups**

Ways to Use Home Groups

- Share learning goals with group members and support each other to meet them.

- Hold weekly check-ins about how things are going with each person in the group.

- Disseminate information and address maintenance and housekeeping issues.

- Share feelings and reactions when a sad event or crisis impacts the school community, before discussing the situation with the whole class.

- Reflect and share what they have learned in a particular activity.

- Apply what you have learned using the group's understanding of a particular topic, problem, or concept.

- Rotate responsibility for explaining assignments to, and reserving sets of assignment materials for, the students in your group who are absent.

- Brainstorm a list of questions and topics that your group wants to address before a major test, exam, or performance assessment.

- Review and study together in order to prepare for a test or exam.

- Support each person in the group to meet a certain level of mastery of a particular skill.

- Correct quizzes, problems, and tests.

- Review homework in preparation for a discussion.

- Have students take responsibility for a particular question to discuss, a topic to investigate, or problem to solve, and have them share what they have learned with the rest of the class.

- Give feedback to each other after they have practiced specific communication, cooperation, and problem-solving skills.

- Create home group team competitions using Jeopardy, Trivial Pursuit, or other game show formats.

Options for Forming Home Groups:

Students Choose Home Groups Within the Limits You Set:

Assign students to one of four colors that each reflects a different group in your class. Students form groups of four by choosing one person from each color group. For example: Red could represent students who are academically able, quiet, reflective; Yellow could be students who are academically able, verbal, highly social; Green could be students who are more academically challenged, verbal, highly social; Blue could be students who are more academically challenged, quiet, reflective. You might also assign equal numbers of boys and girls to each color so students know that they need to form mixed gender groups. This process ensures that each home group includes students with a diverse range of abilities and attributes. Grouping this way also helps avoid having groups that include two students who really clash with each other. If these clashing students receive squares of the same color they won't be able to be in the same home group.

Directions:

Cut up paper squares using the four colors you have selected. For example, if you have 24 students, cut up six squares each of the four colors. Write each student's name on the assigned color square.

The day before students choose their home groups, share some of your hopes and expectations for home groups so that students can consider this information when they make their choices.

On the day that students choose their groups, pass out the color squares to every student. Tell them that they need to form groups that include one person from each color group. Give students about ten minutes to choose and then ask each group to fill out their Home Group Information card. Collect sheets and make copies so that each student has a copy of their Home Group information.

You Choose:

You assign students to home groups, balancing diverse abilities and personalities in each group. The limitation of this option is that students have no choice in forming their groups.

Students Choose:

Students choose their own home groups. The limitation of this option is that students' skills, abilities, strengths, and weaknesses may vary dramatically from home group to home group and each group may have less diversity than you would like.

After the home groups have been formed, have them each fill out a Home Group Information card with the information for the group. Have each group also make a card for you.

Home Group Information

Your Home Group Members
• Name, Color, Phone #, Birthday

• Name, Color, Phone #, Birthday

• Name, Color, Phone #, Birthday

• Name, Color, Phone #, Birthday

Person in charge of assignments and homework (Rotate this role every week.)

Week of _____   Name _____

Week of _____   Name _____

Week of _____   Name _____

Week of _____   Name _____

Create Routines and Rituals That Involve Every Student

A feeling of belonging emerges in part from shared expectations and experiences. Everybody gives and everybody gets. Sometimes, we start relying on volunteers and giving students the option of opting out too early into their adolescence. Inadvertently, this can create a classroom culture where students take on permanent roles of "doers" or "slackers." Try out some of ideas below that communicate to students, "We're all in this together."

Life Skill Connection	**30. Engage in conscious acts of respect, caring, helpfulness, kindness, courtesy, and consideration**
Sample Activities, Strategies, and Routines	• **Sample Routines and Rituals That Involve Everyone**

Sample Routines and Rituals That Involve Everyone

1. Everybody has a birthday. Announce and congratulate students on their special day.

2. Do three minute check-in's with every student on a rotating basis. Students can assess how they're doing and ask questions, and you can give feedback and review students' progress. When check-in's with every student are routine, it becomes less intimidating for struggling students to seek you out when they're experiencing difficulty. Think about doing personal check-in's during the first ten minutes of class, when students are involved in independent learning tasks, when students are involved in sustained cooperative learning activities, or when students are starting on their homework.

3. Keep a stock of cards at school that you can use for different occasions. When a student is ill for an extended period of time, when a student has a suffered a death in the family, even when a student is suspended for an extended period, send a card home that every student has signed that says, "We're thinking of you, we're pulling for you, we hope you're okay."

4. If you generate math or science problems, case studies, or "what if" situations as part of your course work, use every student's name in the scenarios you write up. Just remember to keep problems light and neutral—no personal situations that would feel embarrassing to anyone.

5. Every teacher can use extra hands in the classroom—setting up labs, distributing and collecting materials, helping out with special equipment, making sure the room is neat at the end of the period, etc. Make this an expectation by identifying one person who serves in this role each week. Rather than creating an alphabetical rotation, make it truly random by putting everyone's name in a container and asking a student to pick out a name each week.

6. Depending upon what your school-wide food rules are, when kids eat lunch, and when a class meets, you might want to offer a snack option. If everyone pays a buck, you're willing to keep a snack supply in the classroom, but here's the deal. Everyone contributes a dollar or it doesn't happen. And if students like the idea, let them collect the money and go to the wholesale food store to buy the snacks. When you run out of snacks, students can decide if they want to do it again.

7. Ask each student to contribute a thought or story for the week. If you make this a weekly routine, every student will have a turn before the year is out. Keep books around that students can draw from: *Chicken Soup for the Teen-age Soul*, *Seven Habits for Highly Effective Teens*, *Golden Nuggets*, books of quotations and meditations for young people, etc. This kind of activity does triple duty: Every student chooses something to share with the whole group; every student plays the roles of both speaker and audience; every week you've created an opportunity for quiet listening and reflection.

Recognize and Celebrate the Group's Efforts and Accomplishments

A group starts to become a group when everybody in the group got it, did it, enjoyed it, or endured it! The more you acknowledge what the class has accomplished together, the more students will see themselves as members of a team where everyone belongs.

For the following activities, the word "group" really does mean every student in the class. These activities support high academic and behavioral expectations for all kids, not just some of them.

| *Life Skill Connection* | **29. Encourage and appreciate the contribution of others** |

| *Sample Activities, Strategies, and Routines* | • **Congratulations!**
 • **Create a 100% Club** |

Congratulations!

When every student has completed a project, performed satisfactorily on an assessment, or worked as a team to accomplish something as a whole group—do something special to acknowledge how much you appreciate their efforts. You might consider:

1. Composing a written "Thank you" that you read to the group and post on the class's bulletin board space.

2. Posting a giant "Congratulations" sign when every student in the class has endured and successfully completed a particularly challenging learning unit, task, or assignment.

3. Naming or eliciting from students the qualities and skills the group used to accomplish a task successfully.

4. Passing out colored ball-point pens that you buy in bulk at most office supply stores. You can buy 30 for about four bucks.

5. Declaring a "no-homework" night.

6. Giving everyone "bonus points" toward their quarter grade.

Create a 100% Club

This is a strategy that can be particularly helpful in high schools or classes where students have a tougher time conforming to expected behavioral norms, and where teachers need to be more ... creating structures that encourage more cooperative and self-disciplined behaviors ... nts in the class. The goal is to identify, recognize, and record occasions when all ... he class have met a specific expectation. This is a sample list that one high school ... developed:

- Everyone arrived on time to class.

- Everyone settled in and got to work on the activity with no prompting.

- Everyone focused on completing the task for the entire time allotted.

- Everyone completed the homework assignment on time and satisfactorily.

- Everyone brought all necessary materials to class.

- Everyone contributed to tidying up the room so that it was clean and neat at the end of the period.

- Everyone helped, supported, and encouraged their peers to participate positively in a group activity and complete the task successfully.

- Everyone earned at least a (C) (B) on the test, quiz, or assignment.

- Everyone contributed to a productive discussion by sharing ideas, asking related questions, restating and summarizing key ideas, and seeking and offering more information and evidence.

- Everyone exhibited good listening and observation skills during the presentation/lecture/demonstration.

- No one used abusive, profane, or negative language during the class period.

- No one interrupted the person currently speaking at any time during the class period.

Keeping a tally sheet where you record when the whole class "did it" serves a number of purposes:

- From week to week the class can review and assess how they are doing as a group and set goals for the next week.

- Recording the data shows graphically where the group is succeeding and where the group needs to improve. The data also provides the opportunity for students to discuss what is not working and take responsibility for generating ideas that will help them succeed.

- The 100% Club can also serve as a cooperative/competitive activity that involves all of your classes. For example, when every class you teach has earned 100 points, consider doing something fun in class that has nothing whatsoever to do with your course. Or you might create a competition among your classes to see which class earns 100 points first. The class that earns the first 100 points gets to choose something special they want to do in class. Then the slate is wiped clean and all the classes begin accumulating points for the next round.

Recognize Individual Accomplishments In and Out of the Classroom

Recognizing individual accomplishments is as important as recognizing whole group successes. Our competitive "I win, you lose" culture doesn't always support taking pleasure in the accomplishments of others. Create opportunities that encourage students to appreciate the efforts of their peers.

In addition, we don't often recognize students' talents and competencies if they don't show up in the classroom. When you acknowledge that students do important things in their lives outside of school, you have the power to help students broaden their definitions of success and excellence, as well as breakdown stereotypical views of their classmates. Every time a student says to herself, "Wow, I didn't know that about _____. That's awesome!," something good has happened in your classroom.

Life Skill Connection	**29. Encourage and appreciate the contribution of others**
Sample Activities, Strategies, and Routines	• **Give a Big Hand for...** • **Wall of Fame** • **Did You Know?** • **Appreciations** • **Stick With It**

Give a Big Hand for...

Every week or so, invite students to recognize accomplishments of their peers in class. Invite the group to recognize three or four students and then give all of them a big hand. To make this feel less awkward, you may want to ask some of your best "informers"—who know everything about everyone—to start it up the first time you do it. Use a simple formulaic statement at first to make this easy:

_____, _____ showed a lot of _____ when s/he _____.
  (when)   (name of student)   (quality)   (accomplishment)

Wall of Fame

If you have a bulletin board space for each class, or for all of your classes together, encourage students to post articles, pictures, performance programs, announcements, etc. that recognize what students are doing in and out of school. If you find out about interesting activities your students are involved in, make a small certificate on your computer that you can post. Here's a sample:

Did You Know?

I have never met a kid who didn't perk up when you ask them to talk about their unusual experiences or special knowledge. When you have opportunities to link what students are learning to real world situations and contemporary culture, invite students to share their unique perspectives by saying, "We have a resident expert on _____. What can you tell us about _____?"

Appreciations

Set the timer for three minutes. Tell the students they have the opportunity to say something they appreciated about the class today, about the group, or about individual's contributions. Model by speaking first, then invite anyone who wishes to speak to do so.

Stick With It

Use "sticky notes" to communicate with individual students when you notice that they did something in class that was particularly skillful, responsible, helpful, considerate, etc. In your note be sure to link the specific intellectual, social, or emotional quality that was reflected in the act or behavior you witnessed.

Teach Win-Win Basics

Most of us carry around the myth that conflict is always a contest where one person wins and the other person loses. In fact, many problems can be resolved using a Win-Win process (where both parties are satisfied with the outcome) and nearly all conflicts can be approached from a Win-Win perspective. If believing in the possibility of Win-Win becomes a routine way of thinking, we are more likely to participate in a problem solving process that results in a Win-Win solution.

Life Skill Connection	**24. Use Win-Win problem solving to negotiate satisfactory resolutions to conflicts that meet important goals and interests of people involved.**
Sample Activities, Strategies, and Routines	• **"Kisses"**

"Kisses"

1. Begin the activity by explaining to participants:

    "We're going to play a game now. The name of the game is called "Kisses" because the object of the game is to acquire as many Hershey's Kisses as you can. We need two volunteers to come sit at this table. Each volunteer will represent one half of the larger group."

    Identify two volunteers who are approximately the same size, and share the same handedness. Then identify the half of the group that each volunteer is representing. Position volunteers so that they are facing each other across the table, their right or left elbows are on the table, and they are clasping each others' hands. This is an arm wrestling position but DO NOT use the term. If someone says that this looks like arm wrestling, explain that it's similar, but the rules are different.

2. Continue the instructions:

    The object of the game is for each person to get as many chocolate "Kisses" as possible for their teams in the time allowed. The rules are as follows:

    • From now on the two players may not speak to each other.

    • Every time you get the back of the other person's hand on the table, you will receive a chocolate "Kiss" for your team.

    • Someone from each team needs to keep track of the number of "Kisses" your team receives.

• You will have 30 seconds to get as many "Kisses" as you can.

Note: You can also call the game, "Points" if you don't have or don't want to use Hershey's "Kisses".

3. Say, "Begin", and say "Stop" after 30 seconds. Participants will probably compete against each other and will probably only get a few "Kisses" or none. Discuss what happened.

"What did you see? How many "Kisses" did each team receive?" If the players received very few "Kisses," ask, "What was the goal of the game?"

Ask participants if they can think of another way to play the game so teams can get more "Kisses." (Usually groups will suggest ways that the two students can alternate placing the back of the person's hand on the table.)

4. After the group offers suggestions, play one more 30 second round and ask participants to describe what was different when they played the game the second time. You might also want to ask:

"What words describe the approach you used this time?"

"How do these two approaches to the game reflect ways that you handle conflict?"

Teach the Concept of Win-Win

5. Explain that the game illustrates that conflict doesn't always have to be a Win-Lose contest:

"In a highly competitive society, it's easy to assume that 'For me to get what I want and need, I have to win and you have to lose.' This approach is called Win-Lose. (You might invite students to explore these questions: Think about the society in which you live. Why does Win-Lose thinking have such a powerful hold on people? In what aspects of your life do you experience the strongest Win-Lose messages? Does high school reinforce a Win-Lose approach to problems or life in general?)

Sometimes neither person will get what he or she wants, in which case the result is called Lose-Lose.

AND, like in the game, it's also possible that both people can get what they want or need in the situation. This result is called Win-Win.

The Win-Win approach to working out problems is the one that we will practice here in the classroom. I'd like our first take on classroom problems to be one where we try and seek a solution that works for everyone involved. A Win-Win solution is a solution that is non-violent, meets some important needs of all parties involved, and helps us to maintain positive relationships. We will use this process when we negotiate how and when to do things in class. I also expect students who have a problem with each other to use this process, and we will use it when a student and I are involved in a problem-solving conference around a behavioral or academic situation that needs to be resolved."

Create Opportunities for Negotiated Learning

Negotiated learning is about the "give and take" of classroom life with adolescents. It doesn't mean that teachers relinquish authority or stop teaching the standard curriculum. It does mean that where and when it is appropriate, teachers and students engage in shared decision making and problem solving in all aspects of classroom life.

We know issues around respect, authority, and arbitrary demands cause the most tension in secondary classrooms. And it's true that a significant percentage of adolescents will go along with the program, accommodating each teacher's style, standards, rules, and curriculum without complaint or confrontation. Yet, for lots of other students, disengagement and resentment begin on the first day of school, when teachers lay out "how it's going to be" for the rest of the year with little room for student input and even less room for flexibility.

A key aspect of negotiated learning is shifting orientation from My Classroom to Our Classroom and Your or My Problem to Our Problem. When students are involved in decision making they become more accountable for their own behavior. As you provide more opportunities and support for making decisions, both you and the students reap the benefits of a more productive learning environment. Ultimately, a teacher's role is not to decide things for young people, but to help them see that they have lots of possibilities as they develop the capacity to make good choices throughout their lives.

Life Skill Connection	**24. Use Win-Win problem solving to negotiate satisfactory resolutions to conflicts that meet important goals and interests of people involved**
Sample Activities, Strategies, and Routines	• **Guidelines for Negotiated Learning** • **Ten Ways to Negotiate in the Classroom**

Guidelines for Negotiated Learning

1. There is rarely just one way to do things in the classroom. Negotiated classrooms offer lots of choices and opportunities for shared decision making. Teachers who negotiate are willing to let go of preconceived blueprints and are committed to exploring alternatives that meet important goals and common interests.

2. Most classroom conflicts and disagreements can be handled through problem solving rather than punishment. The disciplinary focus is on how to keep agreements and change undesirable behaviors, rather than on who is breaking the rule.

3. Teachers and students seem to feel better about themselves and each other when everyone is clear about boundaries—identifying what's negotiable and what's not, what's on the "not okay" list for teachers and students, and what special needs, constraints, or criteria must be considered as you negotiate together.

4. Shared decision making means sharing the responsibility—students are expected to take a more active role in their own learning and in the day-to-day functioning of class.

5. Negotiated learning works best in a climate where people are reassured that mistakes are part of the process, that nothing will ever be perfect, and where "good enough" is sometimes enough.

6. Student and teacher assessments, informal check-ins, and discussions about how things are working are essential features of the negotiation process.

7. Teach the language of Win-Win (page 102).

8. Use the A, B, C, D, E problem solving procedure for group negotiations (page 108).

9. Keep these negotiation guidelines in mind:

   • Negotiation is a voluntary process; you can't coerce anyone to negotiate

   • Create a positive climate

   • Clarify positions (what someone demands—it's the only way to get what you want) and interests (underlying needs and concerns—the "whys" behind the position)

   • Identify your goals (short-term and long-term) that satisfy mutual interests

   • Be willing to seek alternative solutions that are different from original positions

   • Develop criteria for a good solution that will meet some important interests of everyone involved

   • Be respectful of value differences—you can't change people's values, but you can change people's behavior

Ten Ways to Negotiate in the Classroom

1. Prioritize and negotiate the topics of study in a particular learning unit, knowing that it's impossible to study every topic you'd like to investigate. Or offer a "my turn, your turn" approach—"I choose one story, novel, topic, or issue and you choose one."

2. When you are required to teach required material that students find exceptionally boring and tedious, negotiate how you will all get through learning it. For example, you could explore how the group wants to attack it—a small dose everyday or an intense marathon.

3. Make class decisions about the sequence of learning units—in many cases, the arbitrary order of curriculum units is just that.

4. Negotiate the number of pages of texts or novels students agree to read per week.

5. Negotiate learning contracts with individual students.

6. Invite students to negotiate a package of review activities before a test or exam.

7. Negotiate test and project deadline days as you and students consider other events and due dates in the next week or so.

8. Negotiate how to use limited resources and equipment in class.

9. Negotiate procedures for how things are done in class. Develop classroom solutions for the mundane problems of classroom life. Example: when students don't have pencils and all materials needed for class

10. After the first quarter, discuss the learning strategies that students found most and least helpful, interesting, and engaging. Negotiate what you will do more of and less of for the next quarter.

Use Class Meetings to Support and Maintain a High Functioning Group

The class meeting is the support structure for the learning community that you and your students create. It's the vehicle for dealing with all things that affect how the group functions. Several features set class meeting apart from other learning structures:

1. Students take primary responsibility for generating the agenda and facilitating activities for class meeting.

2. Students are expected to practice effective communication and problem solving skills as participants and facilitators.

3. Students play a primary role in solving problems and making decisions about issues addressed in class meeting.

Class meeting serves many purposes. One of the most important is creating a special time and space to confront and solve problems that impact the group—whether it's too much noise during work periods, issues around name calling and teasing, or problems with meeting deadlines.

Equally important, however, are class meetings that provide opportunities for students to do things that strengthen their desire and capacity to be a high functioning group.

Life Skill Connection

34. **"Read" dynamics in a group; assess group skills accurately; identify problems; generate, evaluate, and implement informed solutions that meet the needs of the group**
35. **Use a variety of strategies to make decisions democratically**

Sample Activities, Strategies, and Routines

- **Setting the Stage for Class Meetings**
- **Class Meeting Types**
- **Suggested Procedure for Problem-Solving Meetings**
- **Bringing Issues of Concern to a Larger Audience**
- **Help Students Represent Their Ideas Effectively**

Setting the Stage for Class Meetings

- Develop specific, positive guidelines for facilitating and participating in class meeting.

- Meet in a circle or square where everyone can see everyone else.

- Create an agenda that becomes a routine.

- Review the agenda and identify the purpose and specific goals of the meeting.

- Facilitate the meeting (see the seven activity meeting types described below).

- Solicit feedback about the meeting before you close.

- Invite students to take various roles as they become more comfortable: class meeting facilitator, summarizer, note taker, time keeper, feedbacker, activity leader, etc.

Class Meeting Types

1. **Dialogue:** The goal of this meeting is to provide a safe space to raise concerns, share feelings and perspectives, and gain deeper understanding of issues and concerns raised by students or the teacher.

2. **Problem-Solving:** The goal of this meeting is to use negotiation and problem-solving strategies to make decisions and resolve issues of concern and interest that affect the group and the learning environment.

3. **Hypothetical Discussions:** The goal of this activity is to discuss hypothetical situations or case studies as a way to anticipate and generate solutions to problems before they happen. ("If this happens, then _____.")

4. **Skill Building:** The goal of this meeting is to learn or revisit essential communication, conflict resolution, and problem-solving skills that are necessary for effective group functioning.

5. **Group Maintenance:** The goal of this meeting is to provide maintenance and support for the group. These meetings usually involve group goal setting, check-in's, assessment, planning, and celebrations.

6. **School Citizenship:** The goals of this meeting are to: gather, disseminate, and share information about school-wide rules, policies, events, and projects; participate in specific tasks related to official school business and stewardship; and participate in specific tasks that promote school spirit and a positive school climate.

7. **Crisis Meetings:** The goal of this meeting is to address situations that require immediate intervention and attention in a serious, sensitive, and supportive way. Crisis meetings are an important vehicle for reducing tension, restoring order, dealing with a critical concern, or providing caring and support for students impacted by a crisis.

Suggested Procedure for Problem-Solving Meetings

Although you want to communicate your expectation that students will become comfortable facilitating class meetings over time, you will probably want to model this procedure two or three times in the beginning of the course. To make good on this commitment to involve students, you may want to invite three or four volunteers who are interested in facilitating meetings to be part of a class meeting planning group. This communicates that you and your students are partners in class meetings from the beginning; it gives a small group the tasks of reviewing, deciding, and planning agendas; and it allows students to be part of a process that will prepare them to facilitate meetings effectively.

An A, B, C, D, E procedure is used here that is similar to other problem solving protocols in this guide. The teacher, a teacher and student together, or two students can facilitate the problem solving process.

- After you bring the class together, the facilitator reviews the agenda and identifies the purpose of the class meeting.

Assess the situation and Ask, What's the Problem?
- Invite two or three people (teacher and students) to describe how they see the problem and why they think it's a problem.

- Ask the class if they have other thoughts about the problem—how they feel about the situation, what's not working, why it's important to solve the problem, etc. Remind students that this is not a time to point fingers, scapegoat, or criticize individuals. The task is to stay focused on the problem and problem behaviors—not attack individuals. Form a clear statement of the problem and the goal for solving the problem. Write this on the board.

  The problem is _____. A good solution will enable us to _____.

Brainstorm Solutions
- Invite the class to brainstorm potential solutions to the problem. Picture what the situation would look like if it were solved. Do this without criticizing or evaluating anything suggested.

Consider Each Choice Carefully
- Review the solutions with the class. How does each choice meet the needs and interests of everyone involved? What are the benefits of each choice? What are the negative constraints and limitations? Is the choice respectful, responsible, and reasonable? Cross out the choices that the group feels are the least effective.

Decide on Your Best Choice and Do It
- Discuss the remaining choices and come to agreement on the best solution. Be mindful that the best choice might include a combination of several possible solutions. Invite students to share their preferred solutions and the reasons for their choices. Encourage as many students as possible to speak, even if their comments are in agreement with others who have already spoken. This is the way you begin to get a good "read" on the direction the groups seems to want to go.

- Summarize the comments and state what the group seems to think are the most important things to incorporate in the best choice. Use any of the following decision making protocols to reach final agreement. As much as possible during this process, let the students be in charge. The more they feel like the owners of the solution, the more likely it is to work.

- **Reaching Consensus:** Propose the solution that looks like the people's choice. Say, "This looks like the solution that has the most agreement. If there's anyone who has serious objections, this is the time to speak up and tell us what changes would make this work for you." Solicit any other changes or edits until it looks like you have got the agreement of the group. Do a final consensus check by asking students to raise a hand if they fully support it as the best solution; put one thumb up if it's good enough for now; or thumb in the middle if they're not crazy about it but can live with it.

- **Straw Poll:** If the group has narrowed the field to two or three final ideas, ask people to vote for their #1 preference. If there is a clear winner, modify it until the solution works for everyone.

- **Prioritize Ideas:** If the solution involves a set of recommendations, give each student three sticker dots to place on the three ideas they like the best. The ideas with the greatest number of sticker dots become the highest priority to implement.

- **Small Group Proposal:** If all of the information feels unwieldy—if there are oppositional solutions with strong support—ask for a few volunteers to consider all of the data and perspectives and make a proposal to the group.

Have the class or a small group plan precisely how the solution will be implemented. The class should also be able to suggest ways to evaluate how effectively the solution achieves the goal for solving the problem.

Evaluate Your Choice After You Have Implemented It
- At a later class meeting, or as a gathering or closing, evaluate the decision the group made. What happened? Did it work? What evidence do you have that it worked effectively? Is there anything that would help the group implement the solution more effectively?

Bringing Issues of Concern to a Larger Audience

Sometimes issues come up that students would like to take to a larger audience. I have worked with hundreds of students who have used the following process successfully to prepare their case and present it to faculty associations, student-faculty forums, school leadership teams, parent groups, and student government.

Presentation Steps
1. Identify the problem and the desired goal or outcome. Share five examples (without naming names) that illustrate the problem so other students and adults will understand your perspective. If the problem is solved, what would be different? Example: Problem: Students are suspended unfairly. Desired Goal/Outcome: Rules for suspension are fair and clear to everyone and apply to all students the same way.

2. Why is this a problem? How does it affect students and staff? How does it make people feel? How does this problem get in the way of learning, being successful at school, or feeling positive about school? Offer time for questions from the audience.

3. Develop four or five detailed suggestions that would help the school solve the problem. Make sure your solutions meet the Five R criteria. Is the solution Related to the problem? Respectful to all students and adults involved? Responsible so that everyone involved agrees to something constructive to make it work? Reasonable so that you are not asking anyone to do anything hurtful, illegal, unethical, silly, or offensive? Realistic so you have the time, resources, information, and expertise to make it happen? Offer time for questions from the audience.

4. Name three action steps that need to happen in order to implement your suggestions.

Help Students Represent Their Ideas Effectively

Use the following questions to help your students begin to consider the factors in writing a persuasive speech and defending their ideas. You can use these as a basis for a handout, or read them aloud for them to consider.

1. Do you have an opener (a compelling story, incident, quote that sets the context and personalizes the problem so that the audience understands how this issue affects real people)?

2. Do you define and describe the problem clearly in ways that illuminate the conflict, identify what's not working, or describe what needs are not being met?

3. Have you given the audience the facts (specific examples, data, statistics, comparisons, illustrations, anecdotes, etc. that connect conditions and situations to real individuals and groups)?

4. Have you told the audience why "doing something" is important? What might happen if nothing is done? How does this problem affect the community, the nation, the world?

5. Have you shared suggestions for solutions? Do you compare this solution to other possible solutions? Why is this a better idea? What needs to be done? What is the plan? Who will make it happen? How much will it cost? Where will the money come from?

6. Have you made an appeal to your audience? What do you want your audience to think about, reconsider, or do after they listen to your speech?

Make Group Talk, Good Talk

In a discussion with young people from Maine East High School outside of Chicago, I posed the question, "What goes on in your classes that makes you feel safe, respected, and encouraged to learn and be yourselves? Repeatedly, students identified Socratic seminar (dialogue) as the one thing that dramatically changed how they felt about their course work and their classmates. Students shared that for the first time a teacher actually taught them the skills for how to talk and listen to each other respectfully so they could learn from each other. These students said they loved Socratic dialogue because "we drive the discussion, not the teacher. We get to talk about our own opinions and experiences as we talk about a book. We really get to know each other because we sit around a table—everyone is part of it. And the whole point is to understand everyone's point of view." What was most revealing in this conversation was students' acute awareness that it was the consistent practice of dialogue around serious topics that gave them the space to be honest without being sarcastic, to be curious without being arrogant, and to be reflective rather than reactive.

> **Keys for Effective Group Problem Solving**
>
> • Explore different points of view and make sure there is room for respectful disagreement.

This section describes many structures, tools, and strategies that can help make group talk, good talk. My colleague, Rachel Poliner, co-author of *Dialogue: Turning Controversy into Community* (ESR, 1997) suggests three principles that help students engage in meaningful dialogue. First, the purpose of dialogue is about learning, not about winning debate points. Second, dialogue is about the invitation to speak in order to share ideas rather than defend a position and the patience to listen for understanding, rather than to rebut what another person says. Real practice helps students go beyond surface issues to deeper levels of meaning, assumptions, and underlying concerns. Finally, Rachel points out that a primary focus of dialogue is building constructive relationships, rather than polarizing people.

Students seem to improve their listening and speaking skills when:

1. Adults set aside time to listen to students in a serious way on a regular basis.
2. Teachers let students know ahead of time that listening and speaking for understanding is a vital part of a particular activity.
3. Teachers give students enough time to engage in rich and complex conversations.
4. Teachers encourage students to ask questions intended to seek more information, clarification, and understanding and teachers discourage questions intended to provoke or attack the speaker.
5. Both students and teachers monitor their dialogues, giving feedback that can help improve students' conversational skills.

Life Skill Connection

18. Exercise assertiveness; communicate your thoughts, feelings, and needs to others

19. Listen actively to demonstrate to others that they have been understood

22. Empathize; understand and accept another person's feelings, perspectives, point of view

Pair-Share Dialogues

This is a simple technique to get everyone engaged in conversation at the same time. Ideally it is a way to brainstorm, begin discussion on a compelling question, frame a topic or study, exchange first thoughts, or assess what people know.

Directions:
Students pair up in two's facing each other in order to bring their knowledge, opinions, and experiences to the topic at hand. The facilitator frames the issue and invites one person in each pair to speak for one to two minutes in response to the question. Then the other partner speaks for one to two minutes, thus reversing the roles of listener and speaker.

It is important to remind students that when they are in the role of listener, their goal is to focus their complete attention on the speaker and listen in interested silence.

After the pair-share, invite students to share their own thoughts or paraphrase their partner's thoughts as a way to continue discussion.

You might want to use newsprint to record various student responses that reflect a range of ideas and opinions.

Micro Lab

A micro lab is a structured small group experience in which people deepen their understanding of each other's perspective through speaking and listening. This works particularly well when students are sharing personal feelings and experiences as they relate to an issue from the course or from the group. Students who are reticent to speak in a large group find this format a less intimidating way to share their thoughts with others. It isn't really a time for discussion or dialogue. Instead, it's a time for each person to share her or his thoughts and feelings in response to each question. When a person is speaking, the rest of the people in the group should listen only, without interrupting.

Directions:

Divide students into groups of three or four who arrange themselves in small circles. Here are some guidelines for participating in a micro lab. Tell your students:

1. It's okay to pass if you need more time to think or would rather not respond.

2. This is a timed activity and I will let you know when each person's time is up. You will have about 45 seconds. I will say, "Time. It's time for the next person to speak."

3. Please speak from your own experience and point of view.

4. Be aware of your own comfort zone. Share what feels comfortable to share.

5. Keep confidentiality in mind. Can we make an agreement that what we share among ourselves in small groups will stay within the group?

> **Keys for Effective Group Problem Solving**
>
> • Listen and respond to others empathetically.

Ask for a volunteer from each group who is willing to speak first. Have volunteers raise their hands so that you know when all groups are ready to begin.

State the question. Then clarify the question using an example that illustrates various ways students might respond to it. Set your timer for about 45 seconds. Repeat the question and say, "It's time for the first person to speak." When time is up, say, "It's time for the second person to speak." Continue until each student in each group has had a chance to respond to the question.

The first time you use a micro lab, you might want to ask students,
- What was this process like for you?
- What did you notice about how you were listening?
- What did it feel like to be listened to in this way?
- What made this easy or challenging for you?

> **Keys for Effective Group Problem Solving**
>
> • Ask open-ended questions to gain a deeper understanding of various suggestions.

To explore personal issues and perspectives you might use questions suggested for gatherings, closings, and reflections. Here are some examples:
- What are the pros and cons of having a job during the school year?
- What makes you happy on the weekend?
- What do you do that annoys your parents? What do they do that annoys you?
- What do you do when you're sad? Lonely? Bored?

Here are some sample questions for exploring academic content and learning issues:

- **Literature:** In groups of four, each student takes on the role of a character and responds to a series of questions from the perspective of that character.

- **Social Studies:** Create "If... then..." questions about a particular event or period of history and ask students to imagine what would be significantly different.

- **Science:** Discuss social and ethical consequences of environmental policies.

- **Any subject:** Use microlabs as a way to review essay questions, rehearse and prepare for discussions, share project proposals or project findings.

- **Any subject:** Use a microlab before exams where students can share perspectives on what makes exam time stressful; what they do to relax and focus; what kinds of "self-talk" and beliefs about themselves will help them feel confident and prepared.

Paraphrasing Circles

This is a variation of the microlab format. The goal is to use paraphrasing (accurately restating a person's thoughts in one's own words) to ensure that everyone who speaks is understood. Each group of four or five students sits in a circle facing each other. You might want all groups to discuss the same issue or questions, or you can invite groups to choose which two to three questions they want to discuss from a larger list of questions.

In paraphrasing circles, the first student in the group responds to the chosen question without being interrupted. Then the second student paraphrases what the previous student said and checks for accuracy. The first person can correct or clarify the restatement at this time. Then the second student responds to the same question without being interrupted. The third person paraphrases the second person, checks for accuracy, and shares her/his perspective on the question. This process is repeated until everyone has a turn.

You might want to add one more part to each round. Invite one student from each small group to summarize students' perspectives by reporting out to the larger group. Or you might invite one student to record any questions that arise after everyone in the small group has spoken.

Moving Opinion Polls

Moving opinion polls are a way to get students up and moving as they place themselves along a STRONGLY AGREE to STRONGLY DISAGREE continuum according to their opinions about specific statements.

The most powerful aspect of this exercise is the insight, new to many students, that people can disagree without fighting—in fact, people can listen to various points of view respectfully and even rethink their own opinions upon hearing the views of others.

Create a corridor of space in your room, from one end to the other end, that is long enough and wide enough to accommodate your whole class.

Make two large signs and post them on opposite sides of the room:

Strongly Agree	**Strongly Disagree**

Explain to students, "You will be participating in a moving opinion poll. Each time you hear a statement you are to move to the place along the imaginary line between "strongly agree" and "strongly disagree" that most closely reflects your opinion. If you strongly disagree you will move all the way to that side of the room. If you strongly agree you will move all the way to the other side of the room. You can also place yourself anywhere in the middle, especially if you have mixed feelings about the question."

"After you have placed yourselves along the continuum, I will invite people to share why they are standing where they are. This is not a time to debate or grill each other. Rather, this is a way to hear what people are thinking and get a sense of the different ways people perceive the issue."

When you do this activity begin with a statement that indicates non-controversial preferences like, "Chocolate is the best ice cream flavor in the world." Or, "Basketball is the best spectator sport." Then introduce statements related to a topic you're exploring in your course work.

You might want to "muddy the water" by modifying statements slightly, using different qualifiers, conditions, and contexts to see if students' opinions shift. For example, one statement might be, "Local communities should have a general curfew of midnight for all teens under 18." Another statement might be, "Local communities should have a school night curfew of midnight for all teens under 18.

Keys for Effective Group Problem Solving

• Share the "air time" and ensure that everyone's voice is heard.

Structured Class Discussion and Dialogues

Structured class discussions help students pay closer attention to the conversation. These kinds of discussions have the advantage of slowing down thinking, thus, improving listening and encouraging participants to choose more carefully what they say and how they say it. Experiment with these process suggestions to determine what structures and guidelines work best for different groups and different types of discussions.

• Limit the size of the group involved in a dialogue. If you can divide the group in half using two facilitators, there are more opportunities for each person to participate.

• Sit in a circle or horseshoe shape so that everyone can see each other.

- Explore what goes on in a discussion where everyone feels encouraged to speak and comfortable speaking and what goes on in a discussion that shuts down communication and makes people afraid to speak.

- Discuss the differences between dialogue and debate. Many students never talk because they always feel like they are in the middle of somebody else's contest! With the whole class, brainstorm a list of the differences between dialogue and debate. Think about how the goals differ, how people attend and respond differently, and the strengths and limitations of each type of discourse.

- Prepare a set of questions beforehand that students have helped to generate. You might want to prioritize questions or identify three or four that students are eager to discuss.

- Create a rubric for assessing student participation in discussion: Here's one from humanities teacher John Trampesh's Socratic seminar that makes it easy to notice and record the quality and frequency of students' responses. John creates a separate sheet for each seminar recording all student responses using these symbols:

C = comment + very deep − non sequitur   R = redirect or refocus
Q = question + very deep − non sequitur   I = interrupted speaker
T = cite text + very deep − non sequitur   E = energy drain

Assessment Sheet for Socratic Seminar

Assignment #	Seminar Topic											
1. Student Name												
2. Student Name												
3. Student Name												

- Do at least one "go-round" with an open-ended question where everyone who wants to respond gets to speak before the group raises questions or shifts to back and forth dialogue.

- Increase "wait time" before inviting students to speak. Silence encourages deliberative thinking. Use index cards or create a dialogue form that students can use to compose their thoughts before they speak, jot down follow-up questions, and reflect on the dialogue when it's over.

- Encourage self-monitoring so a few people don't dominate the conversation. You might want to introduce constraints that support sharing the air time. For example, limiting comments to one minute so students don't speechify, limiting the number of times each person can speak during a dialogue, or inviting different sub-groups to respond to questions—boys, girls, certain letters of the alphabet, sides of the room, etc.

- Ask participants to paraphrase what the previous speaker has said before sharing their own thoughts.

- Before students rush to argue, ask them first to identify something they agree with that a previous speaker has said. "I agree with _____ and I'd like to add/ask _____ ."

- Emphasize that changing positions or shifting opinions isn't about backing down, but rather involves listeners in reassessing their views after taking in more data and perspectives.

- Encourage students to clarify whether they are speaking from their own experience or making observations about what they have read, heard, or seen.

Keys for Effective Group Problem Solving

• Develop several desirable solutions to choose from.

- Remind students that respectful listening isn't about agreeing or disagreeing with the speaker —it's about taking in what someone says and communicating that you have understood them. Respectful speaking is about communicating your own thoughts and feelings in ways that your audience will hear and understand. Keep exploring how people can disagree and be respectful listeners and speakers.

- Summarize important points before the conversation goes in a new direction. Or take a two minute time-out to pair/share, write about, or reflect as a group on these questions: What issues are clearer for you? What's still vague or confusing? What are the two or three things that have been said that have helped to deepen your understanding of _____? Was there any question or comment that really grabbed your attention and made you stop and think, re-evaluate, or want to find out more? Are there any important questions that haven't been asked yet? Are there any points of view that we've left out?

- If the dialogue starts to feel combative or emotionally intense, stop for a minute and do a feeling/ reality check. Ask how people are feeling about what's being said. How do others see this issue? Who else wants to respond before we move on? Is there anyone else who has another opinion? Is there anyone else who agrees?

- Loaded, provocative, or negative language heats up tensions and sucks positive energy from the room. You may want to encourage the group to think about how they want to call attention to language being used in a respectful way. For example, a student might say, "I'm not sure that language helps us better understand _____" and then request that a word or phrase be replaced with less emotionally charged language. Or say, "That feels like an "ouch." Could you use language that doesn't _____?" Or say, "It's easier for me to hear you if you could say that in another way, so it doesn't sound so judgmental/negative/off-putting."

Fish Bowl

A "fish bowl" is one way to engage the entire class in one small group dialogue. This technique is especially useful when emotions are heated or when students bring vastly different perspectives to a controversial topic.

Invite five to seven students to this "fish bowl" conversation. Ask them to make a circle with their chairs in the middle of the room. Try to ensure that this group reflects diverse points of view on the issue being discussed.

Ask everyone else to make a circle of chairs around the fish bowl (you will have a smaller circle within a bigger circle). Only people in the fish bowl can speak, thus the process facilitates a kind of sustained, focused listening that is seldom experienced in secondary classrooms.

Here's one way to facilitate a fish bowl:
1. The facilitator asks a question and invites the students in the fish bowl to speak to the particular topic or question in a "go-around." Each student in the fish bowl speaks to the question without being interrupted.

2. Then the facilitator designates a specific amount of time for clarifying questions and further comments from students in the fish bowl.

3. After 15 minutes or so, invite students from the larger circle who would like to be part of the fish bowl to join the conversation by tapping a fish-bowl student on the shoulder and changing places with that student. Make a request that students don't join in all at once, but leave a small space of time between "tap in's".

4. Continue the fish bowl, introducing other questions when it feels like the right time to move on.

Assessing Good Talk

Set goals for discussions, generate criteria for what makes a discussion engaging and productive, and brainstorm questions that will help the group assess the quality and process of small and large group discussions.

Invite students to be volunteer "feedbackers" who watch and listen during a discussion, assessing both the substance and the flow of the conversation. Feedbackers can report back to the group, naming specific ways in which the group met the goals and criteria for the discussion and offering suggestions for ways to improve discussion the next time.

Assessment questions might include:
1. Were all points of view heard? Were they all respected? How do you know?

2. What new ideas, questions, and facts were introduced into the discussion that complicated your thinking about this issue?

3. Were there any new insights or information that shifted your thinking during the discussion?

Deconstruct Active Listening

Teachers ask all the time, "How can we practice active listening in a classroom? It feels like it's only an appropriate skill to use in one-on-one conversations with students." The answer is to deconstruct active listening and practice various aspects of good listening within appropriate learning contexts. Active listening involves many discrete skills that include:

- Non-verbal attending—demonstrating your full attention through your body language and facial expression

- Interested silence where you ONLY listen

- Verbal encouragers that invite someone to continue speaking

- Restating what people say so that they know they've been understood

- Checking for accuracy of understanding

- Empathizing by reflecting a speaker's feelings in ways that acknowledge the person's emotional state and the feelings he/she attaches to the issue being discussed

- Asking open-ended questions that give the speaker a chance to clarify his/her thinking, provide more information, or discuss underlying needs and concerns

- Summarizing key ideas, solutions, issues

Here's a list of teacher suggestions that call for students to use specific active listening skills:

- Create guidelines for being a responsive audience before listening to oral presentations or guest speakers.

- Make reading stories aloud a regular practice.

- Ask a student to time your mini-lectures—10 to 15 minutes is about the limit for good retention. Students tend to be far more attentive when they know the lecture will be over soon! Take two minutes after the mini-lecture for students with partners or home groups to review what they understood, fill in the gaps from their notes, and identify any clarifying questions they want to ask. Close by responding to three or four questions from the whole group.

- Help students focus their listening during mini-lectures or group discussions by asking several students to be prepared to summarize key points at various intervals or at the close of a lecture or discussion. Or assign numbers to students so that there are four 1's, four 2's, four 3's, and so on – at the close of the lecture of discussion ask each group to put their heads together

> **Keys for Effective Group Problem Solving**
>
> - Anticipate and predict different outcomes for proposed solutions (If... then...)

> **Keys for Effective Group Problem Solving**
>
> - Evaluate advantages and disadvantages of various solutions—does this solution work for some people at the expense of others? Does everyone get something they need so it feels like it will work for them?

and prepare a response their assigned question. Take three minutes for groups to talk it through and then share responses with whole group.

- Use a talking stick or object when students are involved in a whole group discussion— the only person who can speak is the person with the object.

- Check for understanding by asking students to paraphrase instructions.

- In cooperative groups, notice and post verbal encouragers that students use to encourage each other to speak or ask a person from each group to record at least one idea suggested by each member of the group.

- Use partner paraphrasing to practice listening for understanding. One partner explains a problem or process or shares her/his perspective on a topic or question. The other person write down the explanation as accurately as possible. Then partners switch roles. This strategy is effective when you want students to explain a mathematical solution step-by-step; summarize a lab experiment; rehearse responses to essay questions; describe causal relationships linked to a historical event.

- When students are working with challenging reading material, ask students to do paired reading where one partner reads and the other person paraphrases what the person just read.

- Ask students to pair up to share their understanding about an assignment, directions, a problem that is posed and then ask two or three students to restate the problem, assignment, directions in their own words.

- When it's appropriate, encourage students to empathize with another person's circumstance in a current life situation, in a piece of literature, or in a historical conflict. Ask, "How do you imagine this person feels?" or "How would you feel if you were in that situation?" or "Why might someone feel (frustrated, angry, confused, upset, etc.) in that situation?"

- Use openers and questions that help students clarify their think and provide more detail:

  - Tell us more about that.
  - Can you say more?
  - What other thoughts do you have about _____.
  - Is there anything else you want to say about _____?
  - What do you think that's about?
  - Do you think other people see this the same way?
  - What else should we know about _____?

- At the end of a lesson, ask students to pair up and write down three key points to remember.

CHAPTER 3

Meeting the Developmental and Cultural Needs of Diverse Learners

If we are really serious about improving student achievement, we will need to be as attentive to adolescents' social, cultural, and emotional needs as we are to their intellectual growth and academic performance. Knowing more about the developmental and cultural needs of diverse learners is the basis for creating a classroom and curriculum that connect to who your students are, what they know, what motivates them, and how they learn.

This chapter explores important practices that help you meet the developmental and cultural needs of your students and introduces three key practices:

HH **Practice 5:** Set high academic and behavioral expectations and provide high caring and high support to meet them

 Practice 6: Affirm diversity in your classroom

⌘ **Practice 7:** Integrate multiple ways of knowing and learning

The section for each practice includes sample activities, strategies, and routines that illustrate the key practice.

One of the most curious aspects of writing this guide was discovering just how vast the chasm proved to be between the day-to-day practice I witnessed in high schools and the current research and thinking that illuminate the world of adolescents and how to teach them. In the last two decades we have learned a lot more about how young people experience schooling, how they learn, and what they need to grow up healthy and become good students, good people, and good citizens. This gap between research and practice is all the more astonishing because national leaders and scholars in the fields of education, prevention, youth development, and behavioral sciences have given us a rich picture of adolescents and their needs.

In her book *The Right to Learn*, Linda Darling-Hammond suggests that knowledge of adolescent development is a critical competency for secondary teachers. This understanding should include "knowing how adolescents think and behave; appreciation for the vast range of normal adolescent thinking and behavior; awareness that each students' cultural identity influences their development; and the awareness that an adolescent's intellectual, social, emotional, and ethical development are inextricably linked, although these aspects of development may reach maturity at different times within a single adolescent." (Darling-Hammond, 1997, p. 294)

This chapter provides from some brief snapshots of American adolescents from a variety of developmental viewpoints so that you will be able to reflect on how you see your students.

Some Benchmarks of Adolescent Development
The four major tasks of adolescence are:
- Establishing one's own identity—healthy identity involves a "balance between being with others and being comfortable being alone." (Pruitt, D., 1999, p. 30)

- Becoming more intimate with peers—as students get older they spend increasing amounts of time with friends.

- Developing a mature relationship with one's family—older adolescents see themselves as equals of their parents, and parents tend to recognize that the power balance in family relationships is shifting.

- Achieving a growing sense of autonomy, control, and mastery in the world.

EARLY ADOLESCENCE: 10 – 14 Years, Peer Acceptance
There are big individual and gender differences in the timing and results of puberty. Early maturing girls seem to be especially at risk of emotional, behavioral, and adjustment problems. While most girls have gone through the major transitions of puberty by the time they reach ninth grade, a small minority may lag behind their peers. Most boys entering high school will be in the midst of their developmental transition. Boys who lag far behind are likely to have the most difficulty adjusting and finding acceptance with their peers.

Gaining a sense of their "maleness" and "femaleness" is an important part of their development. Pre-teens are curious about sexual matters. Pre-teens develop new feelings about their own bodies rather than developing sexual relationships with the opposite sex.

Young teens have a huge need for privacy that emerges from what David Elkind calls the imaginary audience—the notion that everyone is watching you all the time. Kids are very self-conscious at this age and "almost die" from fear of embarrassment! This is the stage when children begin to develop their self-awareness, thus feeling more in control of themselves. With this new felt control comes greater challenges to adult authority.

Early adolescents have a desire to have time to engage in same gender activities. Membership in groups is important to the pre-teen. "Heroes" to look up to are important. This may include special people outside the family.

Special athletic, artistic, academic, or musical talents may emerge at this time. Adults should encourage areas of potential success as a means of building the child's self-esteem.

What You Can Do

Emotional security is the foundation of self-concept, self-efficacy, and self-esteem. Teachers can support teens' healthy development by:

- Offering reassurance.
- Offering praise and positive feedback and using criticism sparingly.
- Encouraging students to share their interests and demonstrate their talents.
- Being patient (This will not last forever!)
- Encouraging independence.
- Keeping lines of communication open.
- Encouraging friendships.

MIDDLE ADOLESCENCE: 14 – 17 Years, A Time of Change

Teens struggle with rapid growth, sexual maturation, and desire for independence from their parents. Adults need to keep in mind that their child's hormones have more control over their moods than they do.

Changes in personal habits, manners, dress, and hair, and a pre-occupation (or lack of it) with personal hygiene are normal ways for teens to try on their teenage selves. Adults need to choose their battles on this front very carefully.

Teens have a strong sense of fairness and are judgmental of adults and peers who do not do what is "fair." Teens have a deep need for love and acceptance by parents and peers. Adults should be aware that such a need is often hidden in an effort to act mature.

A physical need for extended periods of rest is normal. Adults often mistake this for laziness. Too little rest can result in moodiness. Adults should depersonalize these ups and downs and look beyond them as much as possible.

Opportunities for drug and alcohol experimentation are common. Once teens become sexually active, they remain sexually active.

Different social influences on boys' and girls' behavior often show up in school settings. For instance, girls are likely to believe that they are not capable of handling challenges and retreat into helplessness, where boys are more likely to feel confident about their problem solving. Girls also seem more likely to take on failure as a personal flaw. On the other hand, on almost every academic measure girls excel more than boys.

Although in childhood girls are more resilient than boys, this flip flops in adolescence where girls appear to be at more psychological risk. Most boys and girls experience negative feelings about physical changes and body image.

Teens find security in structure, although few ever admit it to adults. Adults need to be firm and consistent around a few "bottom-line" rules and expectations. The rules you state need to be enforced, so don't make too many. Adolescents tend to be much more responsible when the consequences are spelled out ahead of time.

By middle adolescence most kids develop what Elkind calls a personal fable, the belief that no one has ever experienced what you're going through and can possibly understand you (except, maybe your best friend). This sense of uniqueness goes hand in hand with feelings of invincibility and wanting to be center-stage for attention.

A teen's sense of self is increasingly shaped by how they see themselves differently from others and where they fit in the social network. Most teens experience more internal conflict than social conflict and most teens don't identify themselves as belonging to just one group of peers. The average teen spends 22 hours a week with friends. Adolescents who have friends report more positive images of themselves and appear to have better relationships with parents and teachers. Attributes of well-liked teens include spontaneity, willingness to try new things, cheerfulness, liveliness, and interest in others. Lonely and shy teens feel more self-conscious —this results in a reluctance to speak, so these kids tend not to be noticed. Shy kids may feel they are perceived as undesirable and may retreat from most social situations.

Part-time work is a positive experience when kids work no more than 13.5 hours per week. Kids who work under 13.5 hours a week have better grades than those teens who don't work at all. (Pruitt, D. 1999, p. 45)

LATE ADOLESCENCE: 17 – 19 Years, Decisions

Mature appearance and behavior may be misleading on all fronts. We may assume that students who "look grown" may be more emotionally, socially, or intellectually mature than they really are. Adults need to acknowledge that most adolescents experience some feelings of frustration and depression during this period due to fears around facing adulthood, school pressures, social life, first time employment, and future planning.

Career choices can be difficult. Schools should help teens explore careers which are suited to them rather than careers which their parents wish they would pursue.

One of the dilemmas of late adolescence is the ambiguity around passage to adulthood. There are few rituals that help teens mark their coming of age. And going to work or going to college result in very different transitions.

What Are Some Important Learning Characteristics of Adolescents?

1. Their learning is both concrete and abstract (formal operational thinking), although it's important to remember that most adults and adolescents use their abstract skills infrequently. Critical thinking, for example, is an abstract ability, but it needs to be taught in a concrete context.

2. Students' learning preferences and styles become even more distinct as they get older. Struggling readers find it more and more difficult to slog through texts; kids who thrive on "hands-on" learning but don't get the chance to learn this way may become restless, resistant, and reluctant learners. Only 23% of kids are linear-sequential learners. (McCarthy, 2000) This means that they are "book smart" and "test smart," with the ability to process large amounts of information. This 23% of students becomes even more savvy at "doing school," while the majority of students find formal, abstract learning (if presented without a real world context) boring and disconnected.

3. Knowledge needs to be relevant; hence, student-centered learning (where students have more choices about what they learn or how they learn it, and more opportunities to link their own interests and experiences to classroom learning) becomes even more important for adolescents, who are always going to ask, "What does this have to do with me? Why do I need to know this? How can I personally express myself in this assignment?"

4. Knowledge is constructed socially. There is a need to process information and check it out with others, so cooperative, experiential, interactive learning works for a majority of kids.

5. Adolescents get better at multi-tasking, yet sometimes overreach their capacity. (I can listen to music, cruise the net, and do my homework at the same time!)

6. Adolescents are immersed in their own culture—they truly live in the here and now of their own lives. This is why history, for example, if it's not connected to their own world or feelings is a challenging subject for most students.

7. Students are questioning adult norms and beliefs—their radar is ultra-sensitive to hypocrisy. They can make better arguments and more critically examine the arguments of others. It is natural for young people of this age to challenge rules and assumptions.

8. Young people gravitate toward controversy. They enjoy a thoughtful argument and like to discuss issues that don't have just one answer.

9. They can hold multiple perspectives; they can use more sophisticated powers of reasoning to examine several perspectives at once rather than looking at problems as an either/or proposition.

10. Students like to create their own theories and test out the theories of others.

11. The more "intelligences" students utilize in a learning experience, the more they will retain. Howard Gardner has defined the intelligences as: verbal/linguistic, logical-mathematical, musical, spacial, kinesthetic, interpersonal, intrapersonal, and naturalist. (Gardner, 2000)

12. Activities that combine cooperation and competition grab most kids' attention and focus.

13. Adolescents' thinking becomes more complicated. They can handle issues that have gray areas; in fact, kids like being challenged to dig around, if the digging around makes meaning for them. Moral dilemmas, ethical questions, "big ideas" around life and death issues are extremely interesting to young people.

14. Most adolescents love contests, games, puzzles, mysteries—most anything that begins as a problem. Whenever possible try to "problematize" the curriculum.

15. Authentic assessment that has an audience is compelling to most adolescents. Think about sports, drama, bands, chorus, the newspaper, art shows, peer education, tutoring, service learning—all of these activities have a real audience where there is a definite product or performance. Kids like to demonstrate what they know and can do.

16. Kids want and need to express themselves—to put their personal stamp on things. This is why what we call electives are critical to a balanced curriculum.

Developmentally Appropriate Practice – Teaching to Adolescents' Developmental Realities

Although educators win as many bad jargon awards as any other group of specialized professionals, "DAP" is actually a useful term, one that should become commonplace among high school staff. DAP means Developmentally Appropriate Practice. Emerging from the field of early childhood education, this phrase is a way of describing the relationship between instruction and the specific intellectual, physical, social, emotional, and ethical development of an individual child.

In other words, DAP is about linking appropriate learning experiences to the developmental stage that indicates what and how a student thinks and feels, what a student can do physically, and how a student perceives and engages with people and the world around her. An important reminder about DAP—a developmental stage of learning and readiness is informed by a child's chronological age and a child's life experience in her family, her culture, and her immediate environment.

Good teaching is occuring when developmental considerations guide decisions about the appropriate learning environment and instructional activities for a particular child or children of a particular age. DAP devotees would say that developmental ages and stages should shape how teachers talk to kids, how teachers respond to various behaviors, how teachers guide children through simple and complex learning experiences.

Here are a couple examples that illustrate what developmentally appropriate practice is all about. Young children cannot recognize letters of the alphabet until and unless they've had plenty of experiences discriminating one shape from another. Consequently, an early childhood teacher provides lots of opportunities for children to explore, identify, and sort two- and three-dimensional shapes. Other reading readiness activities help children develop their imaginations and share stories about life beyond the immediate visible, physical space that they can see and touch. This capacity to imagine something that cannot be seen is crucial for making meaning of the abstract symbols on a written page.

On the social side of things, young children need guided practice that helps them experience how to share, how to play fair, or how to sit in a circle quietly and listen to other children. These are all learned behaviors that only become habits when teachers notice, encourage, and talk with children about how they practice these behaviors on a daily basis. High school educators could learn a lot from watching the interactions between a pre-school teacher and a four year old.

Why is any of this relevant to secondary education? Development doesn't stop when a child becomes fourteen. Rather, the opposite occurs. The intensity and pique of adolescence might, in fact, inspire us to be even more mindful of how we design learning environments and curricula that are more responsive to young people's intellectual, physical, social, emotional, and ethical development. When we overlook asking if and how we engage in developmentally appropriate practice, we risk making high school students endure a lot of things that verge on the developmentally ridiculous, instead of engaging them with effective practices. A few examples will suffice.

**From the Developmentally Questionable to Developmentally Appropriate:
A Few Examples**

School Start Time: Most high schools begin classes between 7:15 and 8:00 a.m. because of bus schedules and adult preferences to start early and leave early.

> **What's developmentally inappropriate?** Adolescents' biological clocks are different—their physiological rhythm of waking and sleeping is later to bed and much later to rise and be fully present.

> **What's more developmentally appropriate?** School start-time would be closer to 9 a.m.

Emphasis on Teacher-Directed Whole Group Instruction: Teachers often determine most of what is taught and how it is learned, requiring all students to do the same thing the same way at the same time.

> **What's developmentally inappropriate?** The desire for increasing autonomy, choice, and independence dominates the adolescent years just when learning in school becomes the most restricted. Most academic courses offer diminishing opportunities for personal expression and engagement with subject matter at the very time when adolescents are most eager to place a personal stamp on what they do. It is ironic that kindergartners usually have more choices and independent learning experiences in one day than a high school sophomore might experience in a week of 35 classes.

> **What's more developmentally appropriate?** Balance whole group instruction with opportunities for students to pursue personal choices, interests, and independent explorations. Even when learning involves the whole group, provide opportunities for students to help make decisions about curricular content and how they go about learning it.

Treating Adolescents Like Adults: It's normal to fret about how best to prepare students for the harsher realities of life after high school. Our worries about students becoming too dependent on second chances can lead to the following declaration to students: "I need to treat you like adults and hold you accountable to adult standards. Otherwise, I'm not preparing you for the real world out there."

> **What's developmentally inappropriate?** The irony is that we are most tempted to hang the adult label on the adolescents who exhibit the most un-adult behaviors, especially when they haven't lived up to academic responsibilities. It's easy to get caught up in the "Big Scold" (much of which is hyperbole anyway) that's usually followed by the "Adult Sanction." It sounds something like this:

"I expect you to be an adult here, so I don't accept late papers. When you have a full time job, there's no room for excuses. You better figure out now how to manage your time, before you're out there in the real world. You're going to have to take a zero on these two assignments." Or "You play, you pay. Next time study harder. This time it's an F. There are no re-takes or second chances in the adult world out there."

The kids who haven't developed the maturity and sense of responsibility we expect of high school students test our patience and best behavior on a good day, much less on a day when we're already stressed. The problem is that the Adult Sanction of punitive grading reinforces irresponsible behavior—the student gets off the hook because he isn't held responsible for completing, correcting, or putting in more serious time and effort to demonstrate a satisfactory level of competence. The Adult Sanction sends another potentially damaging message to students who have the most trouble getting their act together; it communicates to these kids that we care more about punishing the irresponsible behavior than we care about helping them learn how to be better, more responsible students.

What's more developmentally appropriate? Regardless of legal rights, voting status, and growing responsibilities, there are good reasons why the developmental stage of adolescence spans from ages 11 or 12 to about 19 or 20. (Dacey and Kenny, 1997, and Pruitt, D., 1999) Maturity is incredibly personal, depending upon an adolescent's genetic predispositions, physical development, birth order, family circumstances, social experiences, cultural background, and life opportunities in and out of school. In addition, physical, emotional, intellectual, social, and ethical maturity develop at different rates within a single individual. It's only in the early to mid-twenties that all of these aspects of self become fully integrated into an adult personality. High school is the laboratory where young people are learning how to manage their time and responsibilities; it's just that some students are better at this much sooner than others. All of which is to say, it's a risky business to treat kids in high school as if they are already full-fledged adults.

Adolescents are becoming adults; they are not adults yet! Being a teenager means constantly negotiating when you want to be treated like a kid or like an adult to get what you need. One of the biggest challenges for high school teachers is navigating back and forth between adult-to-adult and adult-to-kid learning experiences and communication modes. It's a fine line to get this right and has a lot to do with knowing when our role is more parental and when our role is more like that of a mentor or facilitator with individual students and the group.

If we teach with the assumption that students are not adults quite yet and recognize that the students we teach are at different stages on the maturity continuum, we have another choice. Instead of relying only on grade penalties and punitive responses, we can develop a sequence of consequences and interventions that say we are for serious about insisting that students meet their academic responsibilities. Instructional support strategies can include making an academic plan to complete one's work, daily check-in's, learning new organizational and study strategies, revisions and re-takes on important assignments and tests, tutoring, or early morning study sessions.

And for the zero completion gang who rarely experience the satisfaction of handing in quality work, there is always the friendly but firm call to arms, "Today's the day you and your mother agreed that you will not leave school until this work is completed. It matters to me that you pass this course. You put in the effort, we'll work on one thing at a time, and you'll get out of the hole. I'm confident you can do it." For kids who are immature and the least "adult-like," we need to keep asking the question, "What will help this student learn what it takes to become more responsible? More punishment or more guided support?"

High Stakes Grading: Test grades are final. If homework isn't handed in on time, it's a 0. A student's final grade is the cumulative average of all graded work, regardless of progress or later mastery in the semester.

What's developmentally inappropriate? The current "accountant" approach to grading belongs in the bookkeeper's office, not the classroom. In fact, where else, ever again in a person's life, will an average of tests, quizzes, and homework grades determine the quality and effectiveness of someone's performance? As a result of high stakes grading, millions of high school students spend four years never completing a thing or never experiencing mastery in the academic realm. High stakes grading lets a lot of kids live in the land of the shoddy, where on-time behavior takes precedence over completion, where first time performance is emphasized at the expense of revision and correction, and the sheer quantity of graded tasks forfeits the deeper satisfaction of learning what it takes and what it feels like to master something difficult or produce quality work. High stakes grading devalues the very qualities that help adolescents become life-long learners and support the goal of competency in the work place.

What's more developmentally appropriate? Eliminating obsessive grade calculations is not likely to happen in your lifetime. However, there are plenty of ways to make grading practices more developmentally appropriate.

- Weigh grades differently according to task and purpose. Give less weight to practice tasks; give more weight to assessments that illustrate working knowledge and understanding of a key set of skills and concepts. Example: When students are learning a new skill, practice tasks indicate what a student has or has not learned proficiently at some point in time. The purpose of practice tasks is not to give A's to students who got it and F's to students who didn't. Practice tasks give you feedback on where to go next and what to do to maximize learning for all of your students.

- Provide more time to complete fewer projects and assessments during a grading period; but make sure that these are the kinds of projects and assessments that require students to fully demonstrate in-depth understanding and application of what they are learning.

- Assess effort as well as performance—otherwise, many students will disconnect what they did or did not do from the grades they earn.

- Create opportunities for self-correction, revisions, and re-takes as part of developing proficiency.

- Don't employ grades as a threat, a punishment, or control lever—these tactics never work for kids who are struggling or have chronic problems turning in assignments or reading assigned materials.

- Help students to develop their own goal-setting and self-assessment rubrics.

One of the greatest obstacles to successful instruction is treating students as a homogenous group, rather than appreciating their developmental and cultural differences.

The practices in this chapter help teachers recognize students as unique individuals and foster the positive imaging of all students. By emphasizing differentiated learning strategies and providing differentiated support, teachers can accommodate differences in student interests, learning styles, abilities, and cultural experiences.

Teachers who engage in developmentally appropriate and culturally responsive teaching value the quality of resiliency within young people —the innate "self-righting" mechanism of individuals to transform and change—and believe in each student's capacity and desire to learn and succeed. (Werner, E. and Smith, R., 1992, p. 202)

When we have a better understanding of students' developmental and cultural needs we are more likely to teach, talk, and discipline in ways that increase student motivation and cooperative behavior. Moreover, a greater understanding of what different groups of adolescents need to be successful invites us to take an unsentimental look at traditions, policies, and practices within our schools that may actually harm rather than promote a student's academic success. School faculties who are committed to reducing personal, social, and cultural barriers to learning and development are more likely to implement changes in classroom practice that reduce school failure and narrow the achievement gap among various groups of students.

PRACTICE 5

Set High Academic and Behavioral Expectations and Provide High Caring and High Support to Meet Them

Setting and communicating high expectations that promote positive social norms and a culture of excellence is at the heart of teaching and learning. Ultimately it is our attitudes towards young people and our beliefs about how they learn and how they can recover and change that will drive instruction and classroom management. Believing that "There's nothing wrong with you that what's right with you can't fix" leads to a very different kind of practice than "Many of you won't be able to succeed in here and there's nothing I can do about it." It is our personal interest and support, feedback, encouragement, and inspiration that make the biggest difference for struggling students.

Current research that focuses on reducing problem behaviors and enhancing academic achievement and resiliency confirms the role that high expectations play in the lives of adolescents. Holding high expectations, however, is about more than holding high standards. High expectations communicate your beliefs about what students are capable of doing and achieving; they convey your confidence in students' ability to be successful and let students know that their efforts will make a difference in their performance. High expectations are student centered; they are linked to the support and encouragement you provide so that all students can achieve some measure of academic success.

High standards, on the other hand, focus on subject matter, comparing and evaluating student performance in relation to that one standard of academic excellence. In addition, high standards usually come with the assumption that some students will meet them, making stars of a few while many others inevitably fall short. Consequently, a lot of kids perceive standards as barriers that sort and separate them into groups of winners and losers.

Consider for example, how a greater emphasis on high standards or high expectations can lead to very different outcomes. When a single standard of excellence drives assessment, students are evaluated on how well or poorly they measure up to that one standard—students get one shot to show their stuff. Students take a test, get a grade, look at the results for 30 seconds, and then move on to the next unit, regardless of how they perform. What message does this give the students who earn the C's, D's, and F's? They might come to any of these conclusions: "I guess it doesn't really matter if I learn this or not" or "If I didn't learn it this time, I guess I never will" or "If I can't get an A or B, why put in a lot of effort?" or "I'm not good at anything in this class."

When high expectations are at the center of assessment, teachers are more likely to hold the goal that all students are expected to achieve a minimal high standard of proficiency, mastering essential skills and competencies. For example, students might be required to complete a certain number of tasks that indicate proficiency or demonstrate mastery of key sections of a test or polish one essay to high quality every quarter. Thus, the big test is not the big marker of achievement. Some students may need more time, practice, or instruction to meet minimal high standards that you set for the whole class, but there is a big pay-off for refusing to settle for failure or shoddy work. Everyone gets to feel the pride and pleasure of their own accomplishments.

If you believe that every student can succeed through their own efforts, you are more likely to create a learning environment that encourages and supports all students to become successful learners. Expectations don't have to be dramatic or complicated but they do become the mantras that students know will drive what happens in class.

Here are a few examples:

- "I expect all of you to pass this course. If you put in the effort, I can promise you will pass."

- "All of you can be successful learners in this class. I know you have what it takes to do well." (You may want to name specific examples of academic expectations that you hold for everyone, explaining that failure is not an option for some things that you expect everyone to learn and be able to do.)

- "I expect all of us to treat each other with respect and consideration."

- "I'm counting on everyone to encourage and support each other to participate and do their best."

- "I expect everyone to try to do your best and be your best. Your effort counts for a lot."

- "I don't expect anyone including myself to be perfect at everything all the time. We all make mistakes and we can learn from them and right them."

- "I know that there will be times when you may feel challenged and struggle a bit. Sometimes you might make poor choices. And I'm confident that you can recover and get back on track."

- "Working with each other collaboratively is a big deal with me. It's something we will spend a lot of time doing, and I expect everyone to get pretty good at it."

Give Students High Support to Meet Your Expectations

High support provides students with a road map and an emotional compass to meet high expectations. It's the catalyst that can trigger an individual's positive motivation and meaningful engagement in learning. Meeting the emotional needs of adolescents is at the heart of support and encouragement, in fact, the feelings students bring to any learning experience are the greatest determiner for whether they will learn or not. What you do and say has the power to change how students feel and what they choose to do. Think about teacher support in this way:

Adolescents' Emotional Needs →	**High Teacher Support**	→	*Learning Can Happen*
	When teachers provide provide a learning environment and personal support to meet these needs, most kids feel positively motivated.		

Adolescents' Emotional Needs →	**Low Teacher Support**	→	*Learning Can Happen*
	When teachers don't provide a learning environment and personal support to meet these needs, most kids are likely to feel resistant, angry, hostile, rejected, alienated, invisible, or disinterested.		

Adolescents' Emotional Needs →	**Students with High Motivation**	→	*Learning Can Happen*
	Some students are the exception—their needs are met or unmet in ways that spark so much personal drive that a supportive learning environment may not be as critical a factor for student success.		

Adolescents' Emotional Needs include:

• Psychological and physical safety

• Belonging, attachment, and affection with peers and adults

• Control over parts of their lives and a voice in decisions that affect them

• Freedom to make choices

• Respect and acceptance for who I am

• Recognition and encouragement for what I do

• Power to achieve, contribute, meet challenges, and participate in meaningful activities

• High expectations, clear boundaries, and high support

What Does High Teacher Support Look Like?

The idea of teaching as delivering content will work most of the time for 30% to 40% of kids. But for the vast majority of adolescents, it's only half the job. The other half of teaching is about creating the environment and providing the kind of support that young people need to learn and mature. For example, student self-efficacy (Bandura, 1997) is enhanced when teachers:

- Create opportunities for different kinds of performance accomplishments that students successfully complete. (Every teacher has their own laundry list of verbs that frame various tasks that students do.)

- Model the behaviors that you want students to use in class and do the learning tasks that you expect students to complete.

- Communicate messages of hope and confidence in a student's present and future.

- Maintain a supportive low-stress/low threat learning environment.

It's understandable that high support might be construed as coddling or viewed as that "touchy-feely" stuff that counselors are supposed do with kids. High school teachers are more inclined to live by a fairly narrow definition of support that's about helping kids in academic trouble; but this misses the mark. All students need to feel supported emotionally.

High support isn't about supplying a little boost here and there or adding something extra once in a while. It's about the hundreds of little things teachers do everyday to:

- Create a learning environment that meets students' emotional needs for safety, belonging, freedom, respect, recognition, and power—this has to be in place before many students will be ready to learn.

- Provide students with the tools and "know-how" that will help them express and manage their emotions and utilize their emotions productively.

- Develop relationships and personal connections that invite students to see you as their ally and partner who will help them to learn and grow.

- Provide the kinds of encouragement and support appropriate for different kinds of kids.

- Provide the tools and "know-how" for every student to become more "school smart."

What would you prioritize as your most important behavioral and academic goals and expectations? What kinds of support will help students meet them?

What behavioral goals and expectations do you have for every student?	What kinds of support from you will help all students meet these expectations?	What kinds of outside support will help all students to meet these expectations?	How would coddling look different from effective support?
1. 2. 3.	1. 2. 3.	1. 2. 3.	1. 2. 3.
What academic goals and expectations do you have for every student?	**What kinds of support from you will help all students meet these expectations?**	**What kinds of outside support will help all students to meet these expectations?**	**How would coddling look different from effective support?**
1. 2. 3.	1. 2. 3.	1. 2. 3.	1. 2. 3.

HH

The Feeling-Learning Connection

The latest brain-based research as summarized by Robert Sylwester confirms the positive relationship between emotions and learning. (Sylwester, R., 1995, 2000) How students feel will determine whether they choose to be open and receptive or resist learning, whether they use their emotional energy to listen or use it to draw attention somewhere else.

When students feel safe, settled, calm, and purposeful, they have the ability to balance their feelings with their ability to think. This sense of balance creates the capacity to use emotional energy to focus and pay attention. Students must be able to focus to remember. And without access to memory, students are unable to learn. For adolescents, this is no easy task in the best of circumstances, and there's an irony here. By educating their hearts, by welcoming their feelings and emotional energy into the room, we are better able to educate their minds. On the other hand, when students are out of balance and feel emotionally flooded, it's hard for them to focus on anything except the unsettled feelings that they're experiencing. When students' emotional needs are ignored or trivialized, their feelings of anger, hurt, hostility, and resistance are going to rule the day.

Embracing this aspect of teaching requires the courage, honesty, and generosity to see adolescents as they really are, not as adults would wish them to be to meet their own needs of comfort and convenience. This also means accepting that adolescence is messy, for both the student who is experiencing it and the adults who are supporting students through this stage in their lives. Students want to believe that you're on their side, that you are there for them, especially when they're having a tough time.

Different Support for Different Students

Different students need different doses and different kinds of support at different points in time. For highly interested, high achieving students, support may mean encouraging them to explore careers where people spend a lifetime working in the discipline you teach. You might tap into their enthusiasm by directing them to other resources or suggesting independent projects that give them an opportunity to share their expertise with the class.

For students who struggle academically, support might involve explicit teaching of cognitive strategies that will help them organize, plan, focus, and study. In other words, your support may focus on helping students to become more "school smart." Developing a trusting and caring relationship may be a critical first step toward accepting support from an adult at school. When you show that you're interested in getting to know students personally, they may start to believe that they can count on your positive regard for them. If they begin to trust that you will listen first, before judging or disciplining, they are more likely to invest the time and effort to do well.

For students resistant to seeing themselves as successful students, support may first mean validating their life experiences outside of school. Inviting students to tell their stories gives you a way to acknowledge the hard knocks they've experienced and encourage them to tell you things they're proud of in their lives. Time to listen gives you a chance to empathize with their pain and affirm what they care about. Some young people may have never talked with an adult in school who can help them to make connections between the skills they use to manage and navigate their personal lives and ways that they can utilize these same skills and abilities to succeed at school. Mirror back the inner qualities you see in them that reveal their capacity to meet the challenges they face.

Resistant students may also need your support in reframing their images of themselves. This doesn't mean asking students to trade one identity for another as a requisite for academic success. That approach will only intensify resistance and resentment. It does involve giving students feedback and encouragement that can help them to hold a more inclusive picture of themselves, one in which they can be a successful student, without giving up loyalty to friends or sacrificing their sense of self and racial and cultural identity.

For kids who really think school stinks, normalizing the stance of being a reluctant or resistant learner can reassure students that they're not failures for life, just because school is not working for them right now. Share stories about people who hated school but found a life long passion despite earlier setbacks. Or bring up examples of people who turned their lives around by early adulthood or who failed many times in life before finally achieving personal success.

Support won't always be easy for you to give or for students to accept—a negative school history can make kids justifiably suspect of any teacher's motives and intentions. Timing and pacing can make a big difference for kids who may be hesitant to believe that you are really there for them. Be conscious of a student's readiness or reluctance to be engaged with you, with other students, and with the subject matter. Small doses of support over a few months can be more effective in the long run than intrusive attempts to get everything out in the open and push too soon. Hard to reach students need to see you in action for a while before they will risk making connections and accepting your efforts to support them. Finally, it's good to remind yourself and communicate to these students that every small improvement and every sign of progress spells SUCCESS.

Sample activities, strategies, and routines:

Identify Your Big Goals, Daily Learning Objectives, and Specific Expectations Around Completion

HH

Students bring fresh hope and old hesitations to every new learning situation. Teachers often bring a short list of critical skills, experiences, and understandings that they want every student to leave with by the end of the class. This is the time to give students an idea of the big picture, the big questions, and the significant experiences that will mark the year. It's also a way to communicate your confidence that everyone can achieve these goals.

In addition, think about the different ways you want to communicate learning goals and objectives every day.

Life Skill
Connection | **13. Set big and little goals and make plans**

- **Lay Out Your Big Goals for the Year**
- **Daily Learning Goals and Objectives**
- **Use "Doing" Verbs to Frame Classwork and Homework**

Lay Out Your Big Goals for the Year

Right from the beginning, kids need to know what really matters to you, and they need to know the standards and basic requirements that they are expected to meet in your course. Put this information on posters, so that it's easy to refer to at any time. You might want to insert metal rings through the posters, so that you can hang them from a dowel or wall hooks. This way your posters are accessible and easy to flip over and review. Here are some examples:

Poster Title	Goal	Example
Skills for Learning and Working Together	Identify five or six social skills that you expect everyone to learn and practice in the classroom.	Active listening; expressing and managing feelings; negotiation; using "I~Speak;" and group cooperation skills
Requirements Everyone Needs to Meet	Identify the five most important requirements, exhibitions, or demonstrations that you expect every student to meet in this course. Let students know that you expect them to help each other to meet these essential course requirements.	First semester requirements in English: 1) revise and polish three of your best writing pieces 2) correct all spelling errors, run-on's and fragments on all of your writing 3) explore an issue of your choice using fiction, non-fiction, interviews, art, music, drama, or dance 4) synthesize your findings in a written document 5) prepare a seven minute presentation for class
When You Leave this Class You will be Able to...	Give students a "heads-up" about what matters most to you by asking yourself this question: Before students leave, what are the things that you are determined that everyone will be able to do successfully?	English: You will be able to write paragraphs and papers without using run-on's or fragments. Chemistry: You and a partner will conduct and explain a lab experiment for the class. History: You will be able to defend and illustrate how one individual changed the course of history. History: You will be able to defend why it's important to learn history using your own stories.

Poster Title	Goal	Example
		Math: You will be able to create your own _____ problems and explain your solutions. Any Course: Each one of you will work with every student in class. Any Course: You will be able to meet important deadlines on time.
How I will Grade You?	Give students a clear explanation of how they earn their grades by identifying the percentage value of each grade component.	How Do You Earn Your Grade? ___% Major Tests, Projects, & Performance Assessments ___% In-Class Tasks ___% Homework ___% Successful Work Habits ___% Class Participation ___% Life Skills
Big Picture Questions	Every course has a few key questions that you probably want students to think about throughout the year: Questions that connect one learning unit to another Questions that reflect the big ideas that are at the heart of your course or investigation Questions that inform major student projects and exams	Use these questions informed by the "Habits of Mind" developed by the faculty of Central Park East School: (Perspective) From whose viewpoint are we reading, seeing, hearing? (Evidence) How do we know what we know? What is the evidence and how reliable is it? (Connections) How are things, people, events connected to each other? How do they fit together? (Speculation) What's old, what's new? Have we run across this before? How else might we look at this? What if...? (Significance) What does it mean? So what? Why does it matter? What difference does it make?

HH

Daily Learning Goals and Objectives

Consider which questions are important to answer given your goals and objectives for the day:
- What do you expect students to learn, practice, demonstrate in a particular learning activity?
- What do you expect students to do as a result of a specific learning experience?
- What will students do that provides evidence of what they have learned, accomplished, or practiced?
- How do you expect students to learn in a particular activity?
- What academic skills do you expect students to use?
- What self-management skills do you expect students to use?
- What communication and problem solving skills do you expect students to use?
- What group skills do you expect students to use?
- How do you expect students to connect what they do today with what they did yesterday and what they do tomorrow?

Use "Doing" Verbs to Frame Classwork and Homework

An important way to link effort to achievement and performance is to use concrete "doing" verbs to frame all work that students do. Communicate to students the specific learning processes they are expected to use to complete a task. You might want to refer to Anderson and Krathwohl's A Taxonomy for Learning, Teaching, and Assessing: A Revision of Blooom's Taxonomy of Educational Objectives, Marzono's Dimensions of Learning, and Baron and Sternberg's Teaching Thinking Skills.

A Short List of "Doing" Verbs

Choose	Translate	Decide	Formulate
Define	Classify	Illustrate	Explain
Describe	Draw	Debate	Write
Identify	Apply	Differentiate	Produce
Indicate	Compute	Analyze	Assess
Locate	Demonstrate	Solve	Conclude
Outline	Participate	Diagram	Evaluate
List	Perform	Arrange	Provide evidence
Convert	Plan	Combine	Critique
Defend	Predict	Compile	Judge
Infer	Categorize	Organize	Prove
Interpret	Compare	Summarize	Trace
Paraphrase	Contrast	Rearrange	Discuss

Create a Culture of Excellence Where Every Student Is Expected to Succeed

HH

Creating a culture of excellence is not an easy sell to most teenagers who are immersed in a FedEx'd world where fast gets more play than well done. Even defining academic excellence, proficiency, and mastery can be an elusive proposition for students. It's worth exploring examples of excellence that young people experience in their own lives and solicit from them the criteria that make a sports team, a piece of clothing, a movie, or a meal excellent. In the classroom, develop rubrics for important assignments that describe explicit criteria for proficiency.

For many students recognizing the differences between excellent and mediocre end products or performances is blurry at best. Ask students to share something in their lives that they have mastered successfully or a skill or talent where they have increased their level of competence. Explore the differences between a personal performance they would describe as lousy and a personal performance that indicates a high level of proficiency. This kind of critique requires lots of practice and the patience to observe and compare different results systematically with an eye for detail. Students need to look at and discuss a variety of work samples that run the gamut from shoddy to superior quality.

Students also need to develop an accurate assessment of their efforts. What will it take for them to reach a level of proficiency or high performance? Ask students to spell out what specific efforts they think are necessary to earn an A and what kind of effort earns a D.

The point here is many students will never experience the personal satisfaction and pride that accompany a high level of proficiency unless we create an environment that expects excellence from everyone and we provide the push and support to help them get there.

Life Skill Connection

16. Work for high personal performance and cultivate your strengths and positive qualities

Sample Activities, Strategies, and Routines

- **Require All Students to Reach a Standard of Mastery on Imporant Assignments**
- **Insist on Completion**

Require All Students to Reach a Standard of Mastery on Important Assignments

Choose one project, problem, performance, or product each quarter that every student must complete at a level of excellence. Develop criteria for completion; ask students what they will need in the way of support; block out time to meet with students individually; create a way for students to indicate the status of their work; develop ways for students to share and critique their work with other students; choose how the class will celebrate everyone's successful completion.

Insist on Completion

Many teachers share the opinion that students who choose not to complete work must accept the consequences of this choice—a lot of zeros in the grade book. Unfortunately, this policy makes it difficult to help students acquire the tools that make completion a consistent habit.

Failing or marginal students often attribute their turnaround to teachers who "dog" them, who won't allow them to do nothing. Develop a set of strategies that back up your expectation of completion. These strategies might include:

- Required conference hour (the day you stay late after school) for students who have more than two assignments missing.

- A system of partial credit for completing work late and retaking tests.

- Establishing a required "homework" hall with other teachers so that a group of you can rotate monitoring these afterschool sessions.

- Learning contracts that you, the student, and a parent/guardian sign that state what each person will do to support student's completion of school work.

Provide Steady Doses of Encouragement

HH | Small doses of encouragement take very little time but pack a big pay-off when they become part of your daily classroom routine. What counts for kids is your honesty. Encouragement rings false when it flatters or overstates.

Life Skill Connection	**20. Give and receive feedback and encouragement**
Sample Activities, Strategies, and Routines	• **Daily Check-in's** • **Encourage Students to Tell You What They Need** • **Saying It Out Loud So You Believe It** • **You Change — I Change** • **Develop an Informal Mentoring System**

Daily Check-in's

Quietly seek out hard-to-reach students personally on a daily basis, saying something that says to them "I notice you"; offering words of encouragement; checking out how they're doing; or asking them a question about something that interests them.

Encourage Students to Tell You What They Need

For many students, one of the best ways to be supportive is to ask them directly to tell you the kind of support that will help them to do their best or get back on track when they've experiencing difficulties. You might want to ask students to give you their ideas in a journal entry.

Saying It Out Loud So You Believe It

When students have completed a task or mastered a skill, ask them to tell you what internal qualities helped them to be successful.

You Change — I Change

Let students know that when you ask them to make a change in their behavior that they can count on you to do what it takes to support that change. Sometimes this can may mean changing something you do in class or saying things in a different way. It can often mean deciding together on the best ways to check-in, call attention to inappropriate behaviors, or give students feedback on how they're doing.

Develop an Informal Mentoring System

Meet with teachers who work at the same grade level and make a list of students whom you feel would benefit the most from having an adult mentor who is on their side as an advocate, someone who checks in with them on a weekly basis, provides an extra dose of support and encouragement, listens, does little things that show they notice and care. Each teacher chooses to be a mentor to one or two students. Check in with your teacher group to share information, successes, etc.

Giving Specific Feedback

Link students' personal qualities to specific behaviors and academic efforts that you notice and appreciate. Here are some examples: "I noticed how you completed your last three labs. You tackled every part of each lab. That showed real perseverance." "I saw how you encouraged other students in your group to come up with more ideas. I appreciate your leadership." "Before you started on your project today, I noticed that you took the time to check the machinery and get all of your tools out before jumping in. That shows me you've got great self-discipline. You know what to do without being told."

• **Guidelines for Giving Feedback**
• **Praise and Criticism versus Feedback**
• **Link Personal Qualities to Specific Behaviors and Accomplishments**

Guidelines for Giving Feedback

Feedback is an essential tool for creating and sustaining successful classrooms. Feedback gives us a process to share what we've experienced, positively or negatively, without being punitive or judgmental. More than anything else, feedback allows teachers and students to let go of perfection and makes it okay to discuss feelings and reactions honestly and openly without fear of reprisal or recrimination. By sharing observations about concrete, specific behaviors, constructive feedback separates the person from the problem, providing information and insight that people can use to change what's said and done the next time. Here are some guidelines for giving feedback.

Before giving feedback to individual students:
• Make a request and ask for permission.
• Consider issues of timing (now, later, much later).
• Find a private place to talk.
• You might say, "I'd like to give you some feedback about _____. Is now a good time or would you feel more comfortable if we talked at _____."

When you are giving feedback:
• Encourage the person to do some self-assessment and reflection first.
• Describe your experience, your observations, and your reactions.
• Give feedback that provides specific information that might be helpful to the other person.
• Be sure to provide positive comments about what's working as well as constructive suggestions.
• Link students' positive behaviors or efforts to the personal qualities that enabled them to do what they did or invite students to identify the personal qualities that enabled them to do what they did. (See page 147)

If the feedback is about incomplete or unsatisfactory work or negative behaviors:
• Express your feelings and spell out the specific problems: For example you might say, "I'm concerned about the three missing assignments on _____." Or "I'm disappointed when I noticed you made several starts on this project and haven't yet turned in your outline." Or "I felt upset when I heard you tease Mia about her clothes." Or "I was surprised when I read your paper and I noticed that you didn't defend your arguments citing examples from the text."

• Pause and invite student to comment and provide more information.

• State your hopes and expectations and invite student to generate suggestions for what they can do to make amends, self-correct, or change course. For example: "My hope is that you can complete the outline by Thursday. Tell me how you can make that happen."

• Sometimes you might want to review what happened and discuss what a student could do differently so the problem doesn't occur again.

Praise and Criticism vs. Feedback

Here are some thoughts to keep in mind about giving feedback.

Criticism shuts us down. Criticism usually makes us feel too hurt and defensive to listen, evaluate, and assess what we're hearing. Criticism makes us feel judged as people. Empty praise is praise that is ultimately a judgment of the doer, not the deed, and is too general. Examples of empty praise are, "You're doing great," "Excellent," and "You're terrific." Empty praise often makes us feel uncomfortable and anxious because although the comment is positive, we still feel that we are being judged as people.

Try to give feedback on the deed, not the doer. Effective feedback will let you give your information and opinion to someone while keeping the lines of communication open. Feedback about the deed puts the focus on what a person did or said and how he or she did it, rather than on whether the person is good or bad. Think of feedback as playing back a videotape of what just happened. Feedback also lets the other person know that you're paying attention.

Good feedback begins with a positive response to the event, task, activity, or behavior under discussion. The person giving feedback can then move on to make constructive suggestions.

Give feedback using concrete, specific language that indicates what you saw, heard, felt, or experienced. If you use general words like okay, great, interesting, not good enough, the receiver won't get the specific information that he or she needs. Feedback statements can begin different ways:

- Naming what you witnessed a person say or do. Examples: "You made everyone in the group feel welcome by inviting them all to say something in the beginning." "You spoke loudly enough so that we could all hear you." "You found three different solutions to the problem."

- Giving reactions from your perspective. When someone gives us feedback, he or she is letting you know how our words and behavior affect them. For example, "I liked it when you..." "I noticed that..." "I observed that you..." "I appreciate it when you..." "It would have helped me understand better if you had..."

When feedback is given, the receiver is in control of the data. The receiver of the feedback can assess what aspects of the feedback ring true for him or her. The receiver also decides what to do with the feedback, how to use it, and what to do next time.

Think about feedback as a package you receive in the mail. You can choose to 1) Return it to the sender because it came to the wrong address, 2) Keep the package, open it, and use what's in it right away, 3) Keep it on the shelf for now and think about using it in the future.

Link Personal Qualities to Specific Behaviors and Accomplishments

A

Accepting/Acceptance
Accurate/Accuracy
Adaptable/Adaptability
Analytical/Analysis
Appreciative/Appreciation
Assertive/Assertiveness
Attentive/Attentiveness

B

Brave/Bravery

C

Careful/Carefulness
Caring/Care
Collaborative
Committed/Commitment
Compassionate/Compassion
Concerned/Concern
Competent/Competence
Confident/Confidence
Consistent/Consistency
Cooperative/Cooperation
Creative/Creativity
Curious/Curiosity

D

Decisive/Decision Maker
Dedicated/Dedication
Dependable/Dependability
Detail oriented
Determined/Determination

E

Easy-going
Effective
Efficient/Efficiency
Empathetic/Empathy
Energetic/Energy
Encouraging/Encouragement
Enthusiastic/Enthusiasm

F

Fair/Fairness
Focused/Focus
Forgiving/Forgiveness
Friendly/Friendliness

G

Generous/Generosity
Gentle/Gentleness
Goal-oriented

H

Hard Working
Helpful/Helpfulness
Honest/Honesty
Humorous/Humor

I

Idealistic/Idealism
Imaginative/Imagination
Independent/Independence
Initiative
Insightful/Insight
Intuitive/Intuition
Intentional
Industrious

K

Kind/Kindness

L

Leadership
Logical/Logic
Loving
Loyal/Loyalty

O

Observant
Open-minded/Open-mindedness
Optimistic/Optimism

P

Patient/Patience
Perceptive/Perception
Persevering/Perseverance
Positive
Powerful/Power
Precise/Precision
Predictable/Predictability
Prepared/Preparation
Problem Solver
Principled
Purposeful/Purpose

R

Reasonable
Responsible/Responsibility
Reflective
Reliable/Reliability
Resourceful/Resourcefulness
Respectful/Respect
Responsive

S

Safety-conscious
Self-aware/Self-awareness
Self-control
Self-correcting
Self-directed
Self-disciplined
Self-motivated
Self-regulating
Sensitive
Skeptical/Skeptic
Skillful/Skill
Spirited/Spirit
Studious
Supportive/Support

T

Tactful/Tact
Tenacious/Tenacity
Thorough
Trustworthy

Help Students Become School Smart

HH

Most of us would like to think that high schools provide the opportunity for all kids to learn and achieve a modicum of success. Sadly, the gap between achieving and non-achieving students actually increases between 9th and 12th grades, with already advantaged students becoming more so and disadvantaged students forming an even larger pool of the unsuccessful. High schools tend to reward students who already know how to be smart in school. These kids come to 9th grade with norms, habits, resources, and values that mirror what teachers prize and expect from "good students."

Although all teachers are pretty good at spelling out what will get students in trouble, fewer recognize the importance of discussing and teaching specific behaviors and strategies that will help kids become "school smart." Instead, young people who don't fit the ideal student norm are likely to hear a litany of frustrations and complaints about what they should have learned or known before they arrived. This "sink or swim" attitude is not a big motivator for kids who come to school feeling different, alienated, or discouraged.

Life Skill Connection

7. Make responsible choices for yourself by analyzing situations accurately and predicting consequences of different behaviors

Sample Activities, Strategies, and Routines

- **Have a Conversation About School Smart Strategies**
- **Share Strategies and Habits That Help Students Do School**
- **Habits and Strategies Checklists**

Have a Conversation About School Smart Strategies

One step is making time to discuss this topic in class. Acknowledging that high school is not exactly a "student friendly" environment for lots of kids goes a long way toward building trust with students who can't imagine that any adult knows what school is like for them. Equally important is explaining to students that people aren't born with "school smarts." Anyone can learn what it takes to be smart. We do need to be mindful, however, that students who grow up in white, middle class, educated families, get a lot more practice at this before they ever enter 9th grade. Less advantaged students should be able to count on some adults in their lives who will help them decode what high school is all about.

Reassure students that high school primarily rewards one kind of academic success, giving less attention and recognition to other ways of being successful in the world. Even though students have countless occasions outside of school to show how they are capable, competent, and responsible, it's the satisfactory completion of high school that remains the gatekeeper to a young person's future.

So helping students learn how to "do high school" is a good thing. Being "school smart" doesn't have to remain a mystery, and it doesn't mean students have to give up who they are.

The composition of students in each class will influence whether your conversations occur with the whole group, in small groups, or one-on-one.

If most of your students need to become more "school smart," talking about this openly in class can be positive and supportive. On the other hand, if most kids are already savvy about how to "do school," you may want to share some information with the whole group and discuss other issues privately with students.

How might you begin a conversation about "school smarts"?
1. You might begin by discussing different kinds of "smarts" that students need to survive and succeed. For example, exploring what students need to know to be "street smart" or "work smart" can help them appreciate the need for behaving differently and holding different attitudes in different settings.
2. Brainstorm the benefits of moving successfully from one setting to another, pointing out that people who can do this well usually have more choices and more opportunities in life. How does this ability to move from setting to setting give students more power?
3. Give students information and teach them strategies that help them become more "school smart."

Share Strategies and Habits That Help Students Do School

The following section describes some specific school smart strategies with suggestions for how you might help students develop these strategies and use them more often.

I know how to "read" what really matters from teacher to teacher. For example, I can figure out the bottom line rules I need to pay attention to in each class and I know what to avoid to stay out of trouble.

A Way to Help: Give students a quiz on school-wide rules and consequences and classroom boundaries, non-negotiables, and consequences in your class. And be sure they know that it counts toward their grade

I know what to do and say that will get a teacher's positive attention without "brown-nosing" or "sucking up."

A Way to Help: Let students know five things they can do to get your positive attention. To lighten things up have a bag of mini-candy bars or funky prizes to toss out intermittently when you catch students doing the right thing.

I can adjust to different norms from class to class. For example, I know for one teacher tardy means "not in your seat when the bell rings" and for another teacher tardy means "you've got a minute or two before you will be marked late."

A Way to Help: This is good thing to discuss with students for all kinds of reasons. Are norms consistent or inconsistent from one class to another? Ask students how they navigate this. You might want to explore what's good and what's bad about having different norms.

I know how to become invisible when I'm not prepared or when I'm distracted by a something else going on outside of class.

A Way to Help: This is probably a private conversation. The idea that there are things you can do to disappear or avoid drawing attention to yourself is big news for some kids. In the same vein the idea of pretending to pay attention actually helps some kids to focus.

I know how to talk with teachers privately when I've got a problem learning something, completing an assignment, or meeting a deadline. I also know that if I do this sooner than later, it will probably be easier to deal with it.

A Way to Help: This is so important that it deserves to addressed with the whole class. A good way to introduce this skill is to ask students to present two different role plays, showing ineffective and effective ways to get the help and understanding a student needs. Be sure to do the ineffective role play first so students can discuss what made it ineffective and what they might do and say differently to make it a more effective request. Keep in mind that students who don't have the words might not have the confidence to do this, so rehearsal is extremely helpful.

I can "buddy up" with other students when I think it will help me study or complete an assignment.

A Way to Help: This may merit a discussion about the difference between cheating, copying, and working collaboratively. You might want to establish "home groups" so students automatically have some study buddies they can work with throughout the year (p. 92). Or you might explore with a student who they would imagine to be a good partner to work with.

I can identify the students in class who can help explain or show me how to do something when I don't understand.

A Way to Help: Students ultimately feel more personally powerful when they have strategies they can use that don't always involve going to the teacher for help. One idea is to have students identify two others they feel comfortable asking for help. Have students write the names down for you and for themselves. This way you have the information to suggest when it's timely.

HANDOUT I

Habits and Strategies Checklists

You might use the following check lists as starting points when you conference privately with students. Together you can identify habits and strategies a student is already using effectively and discuss others that a student might want to try out or use more frequently.

Habits and Strategies that Help You Do School – What works for you?	I do this a lot and it works	It would help if I did this more often	I'd like to try this out	This would never work for me
Sometimes I let my parents know what I need to do so they can help me keep my commitments by checking in with me or helping me stick to a schedule that keeps me on track.				
I know how to use my parents as a shield to protect my time and avoid doing things that might get me in trouble. (For example, I can say, "Look, my parents won't let me go out after eight on school nights." or "You know, if my parents find out, I'll be grounded for a month. I think I'll pass this time.")				
I know how to check myself before I say something out loud—I've got a handle on what's okay to say publicly, what's better to say privately, and what's best left unsaid.				
I know when it's not a good idea to "free-style"—I know the times when I need to do things exactly "by the book."				
When I've got a problem at school I've got friends or family I can talk with who can help me sort things through to come up with a solution.				
When I'm upset or angry I know how to "chill out" and not make a major production out of it in class. I can postpone dealing with it until later.				
I can walk away from ignorant comments directed at me, especially when I think there's not much I can do that will change this person's behavior. I have learned, "It's just not worth my time and energy."				
Around school I know the teachers and administrators who will cut me some slack and those who won't.				

Habits and Strategies that Help You Do School – What works for you?	I do this all the time	I do this sometimes – need to do more often	I do once in a while – this is hard to do	I never do this – I need some help on this
I can tell the difference between quality work and work that is shoddy. I know what I do differently when I make an effort and when I don't.				
I manage my time to meet school obligations week in and week out.				
I prioritize tasks and responsibilities.				
I map out plans for completing a complex task. I identify the steps and materials needed to complete it. I "chunk" a big task into smaller parts so it is easier to check what I have accomplished and what I have left to do.				
I make good choices about when and where to do what homework. (For example, I know what is easier to do when I'm tired and what kind of work requires me to be totally focused and alert with no distractions around.)				
I accurately predict how long it will take to do various kinds of school tasks and assignments.				
I know that there will be some peak times during the year when I need to gear up and crank out school work at the exclusion of most other activities.				
I know when it's important to use standard English and when it's okay to use different dialects and slang.				
I ask myself questions that will help me get ready and organized to do work.				
When I'm distracted I use strategies that will help me refocus and pay attention.				

Habits and Strategies that Help You Organize Information – What works for you?	I do this and it's pretty easy	I do this but it's hard	I'd like to learn how to do this	This won't work for me
I use graphic organizers.				
I use Post-It notes for summarizing information, for reminders, for markers of things I need to read over or review.				
I number chunks of information that I need to remember in a specific order.				
I highlight or circle words and concepts that might be hard to remember.				
I create a picture in my mind that includes all the things that are related to the same concept or category.				
I draw pictures and symbols to make connections between concepts and ideas.				
I re-write information on note cards that will help me review and study.				
When I take notes I leave space to correct things, add new information, and write summary points.				

Help Students Develop a Sense of Optimism

HH   Having a positive sense of the future, holding ambitions, and imaging oneself in different circumstances all help foster resilience and help sustain motivation and perseverance.

Included here are a sampling of activities that encourage students to develop an optimistic image of themselves.

Life Skill Connection   **15. Activate hope and optimism and motivate yourself positively**

Sample Activities, Strategies, and Routines   • **Activate a Positive Sense of Self and the Future**

Activate a Positive Sense of Self and the Future

1. Once a quarter or semester, write students' names on brightly colored note cards. On one side, write a quality that demonstrates a student's capacity as a learner and what they did that exemplified that quality. Pass out the cards and on the other side ask students to write another quality and what they did that demonstrates that quality. These cards can become part of students' portfolios.

2. During one round of regular check-in's with individual students, ask students to prepare for their check-in by writing down the following: "Write down something you're good at that has nothing to do with school and then write down the personal skills and qualities that help you to do this well." During your personal check-in with the student, invite she or he to share what she or he wrote and then explore one way the student might use those skills and attitudes at school to get more interested in something, get better at something, do something new or differently in class, take a different approach to something that's not working.

3. As a quick-write, pair-share, or gathering invite students to imaging their future circumstances this way:

   • One/five/ten/fifteen years from now...

   I will no longer be _____.   Instead, I'll probably be _____ .

   I won't see myself as _____.   Instead, I'll probably see myself as _____ .

   I won't view my current situation   Instead, I'll probably view the past
   as _____.   as _____.

4. Ask students to write a journal entry that describes the jobs or careers that hold the most interest for them currently. This can become a starting point for:

- Investigating a career path and learning more about the skills, credentials, and personal qualities necessary to succeed in this career path.

- A gathering go-round where students describe a job that interests them and one quality they have that would help them be good at this job.

- A closing go-round where students link a job that interests them with something they have learned or learned how to do in this course or any other course they are currently taking.

Help Students Navigate When They Get Stuck

HH Kids who get in academic trouble are often the same kids who don't know what to do when they're stuck and don't know how to ask for help. Ask students to think about these issues through written reflections and through small group and large group discussion. The goal here is to give students both the words and the concrete steps that can help them get what they need by relying on their own resources first, and checking in with peers or the teacher second.

| *Life Skill Connection* | **8. Deal with stress and frustration effectively** |

| *Sample Activities, Strategies, and Routines* | **• Problems and Solutions** |

Problems and Solutions

You might want to start with a common problem that many students experience. Solicit ideas to put together a set of sequenced suggestions that you can post. For example:

Problem:
If you don't understand an assignment:

Suggestions:
- 1st, read it over one more time and name what you think you're supposed to do.

- 2nd, name what is still unclear or confusing.

- 3rd, ask someone in class to share their sense of the assignment.

- 4th, if you're still unclear ask me.

You might use the following chart to brainstorm solutions:

Problems that Make You Feel Stuck...	What Can You Do?	Are There Ways Another Student Can Help?	What Can the Teacher Do?
If you don't think you can complete an assignment on time			
If you failed or received a D on a test or exam			
If you're behind in completing assignments and don't know where to begin			
If you forget your books or materials			
If you've lost important papers for class			

Explore How to Give and Get Support

HH   Resilient adolescents are able to reach out to an array of people in situations when another person's wisdom, opinion, or support helps reduce feelings of anxiety, confusion, frustration, or loneliness. They also know how to access resources that will help them get what they need. Equally important, students who know ways to help themselves through rough periods are more likely to face challenging situations with a measure of confidence and optimism.

Life Skill Connection   **11. Seek help when you need it**

Sample Activities, Strategies, and Routines

• **Reflection Tools for Giving and Getting Support**

• **Giving and Getting Support**

• **20 Ways to Support Yourself**

Reflection Tools for Giving and Getting Support

The two surveys presented here (Getting and Giving Support and 20 Ways to Support Yourself) can be used in a number of ways. When you're conferencing with students who are having a tough time, some of the questions might provide useful entry points to explore what's going on in a student's life. In some situations, you might ask a student if she or he feels comfortable filling out the survey and meeting later to talk about her or his responses. Finally, some of the strategies suggested may be appropriate to explore with the whole class during particular times of the year (i.e. holidays, exams) when the general level of anxiety goes up a notch or when a violent incident or national crisis makes everyone feel more vulnerable.

HANDOUT 2

Giving and Getting Support

Everybody needs support. Think about the people in your life right now who can support you to do and be your best, listen to you, have a good time with you, and be there for you when you need them. Then think about how you play a support role with others.

1. I have friends my own age who really care about me, who can talk with me about my problems, and who can help me out when I'm having a hard time.

   Name_____ Name_____
   If there isn't someone like this in your life right now, who would you like to be there for you in this role? _____
   _____

   What are two things you could do to make this relationship happen? _____
   _____

   Are there any friends your own age, or brothers or sisters, for whom you play this role in their lives?
   Name_____ Name_____
   What is one thing I can do to be more supportive to them? _____

2. I have friends my own age who I can study or do homework with, who I can talk to when I'm having a problem in a class, and who are happy for me when I do well in school.

   Name_____ Name_____
   If there isn't someone like this in your life right now, who would you like to be there for you in this role? _____
   _____

   What are two things you could do to make this relationship happen? _____
   _____

   Are there any friends your own age, or brothers or sisters, for whom you play this role in their lives?
   Name_____ Name_____
   What is one thing I can do to be more supportive to them? _____

3. I have a parent or other adult close to me who expects me to follow rules, and who helps keep me on track when things get a little confusing, a little crazy, or just plain difficult.

   Name_____ Name_____
   If there isn't someone like this in your life right now, who would you like to be there for you in this role? _____
   _____

   What are two things you could do to make this relationship happen? _____
   _____

Adapted with permission from Healthy Kids Survey developed by WestEd for the California Department of Education (www.wested.org/hks)

4. I have a parent or other adult close to me who is interested in my school work, who believes I will be successful, who always wants me to do my best.

Name_____ Name_____

If there isn't someone like this in your life right now, who would you like to be there for you in this role? _____
_____

What are two things you could do to make this relationship happen? _____
_____

5. I have a parent or other adult close to me who listens to me when I have something to say and who talks with me about my problems.

Name_____ Name_____

If there isn't someone like this in your life right now, who would you like to be there for you in this role? _____
_____

What are two things you could do to make this relationship happen? _____
_____

6. I have a parent or other adult close to me who counts on me to listen and be supportive to them when they are having a hard time.

Name_____ Name_____

What's one thing you can do to show them that you care about them? _____

7. At my school, there is a teacher or some other adult who really cares about me, who listens to me when I have something to say, who works with me when I need help.

Name_____ Name_____

If there isn't someone like this in your life right now, who would you like to be there for you in this role? _____
_____

What are two things you could do to make this relationship happen? _____
_____

8. At my school, I have several teachers who notice when I do a good job, who believe I will be a success, who always want me to do my best.

Name_____ Name_____

If there isn't someone like this in your life right now, who would you like to be there for you in this role? _____
_____

What are two things you could do to make this relationship happen? _____
_____

HANDOUT 3

20 Ways to Support Yourself

There are good reasons to get good at doing the things for ourselves that can help us keep on track and moving in a positive direction. Often there is no one around to give us the support we would like. At other times we get satisfaction from working things out by ourselves or doing things that build our inner resources and self-confidence. Take a look at these statements and see what you already do in the way of self-support and what you might like to try out.

20 Ways to Support Yourself	I already do this a lot	I'd like to do this more	I'd like to try this	This doesn't work for me
1. I can work out my own problems if I need to.				
2. I'm willing to try new things that can help me achieve my goals.				
3. I stand up for myself without putting others down.				
4. When I'm feeling down, I can imagine myself in a special place that feels safe and calming.				
5. When something is particularly hard for me, I try to picture myself doing that thing.				
6. When I feel overloaded, I can make a realistic plan that will help me get out of the hole.				
7. When friends are pressuring me to do something that's not a good choice for me, I go someplace private and quiet where I can think things through.				
8. I try to understand what other people go through when they are having a bad time. It helps me know that I'm not the only one who has bad days and bad times.				
9. I have some favorite music I listen to that helps me feel calm when I'm upset.				
10. When I've made a good choice for myself that was really hard to make, I go over what I did in my mind so I can use this experience in the future.				
11. Sometimes I write down my thoughts to help me get a clearer sense of what I'm thinking or feeling.				

Adapted in part with permission from Healthy Kids Survey developed by WestEd for the California Department of Education (www.wested.org/hks)

20 Ways to Support Yourself	I already do this a lot	I'd like to do this more	I'd like to try this	This doesn't work for me
12. When I'm feeling pressured, I don't try to please everyone or try to do everything at once. I can feel good about just accomplishing one thing.				
13. Sometimes helping other people or doing something special for someone will lift up my own spirits.				
14. When I can't solve a problem by myself, I know where to go to for help.				
15. When I've made a bad choice, it doesn't mean that all my choices are bad ones. I have confidence that I can make a better choice next time.				
16. When things are bothering me or I don't feel quite myself, I feel okay about letting someone else know.				
17. After I've done something well, I like going over it again in my mind.				
18. I try to understand my own moods and feelings before I jump to conclusions or do something impulsive.				
19. I'm willing to share my opinions about things even when they may be different from others.				
20. I'm willing to change what I'm doing when things are not working out.				
Is there anything else that you do to give yourself support when you need it?				

PRACTICE 6

Affirm diversity in your classroom

Although affirmation, acceptance, and appreciation for diversity are cornerstones of a *Partners in Learning* classroom, these principles are easier to say than to put into practice. Developing the competence, comfort, and sensitivity to teach so many different students effectively can inspire and overwhelm us. For young people, choosing to act on these principles can conflict with the clannishness of adolescent sub-cultures and the pressures of growing up in a "put-down" society where one student's self-esteem may come at the expense of another's. Adolescents bring equal doses of fear and fascination to their growing awareness of the diversity that surrounds them.

This mix of vulnerabilities and attitudes about diversity can build a wall of stony silence among various groups in the classroom. Or we can make the classroom a safe haven where differences are recognized as resources and assets that can add a richness and vibrancy to any learning experience.

Several things can help us better appreciate, learn about, and teach to the differences among our students. First, we need to know ourselves. Teaching is highly personal and subjective. Thus, we need to be aware of the personal and cultural perspectives that shape who we are in the classroom. The more we know about ourselves, the better we can bridge the multiple and different worlds that we and our students inhabit.

Second, we need to know our students and communicate our interest in knowing more about their unique cultural experiences. Knowing our students well also means learning more about how differences of color, culture, class, character, gender, and genes (the physical traits, personality, and intelligences we inherit) influence adolescents' experience of schooling and how they learn.

Third, we need to know the culture of our school, taking a closer look at how the dominant culture of most American high schools continues to advantage some groups of students while disadvantaging others. For students who perceive themselves as culturally different from the high school norm or whom we perceive as culturally different from that norm, high school life can feel particularly discouraging.

Finally, we need to develop a bigger toolbox of strategies and expertise that can help us become more culturally responsive teachers. Specifically, how do we help normalize the vast range of differences among adolescents? How can we teach more effectively to these differences? And how can we help students better understand and "appreciate how individual and group differences complement each other and make the world a much more interesting place?" (CASEL, 2002)

Know Yourself and Know Your Students

"To be effective teachers, you must be fully aware of who you are. What baggage (your ideas of race, gender, class, and so on) do you bring to the classroom? Before you can be "real" with your students, you must "deal" with yourselves."
(Rasool and Curtis, 2000, p. 94)

Our perceptions of reality—what we take in through all of our senses, what we select to respond to out of everything that comes our way—depend on our identity lenses. Our lenses determine the way we make sense of what we see. Take 60 seconds, and without stopping to think, write down all the words that identify and describe who you are:

_____

_____

_____

_____

_____

Look at your list and look for words or phrases that are associated with any of the following aspects of your identity:

- your race, ethnicity, culture

- your core values—the beliefs, things, and ideas you care about the most

- your gender and sexual orientation

- your physical appearance, abilities, limitations, or illnesses

- your past or current socio-economic status

- your past or current family roles and status

- your intellectual qualities, interests, and learning preferences

- your past or current educational status

- your sense of humor

- your experiences of personal trauma

- your age

- your general emotional state, personality attributes, or temperament

- your friendship or partner relationship

- your avocational passions/hobbies/leisure time activities

- your past or current work status/profession

- your religious affiliation or spirituality

- your country of origin, your regional or community affiliation

- your political affiliation

- any other groups to which you belong by birth, by your family background, by choice

These identity lenses help define who we are to ourselves. They affect how we communicate and interact with students and colleagues. They also influence how others define us. Put simply, these lenses shape what we experience in our lives every single day.

While some aspects of your self-identity are permanent, other aspects may vary according to the privileges, disadvantages, passions, and stressors you experience at any given time in your life. Some lenses may change or shift in importance over time. You might choose to keep some aspects of your identity hidden from others. And there may be some descriptors you didn't list because they don't feel important to you, even though they may be obvious to others.

When you think about your identify lenses, which ones have the most influence on who you are as a person and a teacher. People claim different lenses as part of their core identity and there's nothing right or wrong about valuing any one aspect of your identity over another and no one's unique set of lenses are better or worse than anyone else's. It's also important to remember that every lens carries with it a collection of perspectives and biases that affect the classroom decisions you make every day—from the texts and materials you select, to the learning experiences you value, to the kinds of kids you're most comfortable teaching.

Biases are not all bad—they reflect our passions as well as our prejudices. However, becoming conscious of our biases can help us adjust our teaching practices in ways that foster balance, fairness, and equity. For me, this meant teaching students very differently from the way that I personally learn best. As a school kid, putting a book in my hands was the window to learning just about anything. Yet, through my teacher preparation I became aware that this learning preference is the comfort place for less than a quarter of all learners. So I deliberately set out to learn how to teach in ways that emphasized "hands-on" experiences as well as more reflective learning tasks.

A few examples can help illustrate how biases influence our views of students, teaching, and learning with the caveat that the particular biases mentioned are not necessarily associated with all teachers who might fit the description in the example. If I'm a math teacher who came to the educational profession after a lucrative business career, I might be more intentional about exposing students to a variety of career paths linked to the world of numbers. By contrast, the algebra teacher down the hall who's spent thirty years in a classroom may not even think about math in a context beyond four walls and a math book.

If I was a very successful honors student who loved high school, I might know very little about young people who hate school and struggle to get through four years of it. On the other hand, if high school was an alienating experience for me, I might go out of my way to make connections with the kids who are labeled as loners, losers, and outsiders.

If I am a social studies teacher with a master's degree in Women's Studies, I might include gender perspectives in all of my courses while other faculty may never even highlight women in history. If I am a gay man I might have a keener eye for choosing literature that addresses all kinds of issues around tolerance and exclusion. On the other hand, if I grew up in a culturally conservative community, I might avoid choosing any literary works that might be deemed controversial.

Our identity lenses can also affect the quality of our relationships with different people. When we encounter someone who shares similar aspects of identity (physically, culturally, emotionally, socially, intellectually), we are likely to feel an immediate sense of rapport and affinity with that person (Bandler, 1989, 1993). Think about the kids you are drawn to, the kids with whom you feel the greatest affinity. Who are they? What is it about these kids that creates special connections?

Parker Palmer, in his book *The Courage to Teach*, describes good teachers as those who possess "the capacity for connection." (Palmer, 1998) Imagine creating a space that welcomes students' whole selves into the classroom—a safe space that invites students to express and share important aspects of their identity without fear of embarrassment, condescension, or rejection. As teachers, the more conscious we are of all aspects of our identity, the more open we can be to seeking many different points of connection with students. We might find ourselves continually asking, "What is it I like about this kid that I see in myself or that I see in those I love and respect?" The connectedness we feel with another person also tends to prompt positive assumptions and images of him or her and elicit more supportive, accepting, and forgiving responses toward this individual.

The opposite is also true. Perceiving others as immutably different from ourselves can trigger negative assumptions and feelings of discomfort, mistrust, and fear. These feelings can lead to physical and emotional distancing, and perhaps even contribute to negative stereotyping of all people whom we perceive to be different in the same way.

Sometimes our lack of awareness can drive obvious differences underground. Teachers will often declare to students and colleagues, "I don't see color in my classroom—I treat all students alike." In school settings, you're also likely to hear, "I don't treat boys and girls any differently" or "I don't care where you're from or who your parents are—when you come into this classroom you're all the same."

However well intentioned, these sentiments deny the fact that students do experience school differently as a consequence of race, gender, class and other key aspects of their identity. In "Multicultural Education in Middle and Secondary Classrooms", Rasool and Curtis note that this denial can create psychological walls between students and teachers making it difficult to connect with students whose identity is culturally different from their own. (Rasool and Curtis, 2000, p. 36) When teachers neither notice nor appreciate students' multiple identities, kids can easily pick up the message that, "You don't see me for who I really am."

When young people experience messages of invisibility repeatedly in their lives, "You don't see me" can turn pretty quickly into "You don't want to see me—maybe something's wrong with me." During adolescent identity formation, the absence of positive recognition and images of who you are—through direct affirmation or through the faces you see on TV and in the movies, the characters you read about, the people you study, the adults who work with you—is developmentally dicey. What's worse, though, for many young people, is the experience of being bombarded with negative images and stereotypes that target groups with whom students may identify most strongly—racial and ethnic cultures, newly arrived immigrant groups, poor people, religious minority groups, or gays and lesbians.

Kids cope with assaults on their identity in different ways at school. Some suffer in silence. Other students create a bifurcated identity where they take on a dominant culture persona at school and replace it with their home culture identity as soon as they leave school. This strategy often comes at the cost of "always feeling weird and never fitting in anywhere", as one student put it. Poor and working class students are likely to be mistrustful of adult authority, especially when it's heavy-handed, and will often choose defiance as a way of standing up for themselves. Young people who see themselves as members of "out-groups" at school may turn to ridiculing "in-groups."

Sometimes, as a matter of self-protection, a student will reject learning and the values (i.e. being successful at school) of adults and peers within the dominant culture who convey their dislike or disapproval of all things different from conventional white middle class norms and preferences. Herbert Kohl calls this stance, "not-learning."

> Not-learning tends to take place when someone has to deal with unavoidable challenges to her or his personal and family loyalties, integrity, and identity. In such situations, there are forced choices and no apparent middle ground. To agree to learn from a stranger who does not respect your integrity causes a major loss of self. The only alternative is to not-learn and reject their world. (Kohl, 1994, p. 6)

More than anything else, adolescents want to feel normal and be seen as normal. They are preoccupied in the paradoxical search for a unique identity and a sense of connection with others "just like me." A gay colleague shared what his experience was like in high school.

> *I wanted my teachers to respect and appreciate all of me, not just the achiever/leader part of me that I brought to school. I kept asking, 'Am I normal?' It would have meant so much to me if teachers had pointed out, in a positive, joyful way, the remarkable differences among people we read about and talked about, especially people who broke away from the stereotypes of who they were supposed to be and what they were supposed to do. It would have made such a difference if teachers would have shared stories and examples of people who truly represented all of us—men, women, people of all races and cultures, gays and straights, people with different families, religions, jobs, and education. If teachers would have just been a little more conscious of this, I would have felt such relief. 'I could have said to myself, 'Okay, I can fit in here. There a place for me with the differences I bring. There are other people like me she finds worth noticing and discussing.'*

> *With my peers, it was the same deal. I wouldn't have felt so alone if teachers had reassured us that being different was normal—that there were lots of ways that kids were different from each other, the same way there were common experiences that we all shared growing up. If we had known a little more about each other—if teachers had let us know more often that the differences we brought to class made us much more interesting and made us all a better group—I think our acceptance of each other would have felt easier and more real.*

Know Your School and the Dominant Culture That Shapes What Goes on There

Only when we acknowledge that most high schools espouse a fairly narrow set of cultural norms, values, and traditions can we go about creating high school experiences that better serve all of our students. Sometimes it's just a matter of asking some really simple, but critical questions: "Which students get recognized and rewarded? Do the things we teach and do here reflect the needs and interests of all of our students and families, just some of our students and families, or somebody else's students altogether? Do any of our practices and policies favor some groups of students and harm others? Do any of our practices increase separation and divisiveness among student groups?"

Four brief stories illustrate how paying attention can make all the difference between good practices and bad ones.

1. Two teachers in a dialogue group taught the second year of a two year algebra course for lower track students. As designed by the department chair the course was a series of unrelated abstract topics with no practical applications whatsoever. Students who generally performed well in year one (where the curriculum included lots of hands-on experiences and practical problem solving) performed miserably in year two. Only a fraction of these students went on to take geometry.

   As these teachers described their students' frustrations and their own frustrating attempts to change the course, several teachers had a collective "ah hah!" One person remarked, "You've been griping about this for four years. How long do you think it would have taken to get this course changed if it was a class full of AP students and their parents?" The grim contrast between whose needs get attended to and whose needs get neglected sparked a healthy outrage. The group rallied other teachers to the cause, prepared a course change recommendation, met with the principal and department chair, and redesigned the course by the next semester. In the process, they changed how they would teach the course and changed their expectations of students. They took on the goal of preparing every student to take geometry.

2. Another high school was confronting the fact that year after year, student leaders came from the same academic track and the same neighborhoods. So what did they do? Students and teachers personally invited kids attending summer school to be part of their Student Leadership training team. This one decision completely altered the composition of student leaders and led to an annual campaign to recruit student leaders who more accurately represented all groups within the school.

3. I worked with students and faculty in a large urban high school where a majority of students were recent immigrants from Southeast Asia and Central America. For years, the school fielded a losing football team where only a handful of fans showed up. Finally the school spirit squad had sense enough to ask students why they didn't come out in big numbers to field the team or watch the games. A lot of kids shared that they had no interest in football at all. What they wanted were more opportunities to play soccer and

ping pong. The happy solution? The school stopped trying to make square pegs fit into round holes. They abandoned varsity football, enlarged their soccer program, and established intra-mural and inter-high school ping pong leagues.

4. In a high school that takes great pride in its monthly assemblies and celebrations sponsored by various ethnic clubs, the social studies department decided to stage an annual medieval fair that highlighted European life in the 15th century. As it was conceived, no one raised questions about requiring all world history students to participate in a school-wide event that drew attention to one cultural group at the exclusion of all others. Four years later, there is open discussion and some excitement about making this event one that celebrates the life and culture of groups across the continents during this period of history.

It would be easy to assume that high schools create opportunity and provide greater access for those who don't belong to the dominant culture. The opposite is true. High schools tend to reinforce low self-worth among students of color and non-native English speakers. (Nieto, 1998) Furthermore, the achievement gap between students of higher and lower socio-economic status is greater by the end of high school than it is for incoming ninth graders. (Nieto, 2000, p. 40) Class remains the most influential determiner of academic success in high school.

High schools, in particular, are laden with unspoken rules and assumptions about the right way to behave, the right way to speak, the right way to get respect and power, and the right way to learn and be tested. These rules and assumptions are part of the "hidden curriculum" of every high school, although you won't find most of them in an official school handbook. Rather, these unwritten codes reflect the values and dominant culture of the people who make the rules. Historically, high school rule makers reflect the norms of the educated upper middle class families.

Generally, students who reflect these norms physically, socially, and intellectually get more attention, more encouragement, more resources, better teachers, a more engaging curriculum, and more critical and creative learning experiences. Most structures, practices, and activities in high school are designed to support the success and achievement of this group over other groups.

Taken for granted privileges are all too obvious to people who don't have them. Yet, educators and parents from the dominant culture are often reluctant to acknowledge how policies and practices that favor some students will, by definition, disadvantage others.

Advanced Placement courses and the "honors track" illustrate how dominant culture privileges can operate on overt and covert levels. In many high schools it is assumed that parents are at least familiar with the courses students are taking and will play an active role in helping their children succeed in advanced courses—whether it's editing and proofing a paper, taking time to discuss a project, or ensuring that their kids have the right supplies, books, and gear at their fingertips. Upper track students are expected to manage multiple tasks seamlessly and "chunk" their work into discrete tasks that build on one another. It's assumed that students can find all the resources they need easily and use them effectively. Most importantly, when students are experiencing difficulties, it is assumed that they can talk with teachers comfortably or seek out other students to study with. All of these behaviors reflect habits, family values, and expectations associated with upper middle class educated families.

Over the years, I've talked with hundreds of students and adults who saw themselves as culturally different from the majority of their peers in advanced classes. Here's what they have to say about what it was like for them in advanced and upper level courses:

From a young man who recently emigrated from Cambodia:
"I didn't know other kids in the class while they all seemed to be friends. If I didn't know something, it was hard to ask them. I didn't want to feel stupid."

From a Mexican young woman:
"My friends thought I was crazy to take this class. In a way I had to pretend I wasn't me. It was like somebody else was taking this class, speaking and acting in a foreign language."

From a white working class young man:
"I don't have a computer at home so it's hard to keep up. I have a job too. I had to drop one AP class because I didn't have time to do all the reading. I felt so different from everyone else, like I wasn't really good enough to be here. Sometimes it felt like everyone else knew what the teacher was talking about except me."

From an African-American young man:
"I constantly felt like I had to prove that I belonged in this class even though I knew I was smart. Other kids kept looking at me as if they were waiting for me to drop out. It was hard to speak because I was so afraid of making a mistake. Who needs that? No wonder my friends won't take AP classes."

From a Puerto Rican young woman:
"As soon as people heard my name in class I was different to them—and Spanish wasn't even my first language growing up. What was I doing in advanced science classes? Nobody came right out and said this but I knew that they were thinking it. I hated that I had to wear this label when the white kids didn't have to wear any."

From a young woman from Guyana:
"My parents had to push people at my high school so I could be in advanced classes. English was my first language, but everyone assumed that I couldn't speak English well because I was dark skinned and from a different country. No one ever bothered to ask what my education was like before I moved here."

One absolute about high school is that no student feels confident and on top of things three days in a row. On the other hand, the fears about fitting in and doing well don't feel quite so daunting when kids feel supported by friends and adults at school. When I asked these students what kinds of support from teachers and the school helped them succeed and the kind of support they wished they had had, some common themes emerged:

- It was helpful when teachers made an effort to check in with them instead of assuming that they would go to a teacher and ask for help. Countless students remarked that the rule of thumb in upper track classes was, "If you have a problem, see me." For many students, this expectation of assertiveness felt awkward and uncomfortable because it was so different from the way they were taught to relate to adults at home. One student said, "When I was having trouble writing essays the way the teacher wanted them written, I was always hoping he would ask me to come in and work with him on my writing. There were times when the written comments on my papers just didn't make sense to me."

- Students say how much they would have liked to hear from former students who were just like them—students who could give them a "heads up" about what to expect and offer tips on how to survive.

- Students of color often expressed sadness and anger when pointing out how seldom they ever had teachers of color who taught them upper level courses. Students felt frustrated that so many of their teachers couldn't understand why many ethnic minority students see being smart and being "good at school" as a "white thing." One young man remarked, "Take a look around. Most of the teachers, administrators, upper track students, and parents you see in school are all white. My coach is black—how's that for stereotyping? What I wanted was a black physics teacher." In this discussion, students never ran out of ideas for how to invite a more diverse cross-section of men and women into their schools who could share their career pathways and successful lives with young people.

- Words of reassurance that they really could do the work felt particularly crucial to these students. When they felt lost or overpowered by their peers, they longed for words of confidence and a boost of encouragement.

- They wanted teachers to truly understand what it took for them to make it in their classes. None of these kids ever said, "I want my AP teacher to cut me some slack." What they did say is how much it meant to them when a teacher invited them to talk about how it was going for them day in and day out, what was hard to manage, what was getting easier. Students were deeply grateful when teachers took the time to talk to them privately and acknowledged the sacrifices and efforts they were making to hang in.

- Many students said that they wished they could have taken fewer courses during a semester—fewer, but more difficult classes. Students felt that learning the ropes of doing well took so much longer than they ever anticipated. Many said that they would have learned more if they could have successfully completed fewer more difficult courses than ending up with a mediocre record in six mediocre courses. For kids who worked long hours or were slow readers, they felt they could have done much better at juggling home, work, and school if they had had more time to study during the school day. Some students brought up that they never even knew they could take courses in the summer if they hadn't failed anything. Many students would have been willing to adjust summer job schedules to set aside mornings for a course.

- Many students shared stories of not having their academic act together until the second half of high school and didn't want to be written off. "Just because I messed up in the beginning doesn't mean I'm always going to mess up. Sometimes I needed a new start."

Other ways to counter the advantages that some students bring to class include teaching students the explicit codes and rules that are part of being "school smart." This can be as simple as helping a student figure out where to sit to maximize alertness or as complex as learning how to skim a book or chapter when you don't have time to read the entire assignment carefully.

In some high schools where advanced courses are open to all students, faculty and volunteers facilitate study groups to ensure that all students have access to the resources that will help them learn successfully. Other schools have developed mentoring programs where students of color meet regularly in support groups with a mentor who is from their own cultural background. These groups become a sanctuary where students can share success stories, discuss their difficulties, problem solve together, and support one another.

Recently, while discussing the challenges that some kids experience in upper level courses, a teacher shared her reservations about providing too much support. She said, "I worry about coddling kids and not making them accountable to real life expectations. It was good for me to feel a little snowed under and have to figure things out for myself. I had to make some hard choices at times and I learned to deal with 'no excuses' deadlines." I invited her (and the rest of the group piped in) to make a list of all the habits, family traditions and routines, resources, special activities, and types of adult-child interactions that had prepared her to meet the challenges of difficult courses with her head up and her feet on the ground. We stopped at item forty-three, stunned at how easy it was to generate an exhaustive list of assets that gifted her with unflagging self-discipline and encouraged her to take on any intellectual challenge. Here's the list:

1. I had to do homework every night after supper.
2. My parents always told me I could accomplish anything.
3. My parents have friends who all have professional jobs.
4. I have always been expected to go to college.
5. I have played the piano and taken lessons for many years.
6. My parents read to me since I was a baby.
7. Everyone in my family reads for pleasure.

8. Being on time was drilled into me as a kid.

9. If I wanted to do something that was a little weird or different, if I could defend it and had a plan, I could do it.

10. Most of my friends took honors and AP classes, so everyone I hung out with did a ton of homework.

11. My parents made sure they met my teachers.

12. People bought me books and educational toys that I could play with—I knew how to have fun playing or just being by myself.

13. I had a regular schedule for doing chores at home.

14. I was not allowed to work on week nights during the school year.

15. I used a weekly planner during high school.

16. I was on the volleyball team throughout high school.

17. There was a family calendar at home.

18. My parents are big list makers.

19. Both my parents went to college.

20. On vacations we traveled to new places and the kids always got to pick some of the things we did.

21. I watched my mother bring home work from the office.

22. Almost everyone I knew went to college.

23. My parents knew my friends' parents.

24. I had a curfew.

25. If I was stressed out, I could talk with someone at home about it.

26. I had two friends who were in all of my AP classes with me.

27. If I had problems with a class they could help me most of the time.

28. At least once a week we all sat down to a real meal and talked.

29. When I was little if my parents saw mistakes on my papers I had to correct them.

30. If I didn't do something right the first time I was encouraged to keep trying until I got it.

31. My parents, my relatives, and other adults in my life always asked me about school, what courses I liked, and what my future plans might be.

32. My parents showed up at most meetings and events at school.

33. In high school my job was to do well in school.

34. I was encouraged to ask questions as early as I can remember.

35. I was encouraged to ask for what I needed.

36. I was encouraged to be independent and choose activities I wanted to do when I was a kid.

37. I was brought up not to leave something unfinished.

38. Time management was a very big deal—we were always asked about our plans and whether they were realistic.

39. My parents made me watch the news or public TV sometimes.

40. My teachers always expected me to do well.

41. As a kid I knew I could do lots of things well.

42. I was taught to share and take turns when I was little.

43. I wasn't allowed to stay out late just hanging out on weeknights.

This experience left all of us confronting some uncomfortable questions. First, we asked ourselves, "So how many kids really come to school with a comparable set of experiences?" This led us to ask, "So how do we view kids who don't come to school with similar experiences?" As our conversation continued, we gathered up the courage to ask the really hard questions that made us all squirm a little. "Why do we get so frustrated when kids aren't as prepared as we were or would like them to be?" Then, we landed in the pit, asking, "Why is it so easy to punish kids for being different, for life situations over which they have no control?"

Our feelings of frustration and inadequacy reflected the dilemmas of trying our best to teach an increasingly diverse student population in "one size fits all" high schools. One teacher's comment said it all: "I want to get to know all of my students, but there's not enough time to give everyone the attention they deserve. I always feel pressured to keep pushing forward even when I know I've left kids behind."

We all took a deep breath and reminded ourselves that we were already doing an awesome job in the face of awesome challenges. Our group couldn't solve all of the problems of schooling, but each of us could begin tomorrow by reaching out a little differently to just one student. That would be enough for one day.

We ended our conversation by trying on the idea of "no fault learning and teaching." What if we communicated this message to more kids who needed to hear it?

> "I'm not going to blame you because your starting point may be different from other students. I know you want to learn. Everyone wants to feel smart. Your presence, your voice, and your ideas are important to me."

> "I will try meet you where you are. When I miss the mark I want you to understand it's not because I haven't given it my best effort. I can learn more about what you need to feel prepared. I can teach you the hidden rules about what it takes to be successful here."

> "If you can't learn the way I teach, I can try to teach the way you learn. I'm on your side. We'll go the distance one step at a time. You can count on me for that."

Affirming Diversity in Your High School

• Promote awareness and appreciation of differences within the school community—especially related to race, ethnicity, gender, class, physical ability, sexual orientation, religion, learning abilities and preferences, families, and regional culture.

If diversity is perceived as an obstacle or deficit, the divide between who succeeds and who doesn't will only get larger. On the other hand, if we see high schools as pluralistic learning communities, acknowledging all of the differences we bring to the mix, we are more likely to change what we do and how we do it to ensure that all students feel welcomed and all students have a fair chance to succeed.

Becoming a Culturally Responsive Teacher

As defined by Raymond Wlodkowski and Margery Ginsberg,

> [Culturally responsive teaching is] *"an approach to teaching that meets the challenges of cultural pluralism... it has to respect diversity; engage the motivation of all learners; create a safe, inclusive and respectful learning environment; derive teaching practices from principles that cross disciplines and cultures; and promote justice and equity in society.* (Rasool and Curtis, 2000, p. 94)

As suggested earlier, becoming a culturally responsive teachers begins with knowing ourselves, knowing our students, and knowing our school. We are more tuned into the personal and learning differences that make each student unique, and we are more aware and appreciative of how differences in cultural identity impact students' daily experience of schooling and learning. Culturally responsive teaching "capitalizes on students' cultural backgrounds rather than attempting to override or negate them." (Abdal-Haqq, 1994)

From the perspective of teaching and learning—from the classroom environment we create, the assignments we design, the learning experiences we construct, the support we provide, the consequences we enforce, and the ways we grade—it means we're willing to trade in the mantra of "one size fits all" for "one size fits few." (Ohanian, 1999) It means knowing the difference between treating kids the same when it comes to setting high academic and behavioral expectations and treating kids fairly but differently when it comes to the kinds of support and assessment tools we use to help all students achieve. Here's a short list of questions that can inform your thinking about how to make your school and your classroom more culturally responsive:

- How does your school define success? How might a definition of success be broadened to better reflect the aspirations of all of your students?

- How have your life experiences as a targeted person and/or as an ally helped you to connect to young people who are targeted or feel excluded from the dominant culture?

- How does your school (and how do you) encourage students' pride in their home cultures and home languages?

- How can families and respected elders in the community play more vital roles in supporting academic excellence at your school and in your classroom?

- What's already going on at your school that makes all groups feel included and welcomed? What changes in courses and activities would help all groups feel more included and welcomed? What new initiatives would you like to see at your school that would affirm to students, staff, and families that a diverse community is supported and valued?

Affirming Diversity in Your High School

• Broaden opportunities for less powerful and/or less privileged groups of students to participate, to be heard, and to be understood within the dominant school culture.

- What changes in policies and teaching practices would go the farthest to ensure that students who are not part of the dominant culture receive the same treatment and opportunities of those who are more advantaged? In what ways can you provide more differentiated support for diverse learners in your classroom?

- What courses, activities, projects, and events seem to involve the most positive interactions across cultures and different groups? What is it about these activities that attracts a real mix of students (ethnic, gender, social, class, and academic diversity).

- In what ways can you personally encourage and provide opportunities for kids to cross borders in classrooms and school-wide activities?

- How can you encourage students to draw strength and satisfaction from their capacities to cross borders from one culture to another?

> **Affirming Diversity in Your High School**
>
> • Acknowledge the presence of a dominant high school culture and take steps to change the school culture in ways that all students and parents feel welcomed and feel treated respectfully and fairly; recognize how privileges that may advantage one group are likely to disadvantage other groups.

Sample activities, strategies, and routines:

Welcome Diversity Into the Classroom

Appreciation for differences begins with experiences where students can share their own perspectives and enter into the perspectives of others. By taking the time to share personal stories and experiences, young people can begin to sort out and sift through the real and imagined differences they attach to the their peers. While they may learn more about how different they are from some students, they also discover that they have much more in common with others. It is these personal connections that can help a group bond together and feel more comfortable talking openly and sensitively about differences when they become a source of conflict in the classroom. When students identify how they can each help make the group a more caring and effective community, they are more likely to appreciate the benefits that diversity brings with it.

Life Skill Connection

22. Empathize; understand and accept another person's feelings, perspectives, point of view

26. Develop, manage, and maintain healthy relationships with adults

Sample Activities, Strategies, and Routines

- **Cultural Sharing**
- **Share Personal Stories**
- **Make Family Banners**
- **Make Differences Normal**
- **Make Personal Connections**
- **Identity Cards**

Cultural Sharing

Use any of these questions for journaling, pair-shares and micro-labs of three or four students.

- Where was your family born? Where did people in your family grow up?

- Share something that's a tradition or important event in your family.

- Share two values or beliefs that are really important in your family.

- Describe one way you have felt different from everyone else in the past or in the present.

- Choose to focus on gender, race/ethnicity, class/socio-economic status, sexual orientation, or religious affiliation for this question. Think about things you like about belonging to this group and things you don't like about belonging to this group.

- Talk about three groups you belong to by birth.

- Talk about three groups that reflect your cultural identity (ethnicity, family history and status, geographic region and neighborhood, religious beliefs, social and economic background, work experience).

- Talk about three groups that you belong to by choice.

Share Personal Stories

Be mindful of opportunities when you can connect personal stories to what you're studying or to issues that come up in the classroom. Sharing your own stories invites students to share theirs.

Make Family Banners

- The day before doing this activity, give each student a large piece of paper and say, "We're going to create "family banners." Write your full name on your paper and add words, symbols, and drawings that symbolize something about yourself, your family heritage, your cultural background, or something important in your life. We will be sharing them tomorrow."

- At the next class, divide the students into groups of four and give people at least four minutes each to share their family banners.

Make Differences Normal

One way to normalize diversity is to point out people from the past or present who reflect all kinds of differences. During one summer, I worked with a group of teachers from various disciplines who put together lists of people they wanted their students to know about—not only for their accomplishments in their fields and careers, but also for their personal stories that reflected a wide range of cultural backgrounds and experiences; gender and sexual orientation differences; and physical, intellectual, emotional, and social challenges that shaped who they became and their life's work.

> **Affirming Diversity in Your High School**
>
> • Teach students the skills to counter bias, harassment, and stereotyping, and encourage students to become good allies.

Make Personal Connections

Build trust through your personal relationships with individual students. Know each student's correct pronunciation of his or her name. Let students know the ways they can depend on you and the different ways that you will recognize and appreciate each student's contributions in class. Students often reveal that they want their teachers to discover what their lives are like outside of school. Developing a more accurate picture and more sensitive understanding of students' lives also enables the teacher to increase the relevance of lessons and make examples more meaningful.

Identity Cards

Every kid wants their identity affirmed and appreciated. Invite students to create an ID card in which they can self-identify using various descriptors: country of origin, race and ethnicity, gender, groups, organizations, pop culture icons, products, music, media-sports stars with which they identify. Think about how you can bring connections to these groups into your classroom (stories, real people, case studies, Did You Know?, pictures, cross-cultural exploration around one theme); use different youth culture media, topics, and issues as vehicles for problem posing and skill practice.

Become More Culturally Aware of the Students You Teach

 It is important to begin by recognizing and appreciating that everyone has a specific cultural identity. Becoming more culturally aware about the students you teach will help you find more ways to communicate and make connections between the material and their experiences.

Life Skill Connection	**31. Recognize and appreciate similarities and differences in others**
Sample Activities, Strategies, and Routines	• **Connecting to Your Students' Families and Cultures**

Connecting to Your Students' Families and Cultures

- Learn more about their cultures, their neighborhoods, the people who are revered in their communities, and local resources that can be brought into the classroom.

- Establish positive home-school relationships with your students' families. Create ways to help parents know what's happening in your classroom and what their children are learning. Send notes and announcements of upcoming activities to parents. Make a "sunshine call" just to let a parent know the good things you see in their child. Invite parents to bring their experiences and expertise in the classroom.

- Appreciate and accommodate the similarities and differences among students' cultures. Effective teachers of culturally diverse students acknowledge both individual and cultural differences with enthusiasm. They identify cultural differences in a positive manner and are conscious of offering positive examples, stories, models, and contributions from people and cultures that represent the whole range of human diversity. This positive identification creates a basis for the development of effective communication and positive relationships.

Observe What Students Do

Focus on the ways different students learn; observe them carefully to identify their task orientations. Once students' orientations are known, teachers can structure tasks to take students' learning preferences into account. For example, before some students can begin a task, they need time to prepare or attend to details. In this case, the teacher can allow time for students to prepare, provide them with advance organizers, and announce how much time will be given for preparation and when the task will begin. This is a positive way to honor their need for preparation and rituals around getting started.

Life Skill Connection   **31. Recognize and appreciate similarities and differences in others**

Teach Students to Match Their Behaviors to the Setting

We all behave differently in different settings. For example, we behave more formally at official ceremonies. Talk about how people act differently in their home, school, and community settings. Asking students to think in terms of "What's public? What's private?" can help them identify appropriate behaviors for each context. You might discuss differences between conversations students have with friends at home and conversations they have with adults and peers at school or work. How are their behaviors different in each setting? What are the advantages of being able to "code switch"? While some students adjust their behavior automatically, others must be taught and provided with ample opportunities to practice. Involving families and the community can help students recognize the benefits of adapting to different settings.

Life Skill Connection

7. **Make responsible choices for yourself by analyzing situations accurately and predicting consequences of different behaviors**

Consider Students' Cultures and Language Skills in Developing Lessons

Consider students' cultures and language skills when developing learning objectives and instructional activities. Facilitate comparable learning opportunities for students who differ in race, sex, ethnicity, country or region of origin, family background. For example, students might explore a history of number systems from the perspectives of their countries and continents of origin. Or students might be asked to interview someone of their own gender whose career connects to the content of the course. Or when examining the uses of language, invite students to share examples from their first languages that illustrate how words can change their meaning in different contexts.

Make Lessons Explicit

 Tell them how long a task will take to complete or how long it will take to learn a skill or strategy, and give them specific information about what it will take to complete a task or master a certain skill. It may be necessary to provide extra encouragement and support for students who want to achieve mastery but are struggling to do so. They may need you to assure them that they have the ability to achieve mastery, and they may need to know exactly the kind of effort it will take to demonstrate proficiency.

Life Skill Connection

14. Prioritize and "chunk" tasks, predict task completion time, and manage time effectively

Sample Activities, Strategies, and Routines

• **Ideas for Explicit Teaching**

Ideas for Explicit Teaching

• Provide rationales for what you do. Explore and explain the benefits of learning a concept, skill, or task. Ask students to tell you the rationale for learning something and invite them to share how the concept or skill applies to their lives at school, home, and work.

• Use advance- and post-organizers. At the beginning of lessons, give the students an overview and tell them the purpose or goal of the activity. If applicable, tell them the order that the lesson will follow and relate it to previous lessons. At the end of the lesson, invite students to summarize its main points.

• Provide frequent reviews of the content learned and compare and contrast what something is and what it's not, what something does and doesn't do. Take time to briefly review the previous lesson before continuing to a new or related lesson. A good rule of thumb is ten minutes of new material and two minutes of review.

Promote Student On-Task Behavior

Keeping students on-task requires that instruction remain at a level of high intensity. By starting lessons promptly and minimizing transition time between lessons, teachers can help students stay on-task. Try to shift smoothly (no halts) and efficiently (no wasted effort) from one aspect of a lesson to another. Provide a purpose and a specific task for students to do at the same time they are listening or reading.

Life Skill Connection	**16. Work for high personal performance and cultivate your strengths and positive qualities**
Sample Activities, Strategies, and Routines	**• Staying on Task**

Staying on Task

- Monitor students' academic progress during independent and group work. Do informal checks for understanding with individuals and small groups by asking, "What are you doing right now? Why are you doing it? How are you going about doing it?"

- Check with students during independent reading or work time to see if they need assistance before they have to ask for help. Ask if they have any questions about what they are doing and solicit information that lets you know that they understand what they are doing. Also, forecast when and how various skills or strategies can be used and adapted in other situations.

- Require students to master one task before going on to the next. When students are assigned a learning task, tell them (or generate with them) the criteria that define mastery and the different ways mastery can be achieved. When mastery is achieved on one aspect of the task, give students corrective feedback to let them know what aspects they have mastered and what aspects still need more work. Require students to keep logs of what they have learned and mastered in your course.

> **Affirming Diversity in Your High School**
>
> • Develop specific opportunities for young people to cross groups and cultures.

Countering Harassment and Becoming Allies

A big part of making any classroom a safe place is letting students know the words and behaviors that are outside the boundaries of your classroom. Discussing harassment issues serves five purposes.

First, it lets students know that you will be vigilant about listening and looking for words and behaviors that target others and make people feel uncomfortable, embarrassed, or threatened.

Second, it gives you a chance to spell out the ways that you will intervene in situations that look or sound like harassment.

Third, it gives students an opportunity to discuss their perceptions of harassment and to get clear about the school's harassment policy. Most students do not know this information and have a very narrow view of what harassment is.

Fourth, it gives you a chance to introduce the language of aggressor, target, bystander, and ally. Having a common vocabulary makes it easier to link behaviors to the roles we choose to play in any situation.

Finally, this discussion communicates that you expect students to share the responsibility for making the classroom a safe and respectful place for everyone. A sequence of activities that explore harassment is suggested in Chapter 5.

Life Skill Connection	**32. Counter prejudice harassment, privilege, and exclusion by becoming a good ally and acting on your ethical convictions**

Sample Activities, Strategies, and Routines	• **Thinking About Harassment, Bullying, and Bigoted Remarks** • **Define and Discuss Harassment** • **Provide Examples of Harrassment** • **Responding to Harassment**

Thinking About Harassment, Bullying, and Bigoted Remarks

Have students think about your school and choose to write about one of these questions:

1. What kinds of behaviors do you see around school that you think fall into the category of harassment or bullying?

2. Are there any particular groups or types of kids whom you see playing the aggressor /harasser role here at school? Why do you think individual students or groups do this?

3. What groups or types of kids are most likely to be targeted? Why do you think that is?

Thinking about yourself, choose to write about one of these questions in your journal.

1. Think about a time when you were targeted or harassed by an individual or group. What was the other person or the group doing or saying? How did that feel? Did anyone intervene as your ally? If not, what would you have wanted an ally to do?

2. Think about a time when you felt left out or laughed at? What was the other person or group doing or saying? How did it feel for you in that situation? How did you deal with the situation? Is there anything you wish you had done?

3. Think about a time when you witnessed someone else being targeted or harassed? What was going on? What did you do? If you witnessed a similar situation again, what would you say or do differently?

4. If you were targeted or harassed what would you want a teacher to do? What would you want a friend to do?

Ask students to form groups of three or four to share their responses to questions about harassment. Invite students to share some of their stories.

> **Affirming Diversity in Your High School**
>
> • Encourage the use of multiple perspectives and strengthening students' capacities to take on another's perspective.

Define and Discuss Harassment

You might want to make a web chart with HARASSMENT in the center and ask students, "When you hear the word harassment, what words, phrases, feelings come to mind?" Then chart student responses. Clarify the school-wide and legal policies around these behaviors. Explain what you will do if you witness any of these behaviors. Here's a sample sequence of interventions:

• If I hear it or see it once, I will stop and name the behavior and speak to you about it privately.

• If I see you do it or say it again, I will call your family and you will be required to come to a conference hour and write up a report form.

• If it continues, I will notify the dean and school-wide consequences will be enforced. That means...

Provide Examples of Harrassment

Use the following to explain harassment to your students:

Harassment is inappropriate unwanted behavior which disturbs someone. To harass is to insult, grab, aggravate, frighten, tease, taunt, threaten, bully, and/or stalk. Harassment can make us feel uncomfortable, embarrassed, isolated, and angry. Harassment is an act of discrimination based on prejudice. Harassment is mean, harmful, illegal, and doesn't belong in schools or anywhere else.

If someone is doing something to you, or saying something about you, that you are disturbed by or feel uncomfortable about, it's probably harassment. We have the right to be safe. No one has the right to touch us unless we say it's OK. Even if someone is "just joking," if it disturbs the target or spectators of the action, it is still harassment, because mean jokes can be harassing too. If you are disturbed by the cruel way a person is treating someone else, you have the right and responsibility to report the harassment.

Types of Harassment
- Sexual harassment is unwanted, unwelcome sexual comments or actions, including unwanted touching, sexual insults, sexual rumor spreading, staring, unwanted "compliments," and sexual comments or actions with which targets or spectators are uncomfortable.

- Racial harassment includes racist comments and attacks on someone's skin color, native languages, or national origin.

- Heterosexist (also called homophobic) harassment includes anti-gay, anti-bisexual, anti-lesbian, and anti-transgender attacks. Examples include calling someone a "fag" or "lesbo," or calling something you don't like, "gay" or "queer."

- Religious harassment includes attacks on someone's religious beliefs, practices, or group.

- Size-ist harassment means taunting someone because of their height or weight.

- Able-ist harassment means insulting someone based on a real or assumed physical or mental disability. Examples include calling someone, "retard," or insulting them because they use crutches, a hearing aid, or a seeing-eye dog.

- Class-ist harassment includes "making fun" of someone based on how much money they or their family might have. Examples include, "scrub," "Payless," and describing something you don't like as, "welfare."

- Looks-ist harassment means attacks based on someone's looks, including calling someone, "ugly," "greaseball," or "dog."

- Bullying is pressuring someone to do something they don't want to do through physical attacks (pushing, tripping, hitting, kicking, etc.), threats, intimidation, and/or insults.

Excerpted from "What is Harassment?" by Sam Diener, ESR, originally developed for Collins Middle School, Salem, MA.

Responding to Harassment

Talk to students about teasing—when it's fun and when it's not fun. What can we say when it starts changing from the fun version to the nasty version? Explore ways that students can respond to harassment using role plays and/or guided discussion. Whether you know the person well, where the incident happens, how often this has occurred, and how disrespected/violated you feel, will determine what you say, how you say it, and when you say it.

If you are the targeted person, you might try this:

1. Say the aggressor's name and show respect (Sometimes this means saying something like, "Steven, I don't mean any disrespect. I just want you to know...")

2. Tell the aggressor what you don't like, and what behavior is bothering you using any of these suggested responses or rewording a response using language that feels right for you.

   - "I don't like it when you _____.

   - "It doesn't feel respectful when you _____.

   - "That looked and felt like harassment to me. Don't do that again."

   - "Don't go there. That crosses the line."

   - "What you just said felt really uncomfortable. I don't want you to say that to me again?"

   - "You know, I would never say that to anyone. No one needs to hear that kind of stuff here at school."

   - "Look, _____, you're my friend. And I've told you before, I don't like it when you say/do _____. It feels like you don't respect my feelings. Please stop using those words. Can you do that?"

- "I feel disrespected/upset/uncomfortable when I hear you say that to me. I don't deserve hearing that and neither does anyone else."

- "You know, earlier today, when you said _____, I really felt uncomfortable/disrespected. Please don't say that again."

3. Exit (You don't want to wait for a response or a miraculous conversion. Waiting for an apology or change of attitude risks escalating the situation. Leaving the scene, turning around, walking the other way, or focusing attention elsewhere is what you need to do.)

If you see someone else being targeted/harassed, you might try this:
1. Say the aggressor's name and show respect.

2. Tell aggressor to stop, name what you see, and why you don't like it:

- "Knock it off with the abusive language, okay. No one deserves to hear that."

- "I saw that, and it looked like harassment to me. Lay off."

- "If you had said that to me, I would have felt really [uncomfortable/disrespected]. I don't want to hear that kind of stuff when I'm around."

- "You know, if Mr. _____, would have heard that he would have labeled that remark as harassment. Clean up the language, okay?"

- "That really sounds like a stereotype to me. I don't know _____ well enough to make that judgment."

- "Where did that come from? We don't say stuff like that here. That's not what this school is about. Please don't say that here, okay?"

- "I heard that. At this school, that's not okay to say to her/him, me, or anyone else."

- "Hey, that's an ouch. I wouldn't want anyone to say that to me."

- "Watch the language, huh? That's not okay to say to anyone."

- "Look, _____, you're my friend. And I've told you before, I don't like it when you say/do _____ around me. It feels like you don't respect my feelings. Please stop using those words. Can you do that?"

- "You know, earlier today, I heard you say _____ to _____.
   If you had said that to me I would have really felt _____. Please don't
   say that again to her/him or anyone else."

3. Take action
- Help the target leave the scene.
- Go with the target to report the incident.
- Report the incident yourself.

Many thanks to Sam Diener for contributing to this section.

PRACTICE 7

Integrate Multiple Ways of Knowing and Learning

Each of us perceives and processes information differently and favors some ways of learning over others. Consequently, everybody wins when we broaden our definitions of rigor and academic success by providing a repertoire of learning tools, experiences, and assessments in the classroom. This section invites students to think about how they learn and retain information and highlights a variety of collaborative learning strategies that emphasize critical thinking, reflection, dialogue, problem solving, creative expression, and a shared construction of knowledge. These learning strategies provide students with opportunities to learn in ways that are responsive to different communication styles, cognitive styles, aptitudes, and learning preferences.

Sample activities, strategies, and routines:

⌘	**Explore Ways You Learn and Remember**
	The activities in this section help students to explore how they categorize and retain data and to reflect on the kinds of intelligences and learning tasks that they prefer. These activities also provide an opportunity to introduce and discuss three important ideas: 1) There isn't one right way to learn 2) Everyone learns a little differently because each of us brings a different set of perceptions interests, and experiences to any learning situation 3) No one is equally proficient at all learning tasks.
Life Skill Connection	**16. Work for high personal performance and cultivate your strengths and positive qualities**
Sample Activities, Strategies, and Routines	• **20 Things on a Tray** • **Reflections on the Ways You Learn**

⌘

20 Things on a Tray

- Introduce the activity by saying that you are going to explore differences and similarities in learning styles. Place 20 things you have collected on a tray or cloth on a table where everyone can gather around and look at them.

- Explain to the group: "You will have two minutes to look at the 20 objects I have placed on the table. Your goal is to use any strategies you can to remember all 20 objects. Then you will have two minutes to write down as many objects as you can remember when you go back to your chairs. This is not a contest. No one will know how many objects you remembered or not. When you come up to the table, imagine you are in a state of relaxed alertness so that you can focus your attention. When everyone has found a place where you can see, I will uncover the objects and ask everyone to be silent for two minutes as you look. Ready?"

- Set the timer for two minutes and uncover the objects.

- Call time and give students two minutes to write down the objects that they remember.

- Discuss what strategies people used to remember the objects. The sharing will be rich. It is amazing to hear the different ways people organize data (i.e. numbering; alphabetizing; categorizing by color, shape, size, kinds of objects, male/female; making up a story using all of the objects; repeating the names of objects over and over; creating a picture that you walk through touching the objects; studying their placement; dividing objects in rows). Write all of the strategies.

- Here are more discussion points:

  - What objects were easy to remember? Why was that? What objects were hard to remember? Why was that? (The easy to remember objects are usually linked to a personal experience. The hard to remember objects are usually ones that students are unfamiliar with or don't have a name for.) This is an opportunity to explore how we link new learning to prior experiences.

  - Look at the strategies you posted and discuss how students use these strategies in different subject areas to study and retain information. Add other strategies to the list that students use.

  - Invite students to think why people used different strategies to meet the same goal. Point out opportunities in class where they have choices for how to reach a common goal.

Thanks to Rachel Kessler for this activity.

Reflections on the Ways You Learn

This quick guide to Howard Garder's seven different intellegences can be used in the following ways.

- Students can identify strengths, preferences, and "growing edges"—ways of learning that are outside their comfort zone.

- For some independent or cooperative learning projects, you might require students to use at least three intelligences in developing a presentation or creating a product.

- Students might set goals for building new competencies in one intelligence in depth every quarter.

HANDOUT 4

How do you like to learn? What do you like to do?

Are there one or two intelligences where you are a match for almost every statement in the list?
What statements most closely reflect learning tasks that you find particularly appealing or feel like a natural fit for your?
What statements reflect learning tasks that are difficult or boring for you?

Logical/Mathematical
- I like solving logic puzzles.
- I like working with numbers and solving problems with numbers.
- I like to do experiments.
- I like to estimate things and make predictions.
- I like to use tools and equipment.
- I like to reason things out and look for solutions to problems.
- I like to label, order, and categorize information.
- I like working with theories and models.
- I like to design programs on the computer.
- I like things to be logical and orderly.
- I like sorting out and analyzing data.
- I like statistics.
- I like having structures and formulas that will help me get the right answer.
- I like playing games that require strategy.
- I like finding evidence and proving that something is correct.
- I like making lists.
- I like to know how things work.

Kinesthetic
- I like doing things with my hands.
- I like testing my physical strengths and skills.
- I like working with tools and equipment to make and fix things.

- I feel more myself when I'm active, moving, playing, or exercising.
- I like to dance.
- I like to play sports.
- I take care of my body and I'm interested in doing things that keep me healthy.
- I like to perform in plays and skits.
- I like to try out and test things by physically doing something.
- I like to create movements or gestures as a way to remember or give something meaning.
- I like expressing myself physically.
- I prefer doing something rather than reading about it or listening to an explanation of it.

Interpersonal
- I like hanging out with my friends.
- I like to work with others to learn something.
- I'm good at working out conflicts and differences with others.
- I like parties and gatherings with friends or family.
- I like to organize and plan activities and events.
- I'm good at communicating my needs and feelings to others.
- I like helping others.
- I like being a leader.
- I like to figure out what makes people do what they do.
- I like being part of a team or group that has a purpose.

- I'm sensitive to the moods and feelings of others.
- I make friends pretty easily and get along with most people.
- I like to talk to others before making a decision.
- I'm a good participant in a group.
- I like meeting new people in different settings.
- I like learning about different people and cultures.

Naturalist
- I feel more myself when I'm outside in nature.
- I like learning about the natural world.
- I like animals and I like to take care of them.
- I like plants and gardening.
- I'm tuned in to the sensory world outside (water, sky, outdoor sounds and smells, weather, the earth).
- I like to camp, walk, hike, climb, canoe, sail, etc.
- I like to spend time outdoors by myself.
- I like to observe the natural world in different settings in all its detail.
- I connect other things to nature images and analogies.
- I like exploring new places.
- I like returning to the same place over and over to see what's changed.

- I like to see the connections between living things.
- I like doing field studies in the natural environment.

Visual/Spatial

- I like to draw, paint, or create three dimensional forms.
- I like to look at art, architecture, and the built environment.
- I like to work with color, pattern, space, and form.
- I like to present things visually using pictures, charts, graphs.
- I like to do lettering and calligraphy.
- I like to design things.
- I remember things by creating mental pictures and images.
- I like to spend time imagining things.
- I like to transform objects and spaces into something new.
- I can find my way around different spaces and environments easily.
- I notice details about the spaces I'm in.
- I like solving spatial and pattern puzzles.
- I like making maps and diagrams.

Musical/Rhythmic

- I like listening to music.
- I play a musical instrument.
- It's easier for me to remember musical lyrics.
- I find myself looking for a beat, trying to discover the rhythm of things.
- I like to sing.
- I can recognize different kinds of music and different composers.

- I like participating in musical performances.
- I like attending musical performances.
- I remember things by making up a song.
- I like to hum or whistle or have music playing when I'm working.
- I like creating rhymes and sayings that have a beat.
- I like practicing a musical piece until I get it right.

Verbal/Linguistic

- I like the experience of reading.
- I like writing things as a way of remembering.
- I like learning new words and exploring their meaning.
- I like playing with words and making up words.
- I like explaining things to others.
- I like discussing issues with others.
- I like telling stories and making up stories.
- I like poetry.
- I like to write poetry.
- I like creative writing where I can express myself in words.
- I like to write reports and essays.
- I like learning languages.
- I prefer listening or reading about something, rather than watching something or actually doing something physical.
- I like making a good argument.
- I like word games.
- I like listening to stories.
- I like crafting a good sentence.
- I like to analyze and discuss literature.

Intrapersonal

- I like to spend time thinking by myself.
- I am very aware of my own moods and feelings.
- I like being alone.
- I like working independently.
- It's easy for me to make goals for myself and accomplish them.
- I usually know what's the right decision for me without asking others.
- I trust my own judgment.
- I feel comfortable "in my own skin."
- I know who I am and like who I am.
- I have a good sense of what works for me and what doesn't.
- I like sitting back and watching and observing others.
- I like reflecting about what I've done and experienced.
- I like to write my thoughts in a journal.
- I like school work that has a personal meaning for me.

Set the Stage for Effective Cooperative Learning

Although cooperation and collaboration are hallmarks of the new business style, working cooperatively still runs counter to traditional individualistic and competitive school settings where students might even question the value of cooperation. Particularly in high schools, teaching practices and student assessment can often pit students against each other for favored status in the "winner's circle."

In his book, *Nobody Left to Hate*, written after the Columbine shootings, Eliot Aronson makes a compelling case for building collaboration and empathy in the classroom through the use of cooperative learning strategies. He urges us to think about the learning climate we create, noting that how we engage students in learning will influence whether they learn and what they learn. Do we encourage excessive competition where winners and losers are predetermined? Or do we create a learning environment where everyone is expected to work together, look out for each other, and acknowledge the collective talents and insights that each person brings to the task at hand?

Cooperative learning is an intentional restructuring of the learning process where students share a common purpose to complete tasks in ways that include every group member. Especially when activities are structured for "positive interdependence" (Johnson, Johnson, and Holubec, 1994), one student's success is linked to the success of others. A cornerstone of effective group work is the use of the "jigsaw" process where each student brings information, research, or resources to the group that is necessary for full understanding of the problem and successful completion of the task or final product.

Students who work together are learning how to get along together. When students engage in cooperative activities they are developing life long social skills by learning how to:

- Communicate in ways that encourage listening and understanding;
- Deal effectively with people's differences in work styles, skills, interests, and points of view;
- Acknowledge the contributions of others as they help each other and ensure that everyone is included;
- Share leadership, roles and responsibilities, and accountability;
- Practice the kind of "give and take" necessary to make decisions and plans that everyone agrees to implement.

In classrooms, we often assume that students know what collaboration is and we assume that they know how to cooperate. Neither of these assumptions is necessarily valid. Cooperative learning provides the opportunity for teaching and practicing these skills intentionally.

Furthermore, the structure of cooperative learning helps support effective classroom management and discipline. Teaching students to work effectively in small groups helps them improve their self management skills. Secondly, cooperative groups enable you to observe students learning, provide immediate feedback from your observations, and engage in one-to-one coaching while students are working. Finally, when you do have to intervene with a student and handle a disciplinary problem on the spot, you can do it more privately without an audience and without interrupting the learning activity.

Life Skill Connection	**27. Cooperate, share, and work toward high performance within a group to achieve group goals**
Sample Activities, Strategies, and Routines	**• Guidelines for Cooperative Learning**

Guidelines for Cooperative Learning

These guidelines go a long way to ensure successful cooperative learning activities. When teachers complain about ineffective, unproductive group work, I ask them to take a look at this list and identify the guidelines they used for preparing and implementing the group activity. The most common response is "Maybe I used one or two. I gave the assignment and students got into groups and started to work." Effective cooperative learning requires more deliberate set-up and monitoring, but it also produces a more satisfying learning experience and better quality work.

• Divide students into groups of two to five, depending upon the task, students' prior experiences, and levels of skillfulness.

• Identify specific goals for each group. "During this activity, your group is expected to _____."

• Identify specific academic skills and social skills that you expect students to practice. Let students know exactly what you are looking for and listening for when you observe them working. (See Assessing Cooperation, Group Participation, and Leadership Skills in Chapter 2, page 87.)

• Insist that students discuss and make a plan before they dive into the activity. Ask each group to check in with you and share their plan before they start.

• Either assign roles and responsibilities to every group member or invite students to choose roles (facilitator, time keeper, checkers, recorders, reporters, readers, summarizers, encouragers, supply organizer, etc.) and divide up tasks among group members.

- If it's appropriate, frame the activity as a problem to solve. (See collaborative problem solving sidebar on this page.)

- For complicated projects, develop proficiency criteria and describe procedures for completing each task so that students can monitor what they've accomplished and identify what remains to be done. You might also suggest general time frames for completing each task or stop groups at mid-point to review progress.

- Incorporate positive interdependence and group accountability by designing a sequence of tasks where the work of one group member can only be carried out when another group member has completed a previous task. Or "jigsaw" resources where each student receives different information that s/he must share or explain to others in the group in order to complete the task. Or distribute limited resources that students need to share, such as one response sheet for per group. Or assess students on their collaboration skills, taking points off if some students didn't contribute. Give each group a grade for their final product or presentation.

Step-by-Step Jig Saw

Sequence of Steps	Purpose
1. Clarify goals and tasks for all groups.	Focusing
2. Divide tasks in sections and divide students into teams.	Structuring
3. Assign each member of the team one part of the total task. Individuals work on their learning tasks.	Independent work
4. Members who are assigned the same part of the task meet together to review, check for understanding, decide what's essential for the rest of their group to learn, and share ways to teach it.	Expert groups
5. Members return to their teams and take turns teaching their parts.	Peer teaching
6. Individual and/or group assessment/demonstration of what students learned.	Assessment
7. Identify effective teaching strategies.	Debriefing

Collaborative Problem Solving

Collaborative problem solving engages small groups of students in a process of:
- Defining a problem
- Gathering information and assessing the steps necessary to solve the problem
- Generating alternative solutions
- Selecting the means and resources to solve the problem in a way that factors in constraints and meets some interests of everyone in the group
- Implementing the plan or solution

Some Guidelines for Collaborative Problem Solving

1. Describe the problem in detail.
2. Set the challenge and the goal. Let students know there are many ways to solve the problem.
3. Ensure that students have enough information to tackle the problem comfortably. Brainstorm possibilities and review the challenge to make sure that students know what they are doing.
4. Set constraints on what you can and cannot do.
5. Limit resources and materials.
6. Set criteria for assessment.
7. Limit the number of students in a group. Group students in a way that ensures a balance of skill abilities, expertise, and learning strengths.
8. Give everyone a role and responsibility.
9. Divide time between planning and doing.
10. Give instructions in several ways and use examples, illustrations, and models to show what to do or how to do it.

- Incorporate individual accountability by expecting all students to be able to explain a solution or present what was learned to the rest of the class. You might identify who's selected to represent the group's work by "cosmic chance," pulling student's names from a basket. Or motivate students to help everyone learn all the material by giving a group quiz where each group member receives different questions or problems. Assess students' individual contributions. You might want to consider assigning more individual points than group points in your grading scheme.

- Make time for reflection of the group process itself. As students become more aware of the skills they are using to accomplish a task, they can begin to ask questions about how they learn and work in a group. Individual and group reflection can take the form of an "exit slip" that the group fills at the end of the activity; a journal response; a paired "quick write"; or a whole group discussion. Here are a few reflection questions. You might also want to look at the section "Assessing Cooperation, Group Participation, and Leadership Skills" (p. 87).

    1. How did your group work together? What was easy? What was hard? Were there obstacles you didn't count on that made it more difficult to complete your task?

    2. Could you have completed this task by yourself?

    3. What would you do differently next time?

    4. Was everyone listened to? How do you know?

    5. How did you make decisions?

    6. What did you do that helped your group accomplish its goal?

    7. What did you learn that can be applied to other situations?

Teachers serve as coaches and observers as well as instructors in cooperative learning environments. When teachers observe groups working, they have opportunities to monitor, assess, and reinforce behaviors that enable students to interact positively with each other. Conversely, teachers can intervene at times to help students identify and practice a social skill that will help a group to function better.

For students who have an unusually difficult time working in a group, try one of these strategies:

- Assign an individual task that in some way connects to the larger learning experience.

- If you have two or three squirrelly group members, make a time to meet with them outside of class and coach them side-by-side through a cooperative activity, stopping throughout so students can describe what they're doing and name the skills they're using at every point.

- Assign a student to be the "feedbacker" for the period, observing groups and writing comments related to particular skills students are expected to use in the activity.

- Give the student a piece of information that every group needs to complete the task. The student's job is to share/explain the information to every group. This strategy allows a potentially disruptive student to participate, but contains the boundaries of a narrowly defined task and limited group interaction.

Think About How You Want to Group Students

⌘ Building an effective learning community means ensuring that students have plenty of opportunities to work together on different kinds of tasks. No one can force kids to like each other and become friends. However, a crucial life and job skill is the capacity to work with others to accomplish a goal. Let students know this is a basic expectation in your class. You may want to set a goal that by the end of the first month, each student will have worked with every other student. You can create a sheet that students can keep in their notebook that names students they have worked with.

Life Skill Connection

27. Cooperate, share, and work toward high performance within a group to achieve group goals

Sample Activities, Strategies, and Routines

- **Ways to Group Students**
- **Role Cards**
- **Other Grouping Ideas**

Ways to Group Students

Home Groups
You may want to consider forming home groups of four students each who work together throughout the year. (See "Form Home Groups" in Chapter Two)

Random or "Cosmic Chance" Groups
Create random groups of two's, three's, and four's when the "luck of the draw" is least likely to have a negative effect on the quality of group participation. Forming random groups can help change the pace and energy; this also offers the bonus of getting students out of their seats for a few minutes. The potential dread of being grouped with "the kid I can't stand" is less of an issue when students know that random grouping will be used primarily for shorter and less intense activities.

1. Count off. If you have a group of 30, for groups of six, count off 1-5. For groups of five, count off 1-6, for groups of four, count off 1-8, for groups of three, count off 1-10.

2. For pairs, ask students to find a partner who is wearing at least one color that is the same or one piece of clothing that is the same.

3. Have students create composite groups where each group has to meet all the criteria that you have identified. For example: "Create a group of five people that includes at least one male, one female, two people of different racial origins, one person with a younger sibling, one person born between January and June, one wearing glasses, one person wearing athletic shoes, and one person who owns a pet." Remind students that one person can fit more than one category. This is good choice when you need to change the energy and get students to focus in. Ask students to make up some composite groupings.

4. Create laminated puzzles from calendar pictures and photographs. For 30 students, cut 10 puzzles into three pieces each, eight puzzles into four pieces each, and six puzzles into five pieces each.

5. Use playing cards to divide students into four groups having them group according to the face cards.

6. For pairs, find two identical sets of trading cards or art card decks so that matching pairs of the same design can work together.

7. Find interesting wrapping papers that depict multiple variations of the same object (shoes, hats, plants, animals, tools, stars, kids' faces, etc.) for groups of three, four, or five cut out and laminate the objects from identical sheets of wrapping paper.

8. Use different flavored wrapped candies to divide students into groups.

9. For pairs, find a partner who has at least one initial that is the same as yours.

10. For any size groups, keep a basket of students' name that can be pulled to create groups.

Teacher Selected Groups
Sometimes you may want to group students in ways that ensure that students in each group have a balance of specific academic and social skills for a particular task.

Student Selected Groups
There are times when it's good to invite students to select their own partners or groups. This might be the best strategy when students are selecting "study buddies" or when students may be working on a long-term project together. When problems arise in self-selected groups, use the "teachable moment" to encourage students to reflect on what's not working, share what they need to make it work and try to problem solve.

Rotation Groups

If one of your commitments is to ensure that everyone works with everyone else and that students have a stake in supporting each other to do their best, you might want to think about creating different table groups each week, where four students work together for the whole week, and then students move to different groups the next week.

Role Cards

Use colored paper to make multiple sets of 12 role cards. Make at least 10 sets so that you can make groups with three, four, or five roles, choosing the size of the group and specific roles for group members that are best suited for the activity that students are going to do.

Facilitator Gets group started, initiates group discussion, and monitors work process, ensuring that everyone listens and speaks respectfully	**Summarizer and Decision Checker** Summarizes key information and discussion points at each step of the process; checks for agreement on key decisions
Writer/Recorder Records groups responses and/or edits what group has written	**Gatekeeper** Makes sure that group stays focused on goal (tracks time, checks to see if criteria for task are covered, monitors noise level)

Encourager/Cheerleader

Encourages individuals to participate
and makes supportive comments
as people say and do things
that help group meet its goal

Feedbacker

Watches and listens instead of doing;
jots notes about how group is
working together and how group
meets its goals

Reader

Reads the problem, story,
information, or instructions
to the group

Question Asker

Asks questions to seek clearness,
more information, greater
understanding, and alternative
solutions and possibilities

Resource Monitor

Picks up, distributes, collects,
and puts away materials

Investigator/Researcher

Seeks out additional information and
resources to complete the task

Reporter

Presents ideas, solutions,
decisions, and/or insights
to the larger group

Clarifier

Checks with teacher or facilitator
to clarify rules, guidelines, instructions
when the group has questions

Other Grouping Ideas

Academic Grouping Cards

For any academic subject, pair students by:

- Writing key words or terms on cards and cutting cards in half.
- Writing key words or terms and their definitions on two sets of cards that create matching pairs.

For Math

- 2's — two equations that have a common unknown
- 3's — drawn geometric figure, word description of figure, and the degree of angle associated with figure
- 3's — fraction, decimal, and percentage equivalents
- 3's — three equations that equal the same number

For English and Foreign Language

- 2's — antonyms and synonyms
- 3's — words associated with same part of speech (nouns, verbs, adjectives, prepositions, etc)
- 3's — clusters of words that have a similar meaning
- 4's — sets of four characters associated with each book, play, or story
- 4's — attributes, behaviors, and quotes associated with a specific character

For Social Studies

- 2's — Match cities/states; landmarks/countries; famous people/cultures; leaders/countries, etc.
- 3's, 4's, 5's — groups of cities that are located on different continents; groups of famous people who lived in same time period; objects and art associations with different cultures, geographical features (names of mountains, river systems, deserts, lakes, seas, etc)

For Science

- 2's — names of chemical elements and their symbols
- 3's, 4's, 5's — groups of animals and plants that are associated with the same classification
- 3's, 4's, 5's — groups of animals and plants that live within a specific ecosystem or belong to a specific ecological niche
- 3's — features of various systems of the body
- 3's — objects that create different sounds (rice, paper clips, ball bearings, pop corn, tacks, etc.) contained in plastic film canisters.

⌘

Use Collaborative Learning Strategies

The strategies in this section cover a range of learning tasks from activating student knowledge (i.e. brainstorming), to exploring and applying knowledge (i.e. investigation rotation stations), to organizing and integrating what you learned (i.e. Pick Three/Pick Five). Other learning strategies are described in Chapters 1, 2, and 4.

| *Life Skill Connection* | **27. Cooperate, share, and work toward high performance within a group to achieve group goals** |

Sample Activities, Strategies, and Routines

- **Brainstorming**
- **Card Sorts**
- **Concept Synectics/Making Metaphors**
- **Demonstration**
- **Drawing/Mapping/Charting**
- **Interview Rotation Stations**
- **Pick Three/Pick Five**
- **Popcorn Style Sharing**
- **Walk-Abouts**
- **Webbing**

Brainstorming

Brainstorming is a process for generating ideas that foster creative thinking. The teacher proposes a topic or question and lists student responses on the board or on chart paper. The idea is to generate the maximum number of solutions for consideration. Here are some guidelines for brainstorming:

- All ideas are accepted and written down.

- There should be no comments, either positive or negative, on any of the ideas.

- Say anything that comes to mind, even if it is silly.

- Think about what others have suggested and use those ideas to get your brain moving along new lines.

- Push for quantity.

⌘

Card Sorts

To help students organize and clarify content information, you can have them sort and rank cards with information related to the topic you are teaching. Here are a couple of examples:

- Make up sets of cards listing a series of possible titles for a book, story, or play that the group is studying. Each card in the set lists a different title for the same work. Divide students into groups and give each group a set of cards. Ask each group to choose the best title and the worst title. Have them defend their choices to the class. You can also do this type of sorting activity with any problem or controversy where there are multiple factors that influence the situation. Students can rank order factors from least to most important and then defend their choices.

- Make up sets of cards listing a series of historical events—for instance, events leading up to the Civil War—and ask groups to arrange the cards in chronological sequence. Or create cards that describe key experiences and milestones in someone's life, for example the life of Frederick Douglass, and rank these experiences from most to least influential.

Concept Synectics/Making Metaphors

Word version: Connect concepts to objects or pictures, (saying "concept X is like picture Y because..."

Physical version: Teachers and selected students act out or physically represent a particular concept for the class, using only their bodies or simple props that can be made from poster board, tape, string, and markers. You might want to select volunteers and practice the demonstration with them ahead of time, or divide the class into groups of four or five and give each a concept to present to the rest of the class. This can be fun and even silly, and it can help students grasp the essence of a concept, particularly those covered in algebra, geometry, physics, chemistry, ecology, and economics.

Demonstration

Don't forget to use demonstrations when giving directions. Many students need to see how to do it before they can do it for themselves. Demonstrations also offer the opportunity for everyone to see and hear the same information at the same time so that questions and reactions from all students are emerging from the same shared experience.

Drawing/Mapping/Charting

Drawing a concept, charting or mapping a process or problem, and using words, symbols, and pictures to express an idea, offer ways for students to translate their ideas from one medium to another. By personally expressing their ideas on paper, students create their own ways of making meaning, understanding relationships, and organizing information.

Interview Rotation Stations

Rather than presenting a panel discussion (where kids often glaze over after a few minutes), you can use this process for investigating multiple perspectives for any current or historical topic or controversial issue.

1. After you have chosen a topic or issue, use a four question frame or another "door opener" to discover what interests students the most and determine the direction of your investigation. Students can respond to these questions as a whole group or you can divide the class into four groups, having each group respond to one question frame.

What do you think you know?	What do you think you know but you're not sure of?
What do you want to find out? Know more about? Understand more clearly?	What are your sources of information for what you know? What other sources could you use to find out more?

2. Prioritize the questions and issues that are most compelling to students.

3. Brainstorm a list of speakers and organizations that might help you better understand your topic or issues. Select three individuals that will offer different perspectives on your chosen issue or topic.

4. Go back to your four question frame and agree on the three or four questions that you want all speakers to address.

5. Ask for student volunteers to arrange for speakers to come to your class at the same time. Make sure students prepare the speakers by providing them with the questions all speakers will address.

6. Time and space logistics—you will need to reserve a large enough space where you can have one group of students meeting with each of three speakers at the same time. You need to also arrange for at least an hour and 15 minutes of time.

7. Given the questions you have agreed to use, develop an organizing grid that students can use to compare and contrast what each speaker says. The frame could look like this:

Topic or Issue:	Question 1:	Question 2:	Question 3:
Speaker 1:			
Speaker 2:			
Speaker 3:			

Before the speakers arrive:

1. Have students prepare the question grid.

2. Divide students into three groups and identify the speaker who will talk to each group first.

3. Make sure you have students who will introduce the speakers.

4. Let everyone know what the format will be: Each speaker will spend 20 minutes with each group of students. They will spend about ten minutes speaking to the predetermined questions and about ten minutes addressing other questions from students. Then each speaker will move to the next group.

5. Introduce the three speakers to the whole class and give them each about two minutes to say a little more about themselves and/or their organizations. Then have each speaker move to the assigned group and begin.

6. Follow up:
   • Have groups summarize areas of agreement and disagreement among the speakers.

   • Go back to the four question frame and assess what you have learned that you didn't know before.

   • Gandhi said, "Everyone has a piece of the truth." What piece of the truth did each speaker contribute to a more complicated, but deeper understanding of the issues?

   • What did people say that surprised you? "Before, I thought, felt, assumed... Now, I think, feel, know, am aware of..."

   • What new questions do you have now? Are there any areas of confusion that need further clarification?

Now that you have a better understanding of the issue, what do you want to do with your information? How do you want to act on what you learned? How can you share your understanding with others?

Pick Three/Pick Five

This strategy helps students working in small groups to focus attention quickly on the task at hand. When small groups are expected to generate a list of ideas, examples, evidence, reasons, solutions, etc., first give students a few minutes to brainstorm. Then ask them to discuss and evaluate their ideas in the group with the goal of agreeing on the three or five most important, most unusual, most illustrative, most descriptive, most representative, most interesting ideas that they have generated. For example, using a novel or text, students could pick three phrases that best describe a particular character or three pieces of evidence that support a group's rationale for making a specific decision.

Popcorn Style Sharing

In this technique, a set amount of time, usually about four minutes, is allotted for the whole group to share ideas on a topic. Free expression of ideas should be encouraged in a non-judgemental atmosphere. The sharing is "popcorn" style, meaning that rather than going around in a circle one by one, students are welcome to voice their opinions in a random order. There is no pressure for students to share if they don't wish to.

Walk-Abouts

Post lots of questions, problems, pictures, or any other material related to a specific topic all around the room. Give students 3" x 5" cards and ask them to pair up and choose three or five items to respond to. Pairs discuss the item, agree on their response, write it on their card, sign their card, and tape it next to the item they discussed.

Webbing

This strategy gives students the opportunity to visually connect various aspects and levels of a particular topic. It can also be used at the beginning of a unit to help the teacher gauge students' level of familiarity with and understanding of a topic. The key word or concept is placed in the center of the diagram. Students then suggest words, images, phrases, feelings, and ideas that they associate with that word or concept. These associated words are added to the diagram, branched off from the center. Related ideas are clustered together.

CHAPTER 4

Getting Started Step-by-Step

One of the best things about schools is that everyone gets to start fresh in September. The new school year is when teachers are most enthusiastic about trying out something new and students are most receptive to learning new routines. In September, we're primed for putting some extra time into preparation and planning.

Over the years, one of the common frustrations we hear from teachers in our secondary workshops is, "I want to do things differently, but I really don't know exactly what I should introduce when. It's hard to really imagine how I can integrate these ideas into my regular schedule and curriculum."

To present a clearer picture of what it would look like and sound like to establish a *Partners in Learning* classroom, we decided to offer a step-by-step guide in this chapter. It includes suggestions for preparations before school opens, a special focus on the first day of class, and a day-by-day guide for the first month of school. The goal in laying this out is to introduce essential practices during the first month that let students know that community, connection, and cooperation are just as important as the content of your curriculum. As you read this, whether you're a twenty-year veteran or just beginning your teaching career, we hope that these suggestions can help set the stage for creating a positive, productive learning environment that sustains itself throughout the year. The three sections of this chapter are called:

- Before the School Year Begins
- The First Day of Class
- The First Month, Day by Day

Before the School Year Begins

Getting ready for school is a big deal. There's too much to do and never enough time! As you prepare for your classes and incoming students there are a few things you might want to do that will:

- welcome each student and set the stage for clear communication with students and their families;
- set the tone for what really matters in your classroom;
- organize your classroom space to maximize learning, responsibility, and community; and
- help you create a learning environment that communicates organization and focus, and encourages high student participation.

Before the School Year Begins

- Write a letter or create a videotape for families of your students.
- Design an assessment and record keeping system that is standards and learning friendly.
- Stock up on supplies.
- Arrange desks and chairs in a way that makes it easy to see everyone and learn their names.
- Make the classroom "ours."

Write a Letter to Parents or Guardians or Create a Videotape for Families of Your Students

Your first contact with parents and guardians sets the stage for communication the rest of the year. We know that kids do better in school when parents are involved in their children's school. We also know that a parent's influence on their teens is far greater than they think. So you want families to know what's going on in your course. You want families to know how much their support and encouragement can influence both their child's motivation to learn and their academic success.

What do you want parents to know about you, the course you are teaching, and your expectations for yourself and your students? It's likely that you won't see parents at a school open house until several weeks into the school year. Take advantage of "back-to-school" anticipation and anxiety by communicating to parents during the first week of school. Let them know that this is not the last time you will communicate with them. You might want to send a letter home at the beginning of each new quarter, providing a snapshot of last quarter's highlights and a preview of what is coming up. These quarterly communications can also provide the opportunity for students to share their own reflections, self-assessment, and goal-setting as part of letters that are sent home.

Compose a letter to send home to parents and guardians on the first day of school. It's one way to let parents know that their support and encouragement are important to you. Give two copies to each student, so parents and guardians can keep one copy and sign the other letter for students to return to you.

Make your letter one page. This is an introduction and you can always communicate more details later. Choose two or three things that you want to emphasize:

- Describe what your course is about, including requirements, goals, and key learning experiences.

- Describe your hopes and expectations for students.

- Share what might be challenging for students in this class. Have a sense of humor—tell parents if they hear their kids sighing and moaning, it's probably because...

- Let parents know what steps students can take if they are having difficulty meeting class requirements.

- Let parents know how they can communicate with you if they have questions or concerns. Give a school phone number.

- Let parents know what kinds of homework assignments students can expect. Suggest specific ways that they can support and encourage their child's success in this class.

- Emphasize that effort, attitude, and participation really count in your classroom. Identify some of the social skills that you hope will help create a respectful, responsible, and caring classroom.

If some of your students live in families whose parents' or guardians' primary language is not English, you have a couple of options. If all or most of your newcomer families speak the same language, see if someone from your Bilingual or English as a Second Language department can help you translate your letter. If you have students whose families speak a variety of languages, you might invite your students and an English as a Second Language teacher to come in at lunch to work on writing translations of important points in your letter to be sent home with the letter you wrote in English. This activity sends a powerful message to students that you value their family's role in their education and seek their support.

Other Ways to Communicate:
Create a Videotape to Send Home
If you have a communications/video/broadcasting department or your own video cam, introduce yourself by video. Regardless of income, cultural, or social circumstances, most families have a VCR. Create a five-to-ten minute tape in which you introduce yourself and highlight a few important things that you want parents to know. Make several copies of the tape so that three or four students per night can take the tape home, return it, and give it to the next group of families to view.

Introduce Yourself Online
More and more school districts have their own web sites. Check to see if there is a place for teachers to post their own communications to families and students on the web.

Design an Assessment and Record Keeping System That Is Standards and Learning-Friendly

"We need to move from a testing culture to an assessment culture."—Henry Wong

Political scientists frequently use the phrase, "budget is policy," implying that the amount of money legislators are willing to spend indicates how much a particular policy or project is really valued. Similarly, in education, we can say, "assessment is curriculum." What you choose to assess, how you assess students' learning and performance, how you keep records, and how students participate in assessment all determine what kind of teaching and learning will take place in your classroom. Before the school year begins, you might want to think about your responses to these questions:

- What messages do I want to send to students about assessment and grades?

- What are my goals for assessment and grading? (What purpose do grades serve? Do they provide information and feedback so students can improve? Do I want to assess what students already know? Am I using grades as a threat or punishment? Are grades a means for students to draw comparisons among themselves—who's smart and who's dumb? Do grades enable students to assess what they've learned, the quality of their work, their mastery of concepts and skills? Do I want assessment to encourage completion, revision, and correction? Should assessment help students see the connections between effort and performance? Should grades help students monitor their progress and set goals for themselves? Should assessment be diagnostic so that I can make instruction more responsive to the needs of diverse learners?)

- How involved do I want students to be in assessing their learning experience in my class? (Student involvement can include pre-grading-period conferencing, student-led conferences with parents, development of portfolios, student written reflection and self-assessment, peer assessment, etc.)

- What kinds of assessments do I want students to experience? (For example: criterion-referenced tests, essays, presentations, portfolios, demonstrations, projects, papers, written and verbal feedback, rubrics that indicate the use and proficiency of specific skills, self-reflection activities, informal checking for understanding, conferencing, peer review, exhibitions, etc.)

- What do I want to assess? (For example: students' understanding of discrete subject matter concepts and skills, mastery of academic standards and benchmarks, students' ability to use multiple skills and concepts to complete complex tasks that demonstrate learning, students' application and meaningful use of subject matter knowledge, literacy skills, learning-how-to-learn skills, work habits and self-management skills, communication and problem solving skills, group participation skills, etc.)

Your responses to these last two questions will shape what you teach and what students learn more than anything else you do.

Even though research confirms that students whose goals focus on learning for understanding are more receptive and less anxious learners, high school classrooms are, nonetheless, grade driven. All too often, grading can become a sorting device, turning students into grade point averages and the curriculum into an endless series of graded tasks that may or may not be meaningful. The grade on the paper becomes the end in itself, pushing aside other ways of providing information and feedback that can help students know where they stand and what they are learning.

Nearly a decade of conditioning prompts any high school student to ask, "Are we getting a grade for this?" regardless of the task. Students have already received a loud and clear message throughout their schooling that if it isn't graded, it doesn't really count. Asking teenagers and school decision makers to let go of this assumption is probably unrealistic. However, one way to counter this automatic response is to widen the net of what you assess and expand the tools that you use for assessment.

Support Academic Achievement by Assessing the Three L's — Learning to Learn, Literacy, and Life Skills

Semester grades and report cards mostly measure students' performance on written tests and assignments. What they don't measure are "learning how to learn," literacy, and life skills (competencies related to self-management, interpersonal effectiveness, and group participation) that ultimately determine high or low academic achievement in school, and high or low performance on the job. The result is that most students, especially average and low performing students, have little awareness of the connections between personal effort and their academic performance.

You have the power to change this by designing an assessment and record keeping system that includes assessment of the three L's. When you integrate assessment of these skills into daily classroom practice and quarterly and semester grades, you are saying that you value effort and expect students to strengthen skills that will help them become more successful academically. In the bargain, you also provide students and families with more information about who students are as learners. Think about incorporating the following kinds of skills into your grading system.

Assess "Learning How to Learn" Skills

"Learning how to learn" skills, or metacognitive skills as they are sometimes known, refer to one's "self-awareness of cognitive processing strategies and the ability to control them." (Silverman and Casazza, 2000, p. 49) In other words, how much do we know about how and why we think and learn the way we do; how much do we know about the task and the goal in front of us; and what kinds of tools and strategies can we access to meet our goal and complete the task?

metacognition

In a summary analysis of research on factors that influence learning, "a student's metacognitive processes had the most powerful effect on his or her learning." (Walberg and Haertel 1997, p. 202) What is also interesting is that students whose orientation is toward "task goals" (monitoring progress, acquiring skills, solving problems, gaining knowledge) rather than "ability goals" (caring about how smart or dumb one is in relation to others) "are much more likely to believe that effort can improve skills and knowledge." (Walberg and Haertel 1997, p. 345) Yet, these are the very skills that we seldom assess. Here is a short list of learning how to learn skills that lead to student achievement in school:

- following directions and routines
- revising, adapting, and changing learning strategies when one's current strategy isn't working
- discriminating between effective and ineffective learning strategies
- asking questions that lead to deeper understanding
- sustaining effort and persevering until completion of the task
- planning and designing activities that enhance one's learning

- seeking out resources that will enhance one's learning
- thoughtful reflection about what is being learned
- assessing one's effort and performance accurately

More specifically, skills associated with work and study habits fall into this category as well:
- use of multiple strategies to study and prepare for tests
- notebook organization
- bringing necessary materials to class every day
- regular completion of tasks on time

Assess Literacy Skills

For the vast majority of average and low performing students, reading, writing, speaking, and listening deficits become the biggest stumbling blocks to success in school. Consequently, for many high schools, improving student achievement means emphasizing reading, writing, speaking, and listening skills across the curriculum. Think about your academic discipline and your curriculum—what are the literacy skills that are most relevant to high engagement in learning and high academic performance?

You might want to choose three or four literacy skills that you assess continually throughout the year, or you might want to assess different literacy skills that are emphasized during different marking periods. Here are two examples: When I taught a world history/world literature block course, it was critical that students understood that writing coherent paragraphs without run-on's and fragments was a first priority for the first semester, while assessing research skills was a major emphasis during the second semester. Secondly, a friend of mine who teaches math places a huge value on students' ability to talk through their problem solving processes. Consequently, he assesses this skill in dozens of ways during the first quarter.

You might want to look through local and national standards for your content area, highlighting learning standards that relate to literacy skills. Here are some examples:

- **Mathematics:** ability to write and verbalize clear explanations for solving problems

- **Social Studies:** ability to conduct, organize, and summarize research using a variety of sources, including books, periodicals, the internet, and other reference materials

- **English:** use of visual and mapping tools and other reading strategies to demonstrate comprehension and interpretation of texts

- **Science:** use of graphic organizers to illustrate relationships between important principles and concepts

Assess Important Life Skills That Demonstrate Self-Management, Interpersonal Effectiveness, and Group Participation Skills

Self-Management Skills

Self-management skills are another skill set closely related to learning how to learn skills, but these skills deserve a category of their own. Besides reflecting a "readiness to learn," this skill set strengthens students' efforts to be self-disciplined and self-regulating. Self-management skills include the ability or capacity to:

- seek help when needed
- tolerate failure, self-correct, and recover from mistakes
- settle in, focus, and attend
- express and manage emotions appropriately, especially feelings of stress, frustration, and anger
- work independently without constant supervision
- manage time effectively
- stay on task amid distractions

Interpersonal Communication and Problem Solving Skills

Another rarely evaluated skill set relates to interpersonal effectiveness. Students' proficiency with basic communication and problem-solving skills influences their capacity to actively engage in learning and to interact with others effectively in the learning environment. These, too, are skills that not only lead to improved performance, but also reflect the kinds of skills that employers seek in their workers. Here again is a brief list of skills you might want to assess:

- effectively uses problem solving skills to handle personal obstacles and interpersonal conflicts
- understands and accepts differences in perspective, opinion, and experience
- listens to others without interrupting
- uses appropriate language; avoids using profanity and language that has a negative impact on people and the learning environment
- shows evidence of listening for understanding through paraphrasing, questioning, and summarizing
- communicates needs and feelings assertively, rather than aggressively or passively
- gives and receives feedback effectively

Cooperation, Group Participation, and Leadership Skills

You are always teaching individual students and a group of students at the same time. Teachers in high performing classrooms create learning experiences that help students develop the skills to be both effective individual learners and effective participants and leaders in a group. These skills are also associated with the qualities of good citizenship. They include:

- taking initiative and exercising leadership behaviors within the group
- respecting and encouraging everyone's voice to be heard
- encouraging and supporting others to work productively

- gathering information, discussing issues, generating ideas, and reaching consensus in a group
- doing one's fair share in a group
- completing cooperative learning tasks effectively with attention to timeliness and quality
- communicating needs and preferences to the group
- engaging in conscious acts of respect, caring, helpfulness, kindness, and consideration toward other group members
- exercising assertiveness and persuasion within a group
- taking on different roles in a group effectively
- expressing appreciation for the contribution of others
- showing sensitivity and appreciation for individual and cultural differences among group members
- interrupting biased, insensitive, and abusive remarks

How to Grade the Three L's?

You might try setting aside fifteen to twenty percent of your possible grade points for the three L's. (See sample Student Assessment Form p. 218.) For example, if you choose to assess 20 skills, you assign 10 points to each skill for a total of 200 points. Students would then receive 0 to 10 points depending upon how regularly and how well they demonstrate a particular skill competency. Here's what it might look like:

Skill Competency	Using a 10 Point Scale for Each Skill
Effective use of intra- and inter-personal problem solving	10 Student uses the skill naturally on a daily basis and encourages others to use the skill
	8–9 Student uses skill regularly and effectively
	4–7 Student demonstrates effective use of the skill sometimes, but needs more practice for it to become a natural, everyday behavior
	2–3 Student rarely uses this skill and needs to make a more intentional effort to practice it
	0–1 Student's inability to use this skill becomes a major obstacle to learning

Your commitment to teach and model these skills, and the degree to which you encourage and support students to practice these skills, will determine how much students' competency levels improve. At the same time, students also need to develop a greater awareness about how these skills help them become better learners and better people. So you'll need to think about how you and your students assess their use of these skills on a regular basis. Consider these possibilities:

- Students regularly reflect on their use of these skills in their journals.
- You and the students monitor their use of these skills using a checklist.
- You give concrete feedback when you notice exemplary use of a skill or notice how not using a skill is getting in the way of learning.
- Students give each other feedback on the use of specific skills during cooperative learning activities.
- Students choose three or four specific skills to focus on for a quarter, providing an opportunity for you and the student to discuss strategies for improvement and monitor progress.

The more evidence students have that they're using these skills, the more they're likely to continue using them. Self-reflection on their own learning also creates the opportunity to identify and set clear goals from quarter to quarter.

From Developing an Assessment System to Designing a Student Assessment Form

There are three important decisions you need to make before designing a student assessment form:

- What are the five or six categories of assessment that spell out what you will be assessing and grading? (Remember, you are assessing what you want students to learn and be able to do.)
- What percentage and specific number of possible points will you assign to each assessment category?
- What are the individual tasks that you will grade or the individual skills that you will assess within each category? How do these tasks and skills help students learn and meet important academic standards and benchmarks?

The benefits of thinking all of this through before school begins are twofold. First, this creates a way for you to link your expectations to student learning and standards. Right away students and parents will know where you stand; they will know that all kinds of learning tasks and skills count in your classroom, not just paper and pencil tests, quizzes, and homework.

Second, a well thought out assessment system becomes a compelling document, that, in effect, puts on paper your philosophy about student learning, achievement, and assessment. It's a handy way to articulate what you think good teaching and good learning are all about. Given the pressures teachers feel about high stakes testing, it becomes your defense for teaching to the skill and the standard, not to the test. If you work in a high school where the debate over testing is raging, sharing and discussing assessment documents can be a good starting point for thoughtful conversation around testing and evaluation.

Here's one way to assign percentages and points:

Major assessments: 40% (400 possible pts.)

These include tests, projects, essays, products, experiments, and presentations that require extensive study, planning, and/or preparation. These assessments are the ones you want to link to specific learning standards and benchmarks that shape your teaching units. Think about not having more than four or five major assessments in any nine week grading period, 50 to 100 points for each one. Some of these assessments will probably require step-by-step check-in's, editing, revision, and self-correction, so you want to give yourself enough time to check-in regularly with the group and individual students along the way. You want to give your students enough learning time to complete an assessment satisfactorily or perform at a level of proficiency.

In-class tasks: 20% (200 possible pts.)

These tasks include graded practices, notes, and demonstrations associated with newly introduced topics and skills, quizzes and "quick writes" used to check for understanding, specific individual and group learning activities, graded discussions, and written reflections and self-assessments. You might have 10 to 15 of these tasks over the course of nine weeks, each worth between 10 and 20 points, e.g. five quizzes, four reflections and self-assessments, and six learning activities.

Homework: 20% (200 possible pts.)

Homework assignments are the concrete evidence that a student has been reading, thinking, reflecting, experimenting, practicing, collecting data, or problem solving. Homework often includes the following kinds of activities: practices that develop skill competency; logs, graphic organizers, or journals in which students communicate their observations, understanding, and questions about what they are learning and reading; evidence of study, research, investigations, and interviews; creation of questions and problems; and smaller tasks that are part of a major assessment.

The remaining 20% of a student's grade can be distributed among the three L's:

Learning to Learn Skills	5%	**50 possible points**
Literacy Skills	5%	**50 possible points**
Life Skills	10%	**100 possible points**
TOTAL	100%	**1000 possible points**

Using round numbers like 1000 points makes it easy for you and students to calculate grades by adding up the total points and dividing by ten to get an accurate percentage. (873 points = 87% = B+) By assigning every graded item a letter and a specific number of points, you can easily use a computerized grading system to record and print out students' grades. Students should keep a copy of their Student Assessment Form in their portfolio. The form serves several purposes.

- Students can record their grades when they receive them.

- Students can continuously review how they're doing—they can see visually how their efforts make a big difference.

- Students can attach relevant notes and comments to their form.

- Students can review this with you and their parent/guardian.

Look at the sample Student Assessment Form (p. 218). This sample includes six categories of assessment and sample items in each category. When you design your own template, you probably will also want to include some blank spaces for individualized assessment tasks, make-up or extra work, and specific assignments you introduce later in the quarter as you learn more about your students and their learning needs. The sample also includes spaces for post-it note feedback, comments, and contracts as part of your on-going dialogue with each student. When you make copies for students you might want to make them on bright yellow or lime paper so that they are easy for students to find.

Student Assessment Form

Name _____

Course _____ Period_____ Quarter_____

Major Assessments: % of Total Grade = 40% and Total Possible Points = 400

Letter Key/Points	Points Received	Letter Grade	Description	Key Academic Standards
A/50			(Am. Lit) Choice of essay on "The Crucible"	
B/50			(Algebra 2) Test on functions	
C/50			(US History) Project on immigration	
D/50			(Biology) Community toxic waste inquiry	
E/50			(Health) Self-analysis of risk and protective factors that influence your health	
F/100			(Humanities) Exhibition that compares/contrasts arts and letters from two distinct historical periods	
G/50				
TOTAL				

In-Class Tasks: % of Total Grade = 20% and Total Possible Points = 200

Letter Key/Points	Points Received	Letter Grade	Description	Key Academic Standards
H/10			(English 2) Performance of scene from "Raisin in the Sun"	
I/10			(Economics) Global economy simulation	
J/20			(Chemistry) Lab #4	
K/20			Notebook Check #2	
L/20			(Geometry) Problem solving stations	
M/20			(US History) Discussion and small group analysis – 1900 and 2000 – connections, differences, and commonalities	
N/10			(AP English) Editing and wordsmithing thesis statements for final positions papers	
O/10			Reflection and self-assessment #1	
P/20			(Art) Small group critique and feedback	
Q/20			(Science) Quiz on demonstration	
R/10				
S/10				
T/20				
TOTAL				

Homework: % of Total Grade = 20% and Total Possible Points = 200

Letter Key/Points	Points Received	Letter Grade	Description	Key Academic Standards
U/30			Journal Check #3	
V/10			Study card for unit test	
W/10			Analysis of population data	
X/20			Creation of algebraic word problems and their solutions	
Y/20			Reading log check #2	
Z/10			Outline/graphic organizer for essay	
aa/10			Test corrections	
bb/20			Preparation for speech	
cc/20			Role preparation for mock trial	
dd/10			Choice of three vocabulary tasks	
ee/20			Choice of two investigation on motion	
ff/10				
gg/10				
TOTAL				

Learning How to Learn Skills: % of Total Grade = 5% and Total Possible Points = 50

Letter Points	Student Assessment	Teacher Assessment	Final Assessment	Skills
hh/10				Following directions and routines
ii/10				Bringing necessary materials to class
jj/10				Asking questions for understanding
kk/10				Persevering until completion of task
ll/10				Ability to adapt and change strategies for learning
TOTAL				

Literacy Skills: % of Total Grade = 5% and Total Possible Points = 50

Letter Points	Student Assessment	Teacher Assessment	Final Assessment	Skills
mm/10				Use of multiple reading strategies for comprehension
nn/10				Listen effectively in various classroom contexts
oo/10				Verbalize thoughts and opinions effectively
pp/10				Effective use of speech and writing for different audiences and purposes
qq/10				Makes connection between text and personal experience
TOTAL				

Life Skills: % of Total Grade = 10% and Total Possible Points = 100

Letter Points	Student Assessment	Teacher Assessment	Final Assessment	Skills
rr/10				Effective use of intra- and interpersonal problem solving skills
ss/10				Effective expression and management of feelings
tt/10				Capacity to settle in, focus, and attend
uu/10				Seeks help when needed and communicates needs and feelings appropriately
vv/10				Capacity to tolerate failure, self-correct, and learn from mistakes
ww/10				Exercises initiative, leadership, and persuasion in a group
xx/10				Effective use of active listening skills
yy/10				Exhibits cooperation skills within a group
zz/10				Encourages others to work productively, appreciates individual and cultural differences and contributions of group members
AA/10				Exhibits friendliness, kindness, consideration, and helpfulness toward others
TOTAL				

	% of TotalGrade	Total Possible Points	Total Points Received
Major Assessments	40%	400 Points	_____
In-Class Tasks	20%	200 Points	_____
Homework	20%	200 Points	_____
Learning to Learn Skills	5%	50 Points	_____
Literacy Skills	5%	50 Points	_____
Life Skills	10%	100 Points	_____
		Total Points	_____
		Final Grade	_____

Teacher's Feedback, Reminders, Comments:

Student's Goals, Comments, Contracts:

A Final Word about Equity and Assessment and
a Caution about Changing What and How You Grade

Changing the way things are always done is never easy in high schools. So be prepared for the questions that will come your way. The students (and their parents) who may grumble when presented with a more holistic and balanced approach to assessment are most likely to be students who are already school smart and socially adept, self-motivated and self-aware. Indeed, traditional grading and grade reports in high school favor the sons and daughters of highly educated, highly successful baby boomers, and a lot of other kids are left in the dust. The fact is, low grades that measure a narrow range of subject matter knowledge and skills do not serve as a motivator for average and low performing students who have already figured out they can't win the grade game, especially when competing against what an *Atlantic Monthly* cover story describes as "the organization kid." (May 2001)

So why doesn't a system of assessment that seems to disadvantage so many change? For better or worse, the group of parents who are generally satisfied with a standard curriculum and traditional grading are the same parents who are active on school boards and PTO's and exercise political clout in the larger community. If a content, test, and grade driven system works for their kids, why shouldn't it work for everyone else? The undiscussible fear behind the desire to keep things as they are is the fear that their children will somehow be disadvantaged by changes in curriculum and assessment that are likely to benefit other students.

fear

Your job is to make the case—to your students, parents, your department chair, and your principal—that a wider, more participatory, more multi-dimensional framework for learning and assessment benefits all students, supporting academic success and healthy development for everyone. Students who participate in assessing what and how they're learning take more responsibility for their learning. When students know what helps them learn, they are more motivated to persevere and make the effort to excel. The more students are exposed to a variety of learning tasks and assessment tools, the sooner students start getting a sense of what really interests them, what throws them, what requires more deliberate planning and complex thinking, and what makes them feel competent and confident.

Moreover, businesses and employers continue to call on high schools to better prepare young people for the world of work in the 21st century. Integrating learning how to learn skills, literacy skills, and life skills in your assessment system brings students a lot closer to the kinds of skills associated with on-the-job evaluation. As you experiment with changing your system of assessment, think about what you are doing as trading up from a gold standard to a diamond standard. Gold is good—it's rock solid, but it's one dimensional. Diamonds, on the other hand, are multi-faceted, and every single facet contributes to their total sparkle and brilliance.

Stock Up on Basic Learning Tools and Supplies

Having the right materials handy can make a good learning experience an even better one. As you think about stocking your room ask, "What materials will increase student participation? What materials will help me and my students be better organized? And what materials celebrate what we do together?"

1. **Newsprint, Markers, & Masking Tape** – It's good to have large sheets of paper & marking pens available for group work, brainstorming, instructions, etc., so you can record and post important information for as long as you need it. But chart paper is expensive. Instead, order a ream (500 sheets) of 24" X 36" newsprint. This will probably last for the whole year.

2. **Digital Timer** – Timing activities can help improve students' capacity to focus, whether you are taking five minutes to do a quick brainstorm, providing 10 minutes for a small group task, or giving a 15 minute mini-lecture that students know has an ending time.

3. **Note Cards** – Keep note cards (various sizes, lined, blank, and colored) on hand for giving and getting quick feedback, recording small group responses, study and review, signs, games, etc.

4. **Calendars** – Have yearly and monthly erasable calendars on hand to identify important deadlines, events, etc. Use different colored markers for each class you teach.

5. **Camera and Film** – Use these to document what students are doing throughout the year.

6. **Radio/Tape Recorder** – Listening to music can help students focus. You might also want to record small group discussions that you evaluate.

7. **Post-it Notes & Sticky Dots** – Use post-it notes for writing comments about individual students to put in your gradebook, for posting written responses from individuals and groups to specific questions, for posting reminder memos to specific classes. Use colored sticky dots to color code papers and materials for each class you teach.

8. **Folders, Boxes, and Baskets** – Keep work folders, extra copies of handouts, and materials in different boxes or baskets for each class you teach.

9. **Poster Board** – Keep heavier card stock and poster board on hand for information that you want to permanently display.

10. **Steel Clips** – Use clips to organize and separate papers and newsprint for each class.

Have on Hand Examples of the Supplies You Want Students to Buy for Class

If you are picky about what supplies students buy for class, gather a collection of the items that work for you and the items that don't. For example, if the ragged edges of spiral bound notebook paper make you nuts, "just say no" to spiral notebooks. If you want students to have a journal, bring in examples. The same goes for math tools or any other kind of special materials.

Arrange Desks and Chairs in a Way That Makes It Easy to See Everyone and Learn Their Names

You will probably want to assign seats for the first couple of weeks so it's easier to learn everyone's name. In the beginning of the year, think about a seating arrangement that will enable you to to see everyone, see the door, and move easily from student to student. Assign seats alphabetically by first name or last name. You might also want to reverse tradition and start with Z instead of A.

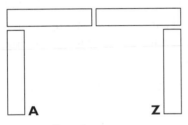

If you have space, arrange tables so everyone can see each other.

You might want to create a V shape with desks or tables, though it's less desirable, since students can't all see each other and it's hard to work with students in the middle rows.

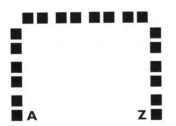

Place desks around three sides of the room so that everyone can see each other. This also gives you a space to do activities in the middle.

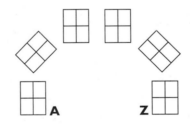

Create working groups of four desks each, so students can turn their chairs around to see each other.

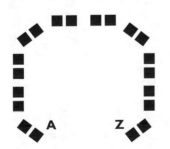

Group chairs in pairs around the room. Everyone can see each other and students can easily work in pairs.

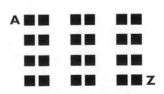

If you need to place students in rows, try placing desks in pairs.

Make the Classroom "Ours"

Turn Walls into Teaching and Organizing Tools

1. Keep notes and work in progress for each class on newsprint. String clothesline across the length of a wall for hanging newsprint from large steel clips. I call this one "Power Newsprint."

2. Post important goals, routines, and procedures around the room. Identify big goals and the basics that every student needs to know.

3. Keep a place for questions that students want to discuss related to an assignment, prepping for a test, etc. Remember, "There's never a stupid question."

4. Post the agenda every day for class, including what you expect students to do as soon as they arrive for class.

5. Whatever your discipline, find provocative articles, quotations, and news clips that make connections between the world students live in and the course you're teaching.

6. Create a space to keep extra homework assignments, study guides, and other important papers in one place.

Make a Wall Space for Students

Organize a wall space that includes a place to post important information about class and that also provides space for you and students to post other things of interest. Take photographs of students doing activities in class. Kids love to see pictures of each other and pictures are a way to affirm community.

- **Put up a provocative quote.**
- **Create a provocative question to post with a controversial news story.**
- **Post a hypothetical question about a classroom issue that you can discuss in a class meeting.**
- **Post interesting articles that relate to your subject matter content.**

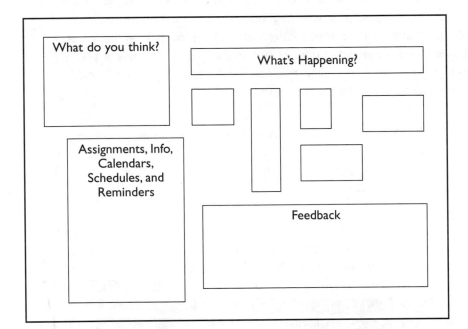

- **Post articles from the school newspaper that are about or by students in your classes.**

- **Post articles about young people or that focus on issues that kids care about. Put up pictures you take of students in class. Invite students to bring in interesting things to post.**

Use a metal clip and a push pin to hang extra copies of information that students who have been absent need to take. Post major deadlines and assignments. Post big picture questions and learning goals that help focus attention on what you are currently learning.

Have post-it notes nearby so you and the students can give feedback on what's happening in class (things students do that you appreciate and successes you notice; student comments; and questions/topics students want to review.)

The First Day of Class

The first day of class is the one day in the entire year when students will come home and actually share their impressions of classes and teachers with their families. Your heartfelt hope, no matter how many years you have been teaching, is that more kids leave your class saying, "This is okay. I can handle this," than muttering, "This really sucks. This is going to be bad!"

You get a lot of mileage out of the first day. Think about the start of a school year like the start of a cross-country trip in a brand new car. Everything feels new and fresh, even your favorite old traveling clothes. You're packed and organized with the right maps at your fingertips. There is nothing quite like the sense of anticipation before you take off. You're excited about the journey ahead, but still worried about what you might have forgotten to shut down, cancel, or put in the car. So you're careful and a little low-key on the first day out. You're not hell-bent on zooming from 0 to 70 mph in the first ten seconds of your trip. Instead, you're checking out how the car hugs the road, you're testing out the brakes. There's plenty of time later to cruise flat out on the interstate.

Long road trips are a lot like the school year. Both have a beginning, middle, and end, and both benefit from good planning and preparation. But what makes both of these experiences fun and scary, deeply rewarding and demanding, is that you really don't know the shape the trip will ultimately take when you start out.

Some First Day Goals

Nevertheless, there is a lot you can predict and prepare for during that first class period, a period that is always over sooner than you would like. This is not the time for lively pro-social bonding, intense conversation, or a high powered learning activity. Students will spend what little time there is fully occupied in four activities: checking out who's in the room; checking you out; getting a quick impression of what it feels like to sit there for 50 minutes; and most important, hoping that, armored with a lot of vigilance and a little cool, they will get through this class and six others without self-destructing or being embarrassed in front of their peers.

Having said this, the goals for your first day with students are more or less the same as the goals that guide your preparation before the school year begins:

• Do something that makes each student feel welcomed and invited but not exposed.

• Do something that makes students feel respected as young people, but not at the expense of your own authority and presence as the adult in the room. Kids want to feel respected and they want to know you're in charge.

• Do something that sets the tone for what matters in your classroom, but don't overwhelm them with a huge laundry list of rules and expectations.

- Do something that lets students know they have entered a learning environment—not their living rooms, not a basketball court, not the local mall, and surely not a police station.

- Engage students in some practices and procedures that will become daily or weekly routines.

- Do something that communicates organization, purpose, and focus, without being fussy or complicated.

- Do something that encourages high student participation, but with a minimum of noise and physical movement.

- Do something that encourages student voice, but does not sanction silliness or cynicism.

- Do something that is unexpected; the element of surprise goes a long way toward grabbing students' attention.

- And finally, do at least one thing that shows your humor and your heart.

Your first day of class is your first chance to invoke the state of mind you would like learners to inhabit every day. Call it anxious anticipation, relaxed alertness, or hopeful expectation; whatever you name it, you want to do things on the first day that will bring that feeling into the room.

What Is Your Most Effective Teaching Stance for the First Day of Class?

Your teaching stance is the combination of attitudes, outlook, and demeanor that you wear most often and most visibly. Your stance communicates "first principles"—the things that matter to you the most. It is about how you present yourself to your students, about what you prize and what you want to protect. Some aspects of your teaching stance are like a second skin. Others are harder to come by, requiring time and practice before you can express that aspect of your teaching persona with authenticity and confidence. If you were to ask your students at the end of the year to write down five words or phrases that they think describe what you stand for, their responses would give you a pretty good sense of whether they took in what you tried to convey in the last nine months.

There isn't one right teaching stance, but there are some wrong ones, especially on the first day of class. The question you need to ask is this: What is the most effective teaching stance that will help you put your best foot forward with a group of young people whom you may never have met?

The dilemma is choosing what to play up and what to tone down on the first day. You do want to respond to students' first day anxieties about what to expect. But you don't want your teaching persona to overwhelm students before they've had a chance to watch, listen, and settle in. Some qualities that you prize most about yourself as a teacher and a learner may need to take a backseat that first week.

Most adolescents are justifiably cautious and a little subdued when they encounter new adults in their lives. They don't want to be caught in a position of giving away too much or appearing too vulnerable, and they are rightly suspicious of adults who want to be "up close and personal" during a first encounter. (What you'll need to be ready for is the one kid who walks in as if he's known everyone, including you, for his entire lifetime.) A handy rule of thumb for meeting a group of adolescents for the first time is to avoid extremes. This is the one time when going all out for the middle ground is a good thing. Your first day is about creating the foundation for building the learning community that you and your students will become in the next month or so, and your teaching stance should reflect the attitudes, outlook, and demeanor that will help get you there.

A First Day Teaching Stance Might Look Like This

Respectful: You can do four things on Day One that let students know you want to be thought of as an adult who is respectful to young people: your preparation of materials and the readiness and attractiveness of the classroom space will tell students they are worthy of your time and effort; your interest in learning all of their names as quickly as you can; your attentiveness to their questions and concerns; and your interest in getting to know them as individuals.

Serious, But With a Touch of Humor: Students will shut down if you present yourself as a stern taskmaster, but don't try to be an MC on Comedy Central, either. Balance and timing are everything.

Friendly: Forget about that "Don't smile until Christmas" baloney. Nobody turns down a smile and a little warmth as a way of saying, "Welcome back." On the other hand, being over-familiar and too personal are about as effective as being cold and detached.

Invitational: You can't demand much of anything from adolescents without risking passive resistance. You can, however, invite students to cooperate and work with you. Use phrases like, "I'd like us to...," "I have a request to make...," "For today, it would be helpful if everyone...," "For the next five minutes, I'd like you to...," "Because we need to... I'm asking if everyone will...," and of course, "Please" and "Thank you."

Knowledgeable: Have something in the room (a curious object, a stack of books, an interesting piece of equipment, a compelling photograph, a provocative quotation, a list of puzzling terms that are specific to your content area, a poster or article linked to your discipline or people who practice your discipline in the work world) that indicates your passion, curiosity, and knowledge of the course content.

A Few Words About Developing a Culture of Caring

A culture of caring develops over time through the sharing of critical events and experiences. Sending the message that you care about your students on the first day sounds and feels phony to adolescents. Your actions during the first month will speak louder and more effectively than words.

Organized: Feeling flustered when you can't find what you need is the daytime version of your worst nightmare. Label, color code, and box everything for different classes; make more than enough copies; make a special tray for all the tools you need for the day; and don't use any electrical equipment if there's even a minute chance that it might go haywire.

Sequential: This is not the day to skip around randomly from one thing to another and hope that "all will be revealed" in the last five minutes. Students should be able to see the connections among the activities you do the first day.

Clear and Succinct: No long winded speeches, no confusing instructions, no complex tasks—keep it simple.

Calm and Low-Key: If quiet, uneventful, and smooth are words that come to mind at the end of your first day, you're good to go.

A Sampling of Activities and Procedures for the First Day of Class:

If your teaching schedule entails fifty-minute periods, it's an even greater challenge to choose what to do and what to leave out on the first day. The fifty-minute agenda that follows is a sample, and only a sample, plan. It includes, however, some essential procedures and activities that can help you get off to a good start. As you read this and develop your own first day plan, think about capturing the spirit of this agenda, rather than implementing it verbatim. Keep asking, "what are the words and ways of expressing myself that will work best for me?"

Procedure 1: I'm in the right place—are you? Post a sign on your door or next to it that gives the basics—your name, the course, the class period, and the room number. A little humor, a picture, or a bit of bold graphics never hurt a sign!

Procedure 2: Post the agenda for the day in the place where you will post it everyday. Agendas may vary according to what you are doing and what you want to emphasize each day. Here is a First Day example:

First Day Agenda

Goals:
- To introduce ourselves
- To become familiar with classroom procedures and course basics
- Getting to Work: Complete your student profile forms
- Introductions
- Classroom and course basics
- Preview of next month
- Homework
- Closing

Other Examples:

Agenda
- Academic Goals:
- Group Goals:
- Personal Goals:
- Skills for the Day:
- Getting to Work:
- Gathering:
- Main Activity:
- Quick Feedback and Assessment
- Homework

Agenda
• Big Goal for the Day:
• Getting to Work:
• Summary of Activities
• Checking Out
• Homework

Agenda
• Aims:
• Skills for the Day:
• Getting to Work:
• Checking In:
• Learning Task #1:
• Learning Task #2:
• Learning Task #3:

Agenda
This is not a regular day!
• Here's the Plan:
• Why?
• Get Ready by...

Procedure 3: Where to sit? You may want to prepare a seating chart ahead of time if you have accurate class lists. I recommend distributing the chart to the entire class. Though teachers receive class rosters, students rarely do. But it is actually a considerate gesture to give students a chart with everyone's name, especially if you expect them to learn each other's names as soon as possible.

If your class list is still incomplete, or if you prefer not to use a seating chart in the beginning of the year, ask students to take any seat and have markers and card stock available so everyone can make a name card to set on their desks. (See Learning Students' Names, p. 37)

Procedure 4: Prepare to pass out a First Day packet as students walk in. Your packet might include the following:
  - A seating chart for the class or instructions for where students are to sit
  - A "First Things First" page of procedures for students to read after they sit down
  - A Student Profile form for students to complete for their "Getting to Work" activity
  - The course syllabus
  - A very brief description of your assessment and grading system
  - A list of materials and supplies that you expect students to bring to class on Day Two
  - Two copies of a letter to parents/guardians (one to sign and return and one to keep) that introduces them to you and the course
  - A page describing the first week's homework assignments

Procedure 5: Meet and greet: Welcome every student at the door. Say hello, say your name, ask their names, and invite them to take a seat and follow directions on the first page of their First Day Packet.

Procedure 6: First things first! The first page of your First Day Packet might be entitled "First Things First." See p. 231 for a sample of what it might look like:

HANDOUT I

First Things First

Please read over these procedures after you take a seat.

> **Read This Now!**
> This classroom is a learning environment and a public place, not your living room (what you do and say there is between you and your family), not the cafeteria (hanging out is not your reason for being here), not the bathroom (this is not the place for personal hygiene care from nails to hair), not the "Fight Club" (no public brawling, cursing, or yelling), not a playing field (no contact sports), and this is not the backseat of a car (please keep your hands and feet to yourself). Thank you.

1. **Walking into the room:** Timely, quietly, carefully, and mindfully are the ways to walk into the room.

   TIMELY — because it's a sign of respect for me to start on time and for you to be here on time. If you have NOT arrived ON-TIME, you've earned yourself a tardy.

   QUIETLY — because everyone needs a minute or two to catch their breath, put aside what went on last hour, and settle in. If you have NOT walked in QUIETLY, I will ask you to re-enter the room.

   CAREFULLY — because there are a lot of bodies and a lot of stuff in this room. Please be respectful of other people's space and other people's stuff. If you have NOT walked in CAREFULLY, I will ask you to re-enter the room.

   MINDFULLY — because when we begin I'd like you to have your materials organized and in front of you and your mind and spirit fully present so we can focus on the task at hand. If it looks like walking in MINDLESSLY is becoming a habit, I will talk with you privately to check out what's going on.

2. **Taking a Seat:** (Please sit_____.)

3. **Getting to Work:** When you walk in the door, there will always be a question, a check-in, or "Getting Started" activity on the board. It will always be posted _____. Please start now. You will have about five minutes.

4. **Gathering as a Group:** After about five minutes, I will call time. I will be ready to have us gather as a whole group. I expect you to show that you're ready by having completed the "Getting to Work" activity, having appropriate materials on your desk, and directing your attention to the front of the room.

5. **Ending Class:** I will make a real commitment to end on time. However, if anyone, either student or teacher, is in the middle of a sentence and the bell rings, I expect all of us to listen until the person finishes their thought. Then I will say, "Time to go. 'Bye for now." That's when you may get up out of your chairs and leave.

Activity 1: 5 min.

"Getting to Work" Activity: In your First Day packet think about including a student profile form that every student can fill in quickly, comfortably, and easily. This might include contact information, some basic family data, brief bio facts, and school history. You can always solicit more personal information using an interest questionnaire a bit later.

Activity 2: 5 min.

Introductions:

1. Acknowledge the "rep" that precedes you: In high schools, most faculty come with some history to the next group of students they teach—some of it is probably positive and some negative, some accurate and some that's more myth than truth. Asking students what they think they know about you is a great way to show students that you have a sense of humor, that you can depersonalize hearsay, and that you want them to hear from you who you are and what you expect.

    So take a few minutes to invite students to say what they've heard or what they think they know about you and this class. Tell them you don't take this personally and explain that it's usually a good idea to check out what students assume or imagine, so that you can clear up any misconceptions or misinformation. Use any of these approaches:

    A. Give them a few minutes to say their assumptions. Don't interrupt or respond to specific things that you hear.

       OR

    B. Ask students to write their assumptions on note cards and you read some aloud to the class.

       OR

    C. If you're uncomfortable asking students to do this or you think students will be uncomfortable sharing with you, say something like, "These are some of the things you might have heard about me." Make what you say light and humorous.

2. **Introducing Yourself:** Afterwards, you might say, "So I'd like you to hear from me a little about who I am." Again, keep it light rather than dramatic or ultra-serious. Leave students a little curious—don't tell them your life history! Share three or four things about yourself—why you decided to teach; where you're from; something about your family; something you love to do outside of school; or maybe something they would be surprised to know about you. Here are some other ideas:

- Pronounce your name and say something about your name if it's unusual or hard to pronounce.

- "You may have heard that I _____. What you probably don't know about me is _____."

- "No matter what you've heard, I have never _____."

- Something you like most about teaching and something you don't like about schools or the teaching profession.

- "You'll probably get tired of hearing me say, '_____ ', so I'm giving you a heads up that you'll hear this a lot because it's really important to me."

- Something about the course you're teaching that keeps you fascinated.

- "I could have been a _____ or a _____ , but I chose to become a teacher because _____."

Close by sharing something about your hopes and expectations:

- "At the end of the year/semester I hope that many of you will be able to say three things: _____, _____, and _____."

3. **Student Introductions:** Usually, you'll want to take roll while students are doing their "Getting to Work" activity. However, on the first day you'll want to take roll by asking students to say their names. Everyone needs an opportunity to start matching names and faces, and you need to hear how students say their names before you mispronounce them.

Tell students that you want to learn their names as soon as possible and learn to pronounce them correctly. Say something like, "If you mispronounce my name, I'd probably say, 'Here's how it's pronounced,' and I'd say it again for you. So I'd appreciate it if you will correct me in a way that's respectful and helps me say it right. Please, be patient—I'll probably be asking you to say your name more than a few times over the next week or so."

Activity 3:
⏰ **5 min.**

What Do You Want to Know? Tell students that you know they have lots of questions and that you won't be able to respond to all of them today. Explain that you would like to take five minutes to answer questions about things that students want to know right away. Be sure to ask students if there is anything they want to ask about First Things First procedures.

Activity 4:
⏰ **8 min.**

What Do You Think This Course Is About? What Do You Think We're Going to Be Doing? Do a quick brainstorm of what students think is going to happen in this class. This is your first opportunity to clarify for students what is and is not part of this course. Try doing this using one of these frames:

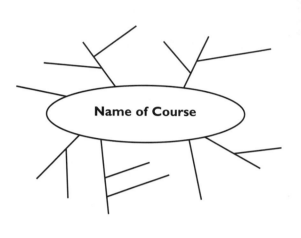

Name of Course	
What's it about?	Skills you'll be learning?

Take about five minutes to do the brainstorm and about three minutes to clarify students' responses or fill in some information gaps.

Activity 5:
⏰ **5 min.**

Big Goals for the Year: Have a few of your big goals and/or expectations posted on a large chart or transparency. Or you might choose not to discuss any detailed goals and/or expectations today. Instead, you might want to share a more global belief or hope that speaks to what you value most about teaching young people. It could be something like this:

"You can count on me not to confuse who you are as a person with the grade you earn on a report card. I know you have a life outside of this course. There are 168 hours in a week. You give this class 5% of your time and effort during the week, and I'll give you 100% of my effort and my support."

OR

"All of you can learn to be successful in this class. I don't start out the year assuming some of you will "get it" and get A's and some of you will just "get over" or "get by" with C's and D's. I have confidence that each of you has what it takes to do well over the long haul."

Activity 6:
⏰ **3 min.**

Materials: If you expect students to purchase specific materials and supplies, include them on a page in the First Day packet. Show students examples of required supplies and materials that meet your criteria. Be sure to include examples of what not to buy.

Activity 7: **A Preview of the Next Month:** On the board, post the learning goals that you
5 min. will emphasize during the next month:

- **Learning Goal 1:** Learn Important Policies and Expectations and
  Practice Important Classroom Procedures
- **Learning Goal 2:** Become a Community of Learners
- **Learning Goal 3:** Learn Course Work

Explain that students will experience activities related to each learning goal
every day over the next month. Explain why each goal is important by saying
something like this:

For #1, *"It's much easier to remember what to do if you hear it and discuss it in
small doses over time. One of my jobs in the first few weeks is to make sure you
know what I expect. One of your jobs is to learn what you need to do to be
successful in this class."*

For #2, *"Here in the classroom, you work as individual learners and as members
of a group. During the first month you will have a chance to learn more about
yourselves as learners and I hope to learn more about what each of you needs
to do your best. I also expect all of us to develop good group skills and form
positive relationships so we can work well as a team."*

For #3, *"The last goal is about learning _____."*

(Preview the first course unit and highlight a few skills and learning activities
that are included in the first unit.)

Activity 8: **Homework:**
5 min. ❏ **Course Work:** Have students read the syllabus and circle two topics that,
on first glance, seem most interesting to them. Then have them write down
at least one question they have about what we're going to study and learn
in this class.

❏ **Letter Home:** If you are planning to send a welcome and introduction letter
home to parents/guardians, this is the day to do it. You might want to put two
letters in every First Day packet, one for families to keep, and the other for
them to send back to you signed.

❏ **Getting Started:** List the required materials and supplies for tomorrow's class.

Procedure 7: Ending Class: Wait for the bell. Then say some version of, "Bye for now.
I look forward to seeing you tomorrow. You may go."

The First Month, Day by Day
Focus on Three Key Learning Goals for the First Month

As you plan your first month, consider integrating a balanced combination of learning activities, strategies, and practices that help students accomplish these three learning goals:

Learning Goal 1:   Learn Important Policies and Expectations and
                       Practice Important Classroom Procedures

Learning Goal 2:   Become a Community of Learners

Learning Goal 3:   Learn Course Work

Why These Three Learning Goals?

Although few secondary staff would disagree about the importance of the learning goals suggested here, few teachers get around to implementing a set of intentional activities and practices that will help students achieve them. The time-honored excuse is always the same —these efforts take too much time and involve too much off-task behavior. Since rethinking teaching and learning is this book's raison d'être, here are a few talking points that tackle the "yes, but" excuses and summarize the benefits of integrating activities that support these goals during the first month.

1. **These activities and practices involve on-task learning behaviors at the most fundamental level.**

    Learning how to learn skills are metacognitive skills that involve students in reflecting on these types of questions: What will it take for me to learn this? How do I go about planning, predicting, and strategizing? How do I learn with others? How do I assess my performance? How do I motivate myself? What did I learn? What do I think about what I learned? How did I learn it? How can I use what I've learned? What gets in the way of learning effectively? What do I do when I'm stuck? and What do I need to change to learn more effectively? A student's capacity and inclination to think metacognitively is one of the most influential determinants of student success or failure.

2. **Front-loading these activities and practices in the beginning of the year gives students what they need so they can do what you want them to do.**

    These activities incorporate basic tools necessary to become successful as independent learners and as members of a group. Contrary to popular wish, most high school students are not as "school-smart", self-motivated, and cooperative as we wish they were. Thus, taking the time to establish classroom procedures and routines, discuss the reasons for them, and monitor students' practice of them goes a long way toward providing the kind of support that will help students meet your academic and behavioral expectations.

    You are likely to find more effective training regimens and rigorous practice and feedback in the army, in industry, or at the local firehouse than you will in most high schools. Teaching is not telling. For a vast majority of students and workers (over 70%) effective learning needs to involve the following steps.

- A clear, understandable reason for learning something.

- Modeling by someone who shares their expertise and experience.

- A direct experience involving the skill to be learned and mastered.

- Good coaching and supervision as the skill is being practiced and regular assessment of performance. (This includes self-reflection and self-assessment.)

- Opportunities to make personal meaning of what is learned, so it will stick.

- Positive recognition and appreciation when the skill is being used effectively and regularly.

This process holds true for learning any academic or behavioral skill. In the beginning of the year you want students to learn and use procedures that help create a smooth running classroom. Incorporating these learning steps may take a little more time, but the benefits are worth it. The big pay-off is gaining more time "on-task" in the long run, because you will spend less time repeating, reminding, and reviewing what you want students to do. Right from the first day, notice and appreciate students when you see them doing the right thing.

3. **Students' perceptions of classroom climate and their feelings toward you personally strongly influence their motivation and capacity to learn.**
   There is a direct relationship between the quality of the classroom climate (Do I feel safe? Can I belong here? Will I be respected and accepted for who I am as a person? Will people make fun of me? Will I be listened to? Will I be treated fairly? Will I look stupid in here? Will I get help when I need it? Will my efforts and talents be recognized?) and a student's receptivity to learning. The degree and measure of a student's positive attitude and good will depends on the relationships you develop with the whole group and with each individual. Consequently, it makes good sense to engage students in learning strategies and activities that help forge positive relationships and establish a positive learning climate.

4. **Pacing the introduction of procedures, reducing the quantity of content, and balancing academic and behavioral goals provide a more equitable start for everyone.**
   By pacing and regulating the sheer quantity of what's introduced day by day, all students, not just the deluxe model of adolescent learners, have a real chance to get on board and get on track with your academic program. Too many kids experience information and procedural overload from day one and never really recover. Furthermore, by stressing the importance of academic and behavioral goals, every student gets the message right away that their effort and their classroom behavior count. This is as important for students who "ace" exams and essays, but disparage everything else about the class and classmates, as it is for students who walk in with knowledge and skill deficits, and need immediate assurance that they won't be left out or left behind.

Making Time for "Both-and" Instead of Choosing "Either-or"

Teachers tend to approach new class start-up in one of two ways. Many rush headlong into a whirlwind of academic tasks and testing while a few forgo academic course work altogether in favor of an onslaught of teambuilding exercises and group processing. Neither "either-or" choice is a good way to go.

Instead, consider a "both-and" approach that incorporates "Getting Started" activities and "Course Work" into every class period. This is not as easy as it sounds. For starters, it means shifting your own expectations of what you want to accomplish and what you want students to experience in the beginning few weeks. The biggest challenge may be letting go of school and self-induced pressures to elevate content coverage and content learning above all other learning goals and experiences in the beginning of the year.

It would be a lie to say that you can help students accomplish these three goals (1: Learn Policies, Expectations, and Procedures, 2: Become a Community of Learners, and 3: Learn Course Work) and still be at the same place you were in your curriculum last year on September 15. It's not going to happen. But no one is going to die either if you teach one less unit during the year. On the other hand, the "slow is fast" approach is likely to result in fewer students giving up and acting out, more students remaining engaged and motivated, and, most notably, less frustration and greater satisfaction for you and the students you're teaching.

Teachers maintain that the biggest obstacle to changing old habits is the challenge of imagining what class would really look like, day by day, if they took a different approach. I hear comments like, "I did one or two things that encouraged students to get to know each other, but I never thought about changing my whole teaching plan during the first month. For that to happen, I'd need a much clearer idea of how it all fits together."

Preparing Yourself to Shift Your Teaching Focus During the First Month

The sample four-week agenda that follows fills in the details of what it would look and sound like to shift your teaching focus during the first month. Each class period includes "Getting Started" activities and "Course Work." This is not intended to serve as a prescription, but to serve as a model of how you might integrate and sequence activities that focus on each goal: 1. Learn Policies, Expectations, and Procedures; 2. Become a Community of Learners; and 3. Learn Course Work.

All change is accompanied by doubts, risks, and uncertainty. It is useful, then, to spell out some of the trade-off's you'll need to live with as you try out a "both-and" approach during the first month. You may wince a little as you read these cautions and caveats. It's that hard to let go of doing things the way they have always been done.

• During most class periods, you're not likely to have more than twenty to thirty minutes for "Course Work" if your classes are scheduled in fifty-minute time segments. This means "chunking" your first learning unit somewhat differently and implementing it over a longer period of time. This is the most dramatic change you'll make. You've got to make peace with this or "content coverage creep" will kick in by the third day of class.

- You are likely to allocate a couple of entire class periods to "Getting Started" activities—there are some experiences that just aren't very effective if you short change the amount of time to do them and reflect on what you've done. This model includes four whole period experiences that are spread out over the month.

- Plan for the uncomfortable reality that you will be asking yourself, "So why am I doing this? Is this really worth all the time and planning?" Put into words your most compelling rationale and learn it by heart—to say to yourself, to say to your colleagues, to say to parents, to say to your students. "I'm doing this because..." And then keep saying it to yourself. It might sound like this, "I've made this commitment, and I'm going to see it through because I want every kid to have a real chance."

- You will probably need to defend yourself against attacks of "off-task" guilt. Remind yourself that all learning is "on-task" behavior, not just the narrow definition of learning tasks associated with content coverage. Remember, too, that young people's healthy growth and development depends, in large part, on how adults support the maturity and integration of intellectual, social, and emotional aspects of an adolescent's life. You are modeling just this kind of support by starting out the year in this way.

- You will find yourself spending more time reflecting back and commenting on what you see and hear students doing. Your efforts to do this serve as a model and invitation for students to become more reflective about their own learning and behavior. This reflection /feedback process is a piece of cake for early childhood educators—for high school faculty this particular teaching behavior might feel a little awkward. Try writing yourself a reminder note each day to comment on at least one procedure or skill that you witness the group using well, and privately try giving appreciative feedback to individual students whose behaviors indicate their growing academic and social competence.

- As you move from day to day and week to week, cultivate the habit of PLAN, DO, REVIEW. At the end of the day or at the end of the week, take time to reflect on these questions:
  - How did it go today? What thoughts or questions are in the front of my mind?
  - At what moments were kids most engaged? How do I know that?
  - What do I think worked best? Are there one or two things that happened—that kids said—that I particularly want to remember?
  - Is there anything I'd like to change or do differently next time? Why? What are the benefits?
  - How does today's experience influence my focus and plan for tomorrow? Is there anything I want to shift around or prepare differently for the next class?
  - Finally, don't expect everything to work the way you planned and imagined it. Remember the mantra, "The lesson/discussion/activity wasn't perfect and it was still successful." Nothing you ever do will reach every kid at the same time with equal effectiveness. This "both-and" approach does, however, create a climate and culture that enables you to reach more kids more of the time.

A Day by Day Agenda for the First Month

Each day contains the following format:

Day ___

Getting Started:

Getting to Work: This is the "walk-in-the-door" activity that is posted in the same place every day. These five-minute start-up activities are usually linked to the previous day's agenda or the current day's agenda.

Become a Community of Learners: These activities help students get to know each other, encourage learner self-awareness and goal-setting, help students identify what they need to be effective members of a group, and introduce students to "Gathering" and team-building activities.

Policies, Procedures, and Expectations: These activities provide opportunities for you to introduce and review policies and expectations, for you and students to discuss and clarify important classroom procedures, and for students to learn some basic problem solving protocols for individual issues (the problem solving process) and whole group issues (class meeting and group negotiation).

Course Work:

For each day, this section is left blank for each teacher to sequence in the way that works best for their students. In this daily model, about thirty minutes out of a fifty minute period are set aside for "Course Work."

Homework:

Course Work: Your curriculum will shape these assignments.

Getting Started: Scattered throughout the first month are some ten-minute assignments linked to other "Getting Started" activities.

As you read through this model plan, keep in mind:
- The first two weeks include more "Getting Started" activities than the last two weeks.
- By the third week, most "Getting to Work" activities and Homework assignments should probably be linked to "Course Work."
- This plan assumes that students keep some kind of journal/reflections notebook that you can read and respond to about once a month.
- Issues around cultural diversity and harassment are presented and discussed later in the month when students have a better sense of classroom procedures and guidelines and know each other better.
- Think about what you'd keep, change, or rearrange and be thinking about the wording and language you would craft for openings, instructions, reflections, transitions, and closings.

Day 2
Getting Started:

Getting to Work: Interview Questions
❏ Have students create five questions you would ask another person in class that would help you introduce her/him to the group.

Become a Community of Learners: Partner Interviews
❏ Partner Interviews: Have students pair-up, interview each other using their questions, and then introduce each other to the class, saying their partner's name and two or three things about her or him.

❏ Let students know that you expect everyone to learn everyone else's name by Day Five. Tell them why this is important to you. Let them know you might stop in the middle of the class to check if there is anyone who wants to try naming everyone. You might want to have some pencils, tokens, etc. to pass out to anyone who can do this during the first week.

Policies, Procedures, and Expectations: Classroom Boundaries
❏ Explain your boundaries, why you have them, what behaviors are boundary violations, and what will happen when boundaries are violated (p. 64).

Course Work:
❏ Discuss course syllabus and answer questions.
❏ Begin teaching your first learning unit.

Homework:
❏ **Course Work:** Give assignment to students.
❏ **Getting Started:** Choose to write about three questions from Creating a Classroom Vision (p. 66). Write your responses in your journal.

Day 3
Getting Started:

Getting to Work: Creating a Classroom Vision
❏ Have students choose to write about three more questions from Creating a Classroom Vision (p. 66). Ask students to share responses to one or two questions with a partner.

Become a Community of Learners: Classroom Vision Learning Carousel
❏ Choose eight to ten questions from the Creating a Classroom Vision (p. 66). to post on chart paper around the room. Divide students into three's using playing cards and assign each group to the chart paper that contains the same number as the one on their playing cards. (The three students who have 2's will be in the same group, the 3's will be in the same group, and so on.) Give each group of three students a marker and ask the group to write one or two responses to the question on their chart paper. Remind groups to get ideas from each group member and to take turns writing.

Use a timer and give groups about a minute and a half at each station. When time is up ask each group to move clockwise to the next chart and repeat the process, responding to a different question.

If you do this activity with several different classes, you may want to collate all responses to each question, so you can create one set of responses to hand back to all of your classes.

Let students know that you will type up the newsprint data so that students can review and use it later in the week when the class develops classroom agreements. Or, if you have students who want to type this up for extra credit, a late or free homework pass, or student leadership points, by all means, take them up on it. It's never too early to ask for help.

Policies, Procedures, and Expectations: Procedural Check-in
- ❏ Clarify, teach, and/or review any important procedures that you have not introduced (p. 281).

Course Work
Homework:
- ❏ **Course Work**
- ❏ **Getting Started:** Bring in an article, photo, or anything else that highlights young people in the news, youth issues, popular culture, or interesting events coming up. Post on the board entitled "What's Going On?"

Day 4
Getting Started:
Getting to Work: Youth Culture
- ❏ Post anything you brought to put on the "What's Going On?" board.
- ❏ In your journal, write a response to one of the following questions:

1. What three youth culture icons (things, names, products, music groups, etc.) should every adult recognize, so they at least know what it is?

2. If all adults could see only one movie, and you had to recommend it, what would you choose? Why?

3. If all adults could listen to only one music group or performer, and you had to recommend the selection, whom would you pick? Why?

4. If you had to make a list of five things no teen should be without, what would those five things be?

Become a Community of Learners: Getting to Know Each Other

❏ Play a name game (p. 38) or ask students to share some of their responses to the journal questions.

❏ Do a spot check to see if anyone can remember everyone's name.

Policies, Procedures, and Expectations: Your Assessment and Grading System

❏ Explain your system of assessment and grading by reviewing your handout on grading in the First Day packet (p. 230). Reassure students that they don't need to know every about the grading system right this minute. There will be plenty of time over the next few weeks to become familiar with it.

For overachievers who won't be satisfied until they know how they can attain every point possible, for worriers who are already imagining themselves grounded after the first marking period, and for protestors who are ready to rally about an unfair system—make a compromise. Set aside 15 minutes before school or during lunch in the next day or so when students can come and talk with you about grading and assessment.

Policies, Procedures, and Expectations: Sharing Big Goals and Expectations

❏ Discuss some of your Big Goals for the year. (pp. 139 to 140) Talk about your expectations and goals, particularly around issues of quality and completion, and share the ways you will provide support for students to meet these goals. If satisfactory completion of certain tasks or a specific portfolio of work is a big deal for you (and I hope it is!), the "cruisers" who get by with D's and the "slackers" who may have NEVER completed a thing will be in for a big shock. You will need to tell students exactly what they will be expected to do when they hand in unsatisfactory or incomplete work.

Course Work
Homework:
❏ **Course Work**

Day 5
Getting Started:
Getting to Work: Writing Hopes and Hesitations

❏ Give each person two different color "sticky notes" or two different color note cards to write down at least one hope—something they're looking forward to in class, something that interests them about the course, or something they hope to accomplish in class (orange); and one hesitation—something that concerns them about class, something they don't think they're going to like about class or the course, or something that makes them feel anxious or hesitant about class (yellow).

❏ Or ask students to write in their journals using these questions:

What hopes do you bring to this course?

At the end of the year...
• I will know more about _____.
• I will have learned _____.
• I will be able to _____.
• Our class will be able to _____.

What hesitations do you bring?
• I don't know whether _____.
• I'm a little uncertain about _____.
• I don't want to spend a lot of time _____.
• I think my biggest concern will be _____.

Become a Community of Learners: Sharing Hopes and Hesitations

❏ Take two minutes for students to do a Pair-Share with a partner discussing their hopes and hesitations.

❏ This is the time to reassure students that everyone has some anxieties and dislikes around some aspect of learning or a particular subject. Share a story about yourself and a learning difficulty you've experienced. Then you might say something like this:

"I know some of you hate _____ or have had a bad experience with _____. It's okay to name it and say it. I'm not going to tell you not to feel that way. What I am going to ask you to do is dig around a little to think about where those feelings come from and to consider anything you might want to do differently that will make this year better for you. My job is to support your efforts in any way I can. So let me know when you're frustrated or feel stuck, and we'll work on it together."

Then ask students to post their sticky-notes or note cards on a bulletin board or poster board that you have identified for this purpose. (Place the orange notes under HOPES and the yellow notes under HESITATIONS).

Here is another way to discuss these issues thanks to math teacher, Mehran Divanbaigyzand. Ask students to put their hesitation notes in a small box of three or four drawers. Kids who have really negative, anxious feelings about a given issue can put their notes in the top drawer, while kids who bring fewer concerns or less negative feelings can put their notes in the middle or bottom drawers. Students can take their notes out and move them to another drawer if they sense a change in their attitudes and perceptions of class and the course.

And here's one more idea, thanks to a Carnegie Professor of the Year. Post a humorous Course Subject Bill of Rights that declares: You have the right not to like _____; You have the right to ask questions when you don't understand what we're doing; You have the right to make mistakes and learn from them; You have the right not to get it all the first time you hear it or do it; You have the right to re-do assignments or re-take exams until you achieve a satisfactory level of mastery; etc.

❏ Do a spot check to see if anyone can remember everyone's name.

Policies, Procedures, and Expectations: School-wide Rules and Policies

❏ Remind students that you will be using the data from the Classroom Vision carousel to develop class agreements. In order to do this responsibly, you need to explain the difference between school-wide rules and policies and classroom guidelines and agreements.

This is a good time to see what kids know, don't know, or have questions about regarding school-wide rules and disciplinary policies. If students are really confused, see if you can find some additional school handbooks and make a later time to review school-wide rules and policy. You might even want to invite the dean or vice-principal of discipline to come in and discuss questions and concerns with students. It's not a bad idea to give students a quiz on important school rules and policy sometime in the first few weeks.

❏ Clarify, teach, and/or review any important procedures that you have not introduced (p. 281).

Course Work
Homework:
❏ **Course Work**
❏ **Getting Started:** Bring in one object or picture that reflects your strong point as a learner or (alternatively) reminds you of the way you learn best. Share an object and something about yourself as a learner before students leave for the day.

Day 6
Getting Started:
Getting to Work:
❏ Quick-write: Ask students to write about a time when they messed up in school or at home (academically or behaviorally). Ask them to describe what adults did to help them deal with the problem and get back on track. What happened? What did the adult do that was helpful? Why did it work? Or ask students what they did for themselves to get back on track. How was it helpful? Why did it work?

Become a Community of Learners: Your Strong Point as a Learner

❑ Gathering: Ask students to say their names and share the objects they brought in from last night's homework. Be sure to model the activity again using the alternative question in their homework, and then ask for volunteers. Take about five minutes.

Policies, Procedures, and Expectations: Problem Solving Protocols

❑ Invite students to share their responses to the quick-write and ask for a volunteer to summarize the kinds of adult responses that felt helpful to students.

❑ Pass out the problem solving protocols (p. 306) and explain how you expect to use these procedures when students get into academic and behavioral difficulties.

Course Work
Homework:

❑ **Course Work**

Day 7
Getting Started:

Getting to Work: Reviewing Data from the Community Vision Learning Carousel

❑ Welcome everyone at the door and hand out the collected responses to the Creating a Classroom Vision questions.

❑ Ask students to read the responses and circle the three responses under each question that they think are most essential to making this class a good place for them. Do a pair-share to compare responses with one partner.

Become a Community of Learners: Making Classroom Guidelines and Agreements

❑ Do a spot check to see if anyone can remember everyone's name.

❑ Share your negotiables and non-negotiables, explaining that all policies and agreements have constraints and limitations (p. 65). These non-negotiables need to be considered as students help develop classroom guidelines and agreements.

❑ Give instructions for how you are going to develop classroom guidelines and agreements. Ask students to think about the ideas and suggestions they generated earlier. Encourage them to incorporate those ideas into the agreements you make together. Use the process described on p. 70. This will probably take the rest of the period.

Course Work:

❑ Course work may have to be just a brief check-in today, because you want to complete the process of making classroom agreements in one class period.

Homework:

- ❑ **Course Work**
- ❑ **Getting Started:** Pass out Personal Pathways Maps (p. 49) for students to begin working on. Let students know they will have two days to work on this.

Day 8
Getting Started:

Getting to Work: Personal Pathways Map

- ❑ Getting Started: Keep working on Personal Pathways map.

Become a Community of Learners: Conversation Circles

- ❑ Gathering: Conversation Circles (p. 80)

Policies, Procedures, and Expectations: Being "School Smart"

- ❑ Talk about what it means to be "school smart" (p. 148). What are the benefits of being "school smart?" Share some case study situations and ask students what they would consider a "school smart" response or solution. Let students know if you notice behaviors that appear to get in the way of learning, you will probably ask to meet them privately to brainstorm some strategies that will help them become more successful in class.

Course Work
Homework:

- ❑ **Course Work**
- ❑ **Getting Started:** Complete your Personal Pathways map.

Day 9
Getting Started:

Getting to Work: Personal Pathways map

- ❑ Prepare to hand in your Personal Pathways map.

Become a Community of Learners: "Learning How You Learn"

- ❑ Ask students to share their maps with at least two other students. After this, let students know that these maps will become part of their portfolios. Explain that students will continue to refine and review their goals throughout the year.

- ❑ Do a spot-check to see if anyone can remember everyone's name.

- ❑ Do the activity Twenty Things on a Tray (p. 189) to explore differences and preferences in how we learn and retain information.

Course Work

Homework:

❏ **Course Work**

Day 10

Getting Started:

Getting to Work:

❏ Do a reflection activity related to the discipline you teach. For example, you might choose from one of the following:

- Post several quotations that express different perspectives about the discipline you are teaching: the study of mathematics, history, literature, science, language, etc. The task might be to find one idea that they strongly agree or disagree with and share their reasons for their opinions.

- Ask students to write down three questions that a mathematician, a historian, a linguist, a scientist, or a writer might continually ask as they pursue their professions.

- Ask students to create similes about your discipline with these starters:

  Literature, science, etc. is like (any object) because _____ is like (anything from nature) because _____ is like (any sport) because _____ is like (any specific space or place) because_____.

- Pose the question, "How would your life be different today if no one had ever heard of_____or if _____did not exist. (Think of a common principle, concept, or innovation that is ubiquitous to your discipline. What would life be like without it?)

Course Work

Homework:

❏ **Course Work**

Day 11

Getting Started:

Getting to Work: Reflections about Group Participation

❏ Hand out three different color "sticky notes" or note cards to each student. On the first one answer this question: "For you to be a good group member, what do you need from the group?" They should answer in this format: "I need to be able to count on other group members to _____."

On the second "sticky note" answer this question: "The best quality I bring to a group is_____."

On the third one, answer this question: "I support others to be and do their best in a group by_____."

Become a Community of Learners: Teambuilding

❏ Take five minutes to share students' responses to the three questions. (This is in preparation for the team building activity.) Then ask students to post their "sticky-notes" on three pieces of chart paper where the questions are used as headers.

❏ Team-building activity: Do Chocolate River (p. 85) or any other activity where students work in teams to solve a problem, with the condition that no one can win unless everybody wins (i.e., successfully achieving the goal).

❏ Debrief by using questions included in the activity or by asking how the skills, qualities, and attitudes identified on their "sticky notes" were played out in the team building activity.

Course Work:

❏ Course work may be just a brief check-in today, because of the length of time required to complete and debrief team-building activity.

Homework:

❏ **Course Work:**
❏ **Getting Started:** Ask students to complete the following journal assignment: Define cooperative learning in the classroom. What do you like about learning this way? What don't you like about it?

Day 12
Getting Started:

Getting to Work: Working in Groups

❏ Have student perform the following quick-write: Think about a learning experience you really liked when you worked with a partner or a small group of students. What were you doing? What did you accomplish? What made it a positive learning experience for you?

OR: Think about a time you were involved with a sports team, a music or dance group, a theater production, a newspaper staff, or another team project where you felt good about working with others and what you and your team accomplished was something that made you proud. Why did it work? What did you like about this experience?

Policies, Procedures, and Expectations: Cooperative Learning

❑ Invite students to share their responses from last night's journaling and today's quick-write.

❑ Set the stage for effective cooperative learning (p. 193).

Course Work:

❑ Begin a cooperative learning activity related to your current learning unit. Examples:

1. **Geometry:** Each group receives a different problem. Each group's task is to construct a geometric proof that works, write their proof on chart paper, and be able to explain their proof to the rest of the group.

2. **English:** Using models and criteria that have already been discussed, each group of four students will choose to write opening paragraphs for a newspaper article of their choice: a crime report; an article on yesterday's sports match between two high schools; an editorial piece; an obituary; an analysis of a current crisis; a report of a local town meeting, hearing, or council meeting; a "puff piece" on a current fashion trend; an opinion piece about a controversial issue; a global event that impacts the US, etc. Each group of four will divide into two pairs, and each pair will compose an opening paragraph. When they are finished, the pairs will come back together in their group of four to share the goals of their opening paragraph, identify three things that must be included in it, and explain why the writing style in their opening paragraph needs to be different from the style used for other newspaper articles. Each pair will offer feedback to their partner pair before turning in their final opening paragraphs.

3. **Graphic Design:** Each group must design a brochure for a school club with the goals of doubling club membership and reaching a more diverse group of students who might consider participating in the club.

4. **Physics:** Each group of three must rotate through nine stations that include tools and objects that illustrate principles of simple machines. At each station, each group must agree on the type of machine being illustrated, evidence that supports their description of the machine, and the mechanical principles being illustrated. Each student in the group of three is responsible for recording data at three of the nine stations.

5. **Foreign Language:** Each group of four must choose to create a map or diagram of one room within a house and label at least twenty objects in it. Then the group needs to demonstrate four activities or tasks that different family members might do in this room. While one group member demonstrates the activity or task, another group member describes and explains what the person is doing. Each group member is required to write up one of the tasks or activities.

6. **Economics:** Each group receives a scenario that they will use to explore the concept of "opportunity costs" (when we choose to allocate time and resources for one thing, we are choosing not to allocate time and resources to something else). Scenarios include A) making a corporate decision about offering more family benefits to employees; B) making a school scheduling decision to include more time for advisory purposes; C) making a personal decision to spend the weekend sleeping and hanging out with friends; D) making a family decision to purchase a second car; E) making a Congressional decision to allocate more resources and services for young children; F) making a local community decision to recycle all glass and paper; G) making a personal decision to set aside most of your paycheck for college expenses; and H) making a school board decision to build a new high school and tear down the current structure. Each group must identify three potential opportunity costs that emerge from the decision described in their scenario.

7. **History:** As students explore the implications and effects of a major political decision or the introduction of a new technology or invention, each group picks a card that identifies a specific group or constituency. Each cooperative group must discuss in detail their group's status before and after this decision or technological change and identify three ways that their group or constituency is affected by this event or technology. They will also need to decide on the overall impact on their group (on a scale from –5 to +5, with 0 being little to no impact positively or negatively) and defend the number they choose.

See page 202 for additional suggestions that will help make a cooperative learning activity productive.

Homework:
- ❏ **Course Work**
- ❏ **Getting Started:** Instruct students that they should be ready to pass in their journals tomorrow.

Ask them to write a reflection about their first two weeks in class. Choose questions from Self-Assessment Tools (p. 53) in Chapter One. Ask students to write about a page.

Let students know that during the next two weeks you will meet personally with three students a day during the "Getting to Work" activity to do a personal check-in and see how things are going and discuss work they have turned in.

Day 13
Getting Started:
Getting to Work:
- ❏ Have students prepare to hand in their journals.

- ❏ Check in with three students during "Getting to Work."

Become a Community of Learners: Form Home Groups

❏ Form Home Groups to establish a student support system (p. 92).

Policies, Procedures, and Expectations: Cooperative Learning

❏ Review how you will be monitoring cooperative learning groups. Be sure to give the class feedback about what you are noticing as you walk around and observe. After students have completed the activity, ask them to reflect on a couple of questions that focus on how they worked together as a group.

Course Work:

❏ Continue the cooperative learning activity.

Closing Class:

❏ Introduce a closing at the end of class. Try "Five Words or Less Headlines"

Homework:

❏ **Course Work**

Day 14

Getting Started:

Getting to Work:

❏ Do an activity related to your current learning unit.

❏ Check in with three students during "Getting to Work."

Course Work
Homework:

❏ **Course Work**

❏ **Getting Started:** Invite students to make Family Banners (p. 176). They will need to complete this to share on Day 16. Have your example to show students.

Day 15

Getting Started:

Getting to Work:

❏ Do an activity related to your current learning unit.
❏ Check in with three students during "Getting to Work."

Become a Community of Learners: Cultural Sharing

❏ Introduce micro-lab listening circles using questions that focus on students' family backgrounds and cultural experiences (p. 176).

Course Work

Homework:
- ❏ **Course Work**
- ❏ **Getting Started:** Students should complete their Family Banners.

Day 16

Getting Started:

Getting to Work:
- ❏ Students should be ready to share their Family Banners.
- ❏ Check in with three students during "Getting to Work."

Become a Community of Learners: Sharing Personal Stories
- ❏ Share students' Family Banners.

Course Work

Homework:
- ❏ **Course Work**

Day 17

Getting Started:

Getting to Work:
- ❏ Do an activity related to your current learning unit.
- ❏ Check in with three students during "Getting to Work."

Become a Community of Learners: Countering Harassment by Becoming Allies
- ❏ Read the story "The Most Mature Thing I've Ever Seen" from *Chicken Soup for the Teenage Soul* (Canfield, J., Hansen, M., Kirberger, K., 1997) and debrief the story by discussing the roles of aggressor, target, bystander, and ally. Let students know that tomorrow the class will discuss harassment.

Course Work

Homework:
- ❏ **Course Work**

Day 18

Getting Started:

Getting to Work: Thinking About Harassment
- ❏ Ask students to think about your school and choose to write about one of these questions:

1. What kinds of behaviors do you see around school that you think fall into the category of harassment or bullying?

2. Are there any particular groups or types of kids whom you see playing the aggressor/harasser role here at school? Why do you think individual students or groups do this?

3. What groups or types of kids are most likely to be targeted? Why do you think that is?

❏ Check in with three students during "Getting to Work."

Policies, Procedures, and Expectations: Harassment
❏ Define and discuss harassment, (p. 183). Clarify school-wide and legal policies around these behaviors. Explain what you will do if you witness any of these behaviors.

Course Work
Homework:
❏ **Course Work**

Day 19
Getting Started:
Getting to Work: Thinking About Harassment
❏ Ask students to write about one of these questions in their journals:

1. Think about a time when you were targeted or harassed by an individual or group. What was going on? How did it feel? Did anyone intervene as your ally? If not, what would you have wanted an ally to do?

2. Think about a time when you witnessed someone else being targeted or harassed. What was going on? What did you do? If you witnessed a similar situation again, what would you say or do differently?

3. If you were targeted or harassed what would you want a teacher to do? What would you want a friend to do?

❏ Check in with three students during "Getting to Work."

Become a Community of Learners: Responding to Harassment
❏ Ask students to form groups of three or four to share their responses to questions about harassment.
❏ Explore ways that students can respond to harassment using role plays or guided discussion (p. 185).

Course Work:
❏ Course work may be just a brief check-in today, because of the length of time required to complete and debrief the team-building activity.

Homework:
- ❑ Course Work

Day 20
Getting Started:
Getting to Work: Class Meeting Topics
- ❑ Pass out note cards and ask students to write down classroom or school-wide issues that they would like to discuss or any particular problems that they think require a group solution. Collect cards.

- ❑ Check in with three students during "Getting to Work."

Become a Community of Learners: Introduce the language of WIN-WIN and Class Meeting
- ❑ Learn Win-Win negotiation and consensus (p. 101).

- ❑ Introduce Class Meeting format using a classroom or school-wide issue or problem that you would like students to discuss and solve as a group (p. 105). Let students know that you will use this format for other issues that come up and that your hope is that students will facilitate this process. Read aloud some of the topics that students suggested. Ask for a volunteer to type up the suggestions and later students can prioritize class meeting topics that they want to discuss.

Course Work
Homework:
- ❑ **Course Work**
- ❑ **Getting Started:** One-month check-in. Have students choose two questions from Self-Assessment Tools (p. 53) to write about.

CHAPTER 5

Thinking about Discipline in a
Partners in Learning Classroom

According to the NEA, classroom discipline remains the #1 problem identified by teachers.
In framing this discussion of classroom discipline, I have to own up that I'm a big fan of the
word discipline and its many meanings. I like thinking about areas in my life where I feel self-
disciplined, where I can easily access tried and true qualities, habits, and skills that will lead
to a job well done and a personal sense of well-being. I love the idea of engaging in daily
disciplines that become comforting routines. I grew up in a disciplined household—there were
ways that we did things in our home—but I didn't get disciplined in the punitive sense very
often. Rather, I was mostly shown and taught how to do something and then I was expected
to learn how to do it for myself. The reward was in the doing and the internal satisfaction I felt
from doing it. Disciplined practice of the smallest tasks gave me a sense of control, responsibility,
and competence. As a student and a teacher I also love the notion of learning and practicing a
discipline—whether it's history or science, music or literary analysis. And even though there are
undisciplined corners of my life that I don't much like to visit, I also know that making room
for my undisciplined self can help me think outside of the box and have fun doing it.

Think about yourself for a minute. How would you describe yourself when you feel disciplined
and undisciplined? How were you disciplined at home and at school? When you were growing
up how did adults help you become responsible and learn self-discipline? What kinds of support
motivate you to be disciplined in some areas of your life? When and how has practice helped
you become more disciplined? How do you feel when you have a sense of self-control in your
life? What happens when you don't? Your personal responses to these questions can help jump-
start your thinking about establishing and maintaining effective discipline in the classroom.

I propose that the goal of effective classroom management and discipline is to help all students
to become more self-disciplined—that is, to regulate and manage their behavior in ways that
promote social skillfulness, responsible decision making, and academic success.

Three Approaches to Classroom
Management and Discipline

There are three basic choices we can make when students get into behavioral or academic
difficulties. We can choose to respond with threats, verbal assaults, and punishments. We
can choose to ignore the problem and do nothing. Or we can engage in the practice of
guided discipline where we become partners with students as we work out problems together.

The Punishment Approach

Punitive action are done to a student—the intention is to verbally, psychologically, or physically threaten or inflict sufficient hurt, humiliation, discomfort, or deprivation so that a student will avoid the same behavior in the future to avoid being punished. Punishment is "past oriented" and usually prompted by a teacher's need to exercise control and power over the student. When we operate in punitive mode, the unspoken message is something like, "My will has to dominate your will. You need to be put in your place for what you've said or done or not done." This response is often linked to a choice to personalize the situation. When we interpret a student's misbehavior or unskillful responses as a personal affront to our authority or self-respect—we gravitate toward payback and punishment. It's as if we are thinking, "You chose to make my life unpleasant so I'm going to return the sting."

Among educational researchers, there is remarkable agreement that punishment by itself, without guided instruction and support, rarely changes a student's behavior or improves student achievement. It is important to note how often secondary teachers use grades and assessments as a form of academic punishment in hopes of getting kids to shape up. Punishment may extinguish a negative behavior briefly, but that's about it. A "punitive only" approach becomes problematic because it often intensifies students' feelings of anger, hostility, alienation, resentment, or defiance. Punishment feels adversarial to students and is likely to reinforce "us vs. them" thinking. The final irony is that punitive strategies work least effectively for the kids who get in the most trouble, academically or behaviorally.

The Do Nothing Approach

The Do Nothing approach literally means that a teacher doesn't intervene and nothing is done to, done by, or done with a student to interrupt or change behavior. Sometimes we do nothing out of fear of a confrontation or fear of being disliked. Some teachers are simply disinterested in monitoring and helping kids change their behavior; claiming that their job is to teach, not to discipline high school students. We may feel uneasy about using our authority in some situations or just feel stuck, not knowing how to respond. Taking effective action can also feel draining. Especially when we're tired or overloaded, intervening with care and intention can feel like it requires too much time and energy.

The choice to do nothing can emerge from the best of intentions. We might convince ourselves that, "If I'm low key and don't draw attention to negative behavior, students will gradually stop engaging in these behaviors." Or we might hope that kids get the message, "I won't mess with you if you don't mess with me." Or we might think that if we attend to the rest of the group and keep focused on the task at hand, students with problem behaviors will eventually figure out behavioral norms in the class and right themselves on their own.

This is a risky proposition because the message we think we're sending might not be the message a student takes in. Students may assume that a teacher's reluctance to intervene with problem behaviors is a sign of weakness—some kids may interpret a "hands-off" approach as a free pass to do whatever they want, whenever they want. Other students might think that your avoidance means you don't care enough to notice—these students may opt out and become passive and detached from you and the class. The bottom line is that doing nothing may serve as a temporary holding pattern while you observe the behavior of a particular student. But a do nothing approach to discipline is likely to create more problems and solve next to none.

The Guided Discipline Approach

As its heart, the word discipline has everything to do with instruction. Among its Latin origins are the words, discipulus which means "teacher or disciple" and disciplina which means "to teach." Guided discipline is a combination of guided instruction and support, interventions and meaningful consequences that will help students learn and regularly practice more skillful behaviors and responsible decision making. In contrast to punishment and doing nothing, meaningful consequences are done with and by a student—the intention is to help students take responsibility for their behavior or academic problems, understand the effects of their behavior on themselves and others, and learn and practice behaviors that are more skillful, responsible, and productive.

Guided discipline is "present and future oriented"; it focuses on the student's need to regain control, self-correct, redirect focus, or get back on track. Positive and negative consequences are viewed as natural outcomes of the choices students make. Guided discipline involves a wide range of graduated and differentiated consequences and interventions. The idea is to match appropriate consequences to the frequency and severity of a problem behavior and provide the kind of instruction and support that best matches the needs of individual students. Rather than butting heads as adversaries, teachers' instruction, coaching, and support help students develop greater personal self-discipline and foster classroom habits and routines that create a more disciplined learning environment.

The concept of guided discipline is informed by beliefs that students are capable of reflecting on their mistakes and setbacks and can set goals and develop new strategies that will help them change their behavior. Students who experience guided discipline and support are more likely to feel trusted, cared for, and respected. These positive feelings are more likely to motivate students to improve their behavior and their academic efforts.

Three Different Approaches to Classroom Management

Punishment	Do Nothing	Guided Discipline
Punishment is done to a student and consequences are often arbitrary. Punishment is about rule-breaking and payback without instruction or support.	Nothing is done to interrupt or change current bahavior. Do nothing is about avoidance and reluctance due to fear of confrontation, fear of being disliked, uneasiness of using authority, disinterest in helping students change behavior, or a concern that effective intervention will take too much time or energy.	Guided discipline involves meaningful invitations, interventions, consequences, and problem solving done with a student. It is about support and practice building and maintaining relationships.
Goal: To verbally, emotionally, or physically threaten or inflict sufficient hurt, humilation, discomfort, or deprivation so student will stop engaging in offending behavior to avoid punishment	**Goal:** To ignore misbehavior and hope that students will figure out behavioral norms and right themselves on their own	**Goal:** To help students take responsibility for their behavior or academic problems, understand the effects of their behavior, and learn and practice behaviors that are more skillful, successful, and responsible
Orientation: Past	**Orientation:** Present	**Orientation:** Present and Future
Immediate Focus: Teacher's need to exercise power, control, and authority over student	**Immediate Focus:** Attend to the needs of the rest of the class and keep focused on the task at hand	**Immediate Focus:** Help student self-correct, regain control, redirect, and get back on track
Effects on Student: Likely to intensify feelings of anger, resentment, hostility, alienation, and defiance with little motivation to change	**Effects on Student:** Likely to encourage detachment and passivity or an inflated sense of power to act out, test limits, and challenge authority	**Effects on Student:** Likely to encourage feelings of being trusted, cared for, and respected with motivation to change

Three Different Approaches — Three Different Outcomes

Here are six scenarios that illustrate how punitive, do nothing, and guided discipline approaches to classroom management result in very different student outcomes.

Scenario #1 (This is a boundary violation because some students are interfering with other students' learning)

Two boys are talking across the room to friends in another group during a cooperative learning activity.

Punishment: The teacher responds by demanding in a voice louder than theirs that they stop the side conversations with other groups and get back to work. When the pair continue talking across the room, the teacher says in an even louder voice: "That's it. You've got a zero for the day and a detention after school." The two students quiet down, continue to grumble among themselves, and don't do a lick of work. They don't go to detention and no one realizes they were missing in action until two weeks later.

Do Nothing: The teacher ignores the students and focuses her attention on the students who are on-task. The boys' behavior is not disrupting the class as a whole, but the conversation continues to distract their friends from focusing on their group's task. In the meantime, the two boys are contributing nothing to the efforts of their own group.

Guided Discipline: The teacher moves over to the two students, gets their attention, and talks to them quietly near their group. The goal is to get students back on track, so the teacher asks, "I want to make sure you're clear about what to do. What's your task right now?" One student doesn't have a clue, so the teacher says, "Okay, check in with your group and then tell me two things you need to do during the rest of the period. Got it?" The student checks back in with the teacher and begins working. At the end of class, the teacher checks in again with both students and asks, "Tell me what you accomplished today and what's left to do tonight?" The teacher gives them a smile and thumbs up and closes by saying, "So when you come in tomorrow, let me know what you're going to do to stay focused on the assignment. Okay?"

Scenario #2 (This is a procedural infraction because the student has not yet learned how to follow assignment procedures consistently)

A very bright 9th grade boy named Eric has set new records for disorganization. He constantly loses important papers, his notebook is a mess, he hasn't turned in key assignments, and he leaves his assignment notebook at home. Thus he is unable to write down his assignments at school.

Punishment: Here are the procedures Eric isn't following:

- There are strict guidelines for organizing notes and notebooks. Notebooks are collected and graded every month. Eric has received two F's.

- When students are missing important papers they need to make a copy from a classmate's copy. Eric has not done this so has doesn't have important information to complete a major assignment.

- If students hand in homework a day late they receive 50% credit. After that , it's a zero. Eric is racking up the zero's.

- As part of 9th grade study skills, students are required to keep assignment notebooks. The teacher randomly checks a few students' assignment notebooks everyday. Eric has received two zero's.

Eric is sinking fast. The teacher's message to students is, "I am not your mother, and I'm not going to look after you. You're in high school, so you better figure out how to stay organized or your report card grade is not going to look too good. It's your choice."

Do Nothing: The teacher posts organizational procedures at the beginning of the year, but doesn't follow-through collecting or checking students' work and notebooks except for major assignments, quizzes, and tests. Eric has managed to get a C - because of his test scores, but he is not likely to clean up his organizational problems anytime soon.

Guided Discipline: Here are the procedures Eric isn't following:

- There are a number of options for how students can codify their notes and organize their notebooks. Eric has chosen to do none of them. Notebooks are spot checked on a daily basis and collected once every month. Eric has received two F's because he has not turned his notebook in. This is one of the reasons he's meeting with the teacher today.

- When students are missing important materials they can go to a file to retrieve an extra copy. Eric never remembers this option so when he finally gets around to looking for an extra copy there are none left.

- Students have a week to finish up back-work for reduced credit or they are required to make arrangements to spend time during Conference Hour completing important assignments. Eric insists that he's done several missing assignments but he can't seem to find them. This is the other reason he is meeting with the teacher today. Students must stay after school until they complete a minimal number of class and homework assignments satisfactorily.

- As part of 9th grade study skills, students are required to keep assignment notebooks. The teacher spot checks to see if students are writing down their assignments and notices that Eric can't even find his assignment notebook.

For better or worse the teacher's own son had severe "Eric" tendencies, so she knows that some boys never personally encounter the words NEAT, ORGANIZED, and TIMELY until they finish high school or play on a sports team. She knows this is a developmental issue for some kids AND she recognizes the importance of not letting it go completely. She's willing to fight some battles even though she's aware she won't win the organizational war by the end of 9th grade. Eric fills out his procedure report and he and the teacher discuss some next steps to deal with the big mess.

Here's what they come up with:

- Eric agrees to bring everything he possesses related to class to Conference Hour tomorrow. The goals are to see what he can find that hasn't been turned in and assess ways that he might track and organize his materials.

- Eric agrees to organize the last two weeks of his notebook. Going back further would be futile.

- Eric agrees to set up a phone call with him, the teacher, and a parent to develop some supports and consequences at home to try and sustain the clean-up effort.

- Eric agrees to get a different kind of assignment notebook that fits within his larger notebook.

- Eric agrees to check in on Tuesdays and Fridays with the teacher to see how the plan is working.

Scenario #3 (This is a boundary violation because one student's disrespectful behavior affects the classroom environment)

A junior girl named Cherise has a loose mouth. She is swearing under her breath about the assignment in front of her and announces just loud enough for you and the students around her to hear: "I'm not going to do this stupid ass homework. What a waste of time."

Punishment: The teacher looks up and says, "And you don't think you're a waste of my time right now? Think again." The student sees everyone else looking at her, slams her book down on the desk, and sits for the rest of the period in stony silence.

Do Nothing: The teacher is in the middle of discussing the assignment with a small group of students and notices that almost everyone is involved in some stage of working on the assignment. The teacher ignores the comment. Cherise continues her low-grade mumbling and does nothing.

Guided Discipline: The teacher has already interrupted Cherise twice about making disrespectful remarks today. Cherise has a short fuse, so the teacher wants to avoid confrontation with her. She wants to accomplish three things in next the 10 seconds: 1) she wants the class to know she heard the comment; 2) she wants Cherise to know she heard it; and 3) she wants to remind her of the classroom procedure when kids make disrespectful remarks. So the teacher says quietly, "I heard that, Cherise. So what's it going to be? Ten minutes at lunch or ten minutes after school? You know the routine." Cherise sulks, but grudgingly says, "Okay, fine, at lunch." Students in class know that the first or second time they use abusive language or make disrespectful remarks in class they will need to meet with the teacher. The teacher meets with Cherise at lunch and begins by saying, "It sure sounded like that assignment set you off. What was that about?" At this point Cherise bursts into tears, and confides how long it takes her to read and how frustrating that feels. They talk a bit more and the teacher asks if Cherise would be willing to meet with the reading specialist to learn some new strategies. Cherise agrees to do this. The teacher revisits the earlier outburst in class and gives Cherise a blue form that students are required to fill out for this infraction. They go over the questions together. The form closes by asking, "When you feel like this the next time, what are two things you can do that are better choices?" The teacher reassures Cherise that they will work on the reading problem together and suggests one strategy for Cherise to try tonight. Cherise leaves much less upset and more motivated to hang in there.

Scenario #4 (This is an academic problem that impacts a significant number of students)

40% of your students received D's and F's on a major math test.

Punishment: The teacher's response is "Next time, those of you who received D's and F's might want to reconsider how you spend the night before a test. Some of you have continued to perform on the pathetic side of the grade equation. I suggest you change your ways. Academic warning slips go out tomorrow." Some students feel antagonized by these comments and write off the teacher and the class. Other kids just feel stupid.

Do Nothing: The teacher accepts that a percentage of students will not succeed in this class. Therefore, she makes no attempt to deal with the academic slide of one group of students. If some students are motivated enough to talk to her about getting some help, she'll make the time. The result is that failing students get further behind and become more resistant and reluctant to put in the effort to learn.

Guided Discipline: The teacher is frustrated that the same group of students are consistently having academic difficulty. He says to his class, "Here's what I've observed over the last few weeks. There's a split between those of you who have a good grasp of what we're doing and those of you who are having a tough time passing and doing well. My expectation is that all you can master many of these skills, so I don't like what's happening. Your failure to do well is my failure too. So I'm going to push the pause button today so we can try and sort out what's going on. I want to give my undivided attention to this during the rest of the period. You're not bad students for doing poorly. But it is a bad thing if we don't deal with the situation." Students who have consistently been earning A's and B's receive passes to go to the library. Their assignment is to make solution flow charts for key problems on the test. With the rest of the students the teacher facilitates a class meeting asking students to discuss how they see the situation, identify what they think is blocking their success, brainstorm what they could do to help themselves, and agree on several strategies that they could try out in class, with a buddy, and by themselves. Each student writes a brief reflection and set goals for the next two weeks. The next day is an informal test correction session where students work in pairs and small groups. The teacher spends the period checking in with students and those who created flow charts for key problems share their solutions with their peers. Students have the option of retaking the test and averaging the two grades.

Scenario #5 (This is a boundary violation because the behavior is unsafe)

Three 9th grade girls in one of your classes are friends one minute and enemies the next. Before walking into your class, you hear them outside your door, engaged in an Oscar winning screaming match and it looks like it's escalating to a shoving and pushing match.

Punishment: The teacher steps outside and is seething with anger at having to take time to escort the three of them to the office. The girls spend the rest of the day in-school suspension. ISS is monitored by a teaching assistant whose job it is to ensure that the students remain silent and do some school work. The three girls spend most of their time writing and passing notes to each other when the ISS monitor isn't looking. Students return to class as if nothing ever happened and the teacher is still steamed up about the incident.

Do Nothing: The commotion is outside the teacher's door. He's busy setting up a lab. It's not his problem. Another teacher in the hall intervenes.

Guided Discipline: The teacher steps outside, gets their attention, and says, "Stop. Look at what's happening here. You've created a commotion that's drawn a crowd and you look like you're ready to come to blows. We can't have this in the hallways. It's not safe. The three of you need to deal with this now." The teacher escorts the girls to the Problem Solving Place where the PSP coach signs them in and invites them to sit down and take a few deep breaths. Then he asks the girls why they think they were referred to the Problem Solving Place. Students take a few minutes to fill out their PSP report form and the PSP coach talks them through their responses. The goal of the session is for the girls to come to some kind of agreement that will reduce the chance of another public drama in the halls or in class. The girls talk about the reasons for their "drama queen" behaviors and agree on several specific actions they can take to avoid this in the future. They rehearse what they will say to the teacher who referred them. The PSP coach escorts the girls back to their teacher later in the day. They name how their behavior affected other people and tell the teacher what they're going to do to prevent this from happening again. The PSP coach also arranges a series of one minute check-in's with the girls so they can tell him what they are doing to keep their agreements.

Scenario #6 (This is both a boundary violation and an interpersonal conflict because it is about peer relationships in the classroom)

You have two students in different classes who manifest polar opposites of the same problem—putting down and ridiculing other kids whom they perceive as uncool and not "with it." Mario is a very bright boy who is much too quick to call kids stupid, and sighs and smirks when students don't "get it" as fast or as well as he does. The other boy, Greg, directs his sarcasm and ridicule toward anyone who acts "smart" or expresses any enthusiasm about what they are doing in class. In both classes their disrespectful behaviors have become chronic and they seem to suck the positive energy out of the air. You are worried about the negative impact of their behavior on other students and the learning environment, and you are also worried about the negative attitude you are beginning to have toward them.

Punishment: With both boys, the teacher has warned them about their attitudes, called their parents, and sent them to the office; but nothing seems to be working. Now their hostility toward other kids has rubbed off, and the teacher is increasingly hostile toward them. The teacher is aware that she is increasingly impatient, sarcastic, angry, and threatening with them—she finds herself tossing back zingers to these boys so they get a taste of what it feels like to be personally attacked. This is becoming a grudge match of who can deliver the most cutting verbal blow. The teacher has assigned several detentions to both boys who already have more than three detentions. The next step will be a suspension.

Do Nothing: The teacher has steeled herself to these students' rudeness and has moved students who were the targets of their comments to other seats. The teacher doesn't believe that he can do anything that will change their ingrained insensitivity. Real life is learning to toughen up and live with people you don't like or who bother you.

Guided Discipline: The teacher has already had conferences with each boy, but has decided that a classroom intervention alone won't be sufficient to address what feels pretty serious. He arranges for separate meetings with each boy, a parent, the counselor, and himself. The teacher wants to proceed in this way so that he can be a full participant in the conversations with the boys and their parents. It turns out that each boy feels isolated and different from the other students in class and takes on the same roles of critic and judge at home. For each of them, it appears that their verbal assaults on others are a way of protecting themselves. In each conference the group develops a plan that includes the following:

Mario has agreed to:
- meet with the counselor several more times to talk
- keep a learning log where he will write about positive contributions that he notices that others make in class and write about the ways he is encouraging and supporting other students to be successful in class
- spend one period a week doing peer tutoring instead of attending class

The teacher has agreed to:
- note the changes he has observed in Mario's behavior toward others
- check in with Mario once a week to assess the week and make a phone call home to the parents

Greg has agreed to:
- meet with the counselor several more times to talk
- keep a learning log where he will write about ways that he sees himself as smart in and out of class and write down what's going on when he feels frustrated in class
- spend one period a week helping out in a SPED PE class instead of attending class

The teacher has agreed to:

- note the changes he has observed in Greg's behavior toward others
- check in with Greg once a week to assess the week and make a phone call home to the parents
- develop an academic plan with Greg so that he can improve his performance in class

My hope is that this brief snapshot makes a credible case that a guided discipline approach holds out the best prospect for helping students change their behavior. If there is a downside to guided discipline, it's about the amount of time needed for planning, implementation, and follow-up. For this reason, you might not be able to always implement the ideal solution. But guided discipline can still inform every decision. The upside, however, is huge. You are likely to have fewer disruptions and problematic behaviors and more motivated and self-disciplined learners. The section that follows describes in detail five steps for implementing guided discipline in the classroom.

Implementing Guided Discipline

Guided Discipline is a combination of guided instruction, reflection, support, interventions, and meaningful consequences that will help students learn and regularly practice more skillful behaviors and responsible decision making.

1. **Awareness—Know Yourself, Know Your Students, Know Your School**
   - What is your teaching stance? Where does your authority come from?
   - What are your discipline goals, your "No's," your triggers and reducers?
   - What will help you deal effectively with adolescents' disrespectful speech?
   - What kinds of teacher behaviors will set your kids off?
   - What kinds of teacher support will help your kids become more self-disciplined and engage in more skillful behaviors more of the time?

2. **Prevention**
   - Help students get ready to learn
   - Establish positive group agreements, norms, goals, and expectations
   - Set clear boundaries and explain what makes a behavior a boundary violation
   - Teach and practice procedures and problem solving protocols
   - Build group cohesion and connectedness in the classroom
   - Develop personal connections with each student
   - Practice negotiated learning and group problem solving
   - Model and teach life skills

3. **Invitations**
   - Invite cooperation using verbal and written prompts
   - Give students opportunities to self-correct
   - Offer chances to make a choice
   - Help students to redirect their focus
   - Use two minute problem solving strategies

- Let students know what they can do when they're upset and angry
- When invitations don't work, interrupt and de-escalate conflicts and confrontations quickly and calmly

4. **Interventions**
   - Clarify the differences between (1) boundary violations, (2) procedural infractions, and (3) intra- and inter-personal conflicts and problems
   - Begin student conferences by listening first and defusing students' upset feelings before you problem solve
   - Make sure that problem solving reports, behavior plans, and academic contracts play a central role in follow-up consequences
   - Communicate with parents by phone, e-mail, notes, and conferences
   - Use class meetings to discuss problems and concerns that affect the whole group
   - Refer students to mediation, counseling services, and student assistance programs

5. **Support and Maintenance**
   - Provide immediate feedback when students are trying out new skills and behaviors
   - Create classroom routines and rituals that involve every student
   - Make connections through 10 second "hits"
   - Recognize and celebrate the group's efforts and accomplishments
   - Recognize individual accomplishments in and out of the classroom
   - Provide differentiated support for students who are struggling
   - Create opportunities for students to link personal effort to their successes in the classroom

Five Steps for Implementing Guided Discipline in the Classroom:

1. Awareness – Know Yourself, Your Students, and Your School

Know Yourself
These are some questions you might ask yourself. Your personal responses will influence the kind of discipline policies and practices you develop and the kind of follow through you are willing to do.

- **What is your teaching stance?** What values and principles do you stand for in the classroom? (For more on teaching stance, see p. 227)

- **Where does your authority come from?** Does it come from the personal relationships you develop with people? Your expertise and know-how? Your reputation and experience? Your personal charisma and style? Your physical presence and stature? Your age? Your formal position and status? Your capacity to threaten, punish, and exercise power over others?

- **Are you more authoritarian or authoritative?** People who are authoritarian command obedience and demand respect. They tend to rely on their formal status and position as the primary source of their authority. In other words, "I'm the teacher; you're the student. This is the way it's going to be." In authoritarian classrooms students must usually conform to a narrow set of behaviors, leaving little space to be themselves. Authoritarian teachers need to feel that they are 100% in charge and in control. They have the final say in all matters and students have very little input about what goes on in class. Classroom practice tends to be teacher directed and textbook driven. There is low-to-no tolerance for questions about procedures, processes, or subject matter content. Relationships between students and teachers are usually more formal, distant, and businesslike.

  Authoritarian teachers communicate to students that "it's my way or the highway;" this is often accomplished by dozens of strict rules that usually begin with "No." Student misbehaviors, mistakes, and missteps are viewed as a violation of a teacher's authority; thus some form of punishment must be meted out to offending students. A few teachers can pull this off brilliantly, but most of us can't. The teachers who can often have quirky personae, unwavering standards, and an unusual knowledge base that garner genuine respect, especially from high achieving kids who seek a similar kind of mastery and control. But for most students the authoritarian formula backfires.

  Authoritative teachers know they're in charge too. The difference isn't about giving up power and control—it's about how teachers use their power and control differently. Authoritative teachers use their authority to create a foundation of mutual respect; they model respect rather than demand it. Of paramount importance is creating a learning environment that is first and foremost a safe place for everyone. This means communicating clearly the two or three behaviors that won't be tolerated in any form and letting kids know what will happen if students engage in them. Being in charge means ensuring that every student has the right to learn, the right to be treated with dignity and respect, and the right to be heard.

  Authoritative teachers establish a community of WE rather than US vs. THEM, putting in place practices that invite the teacher and the students to become partners in the classroom. Sharing responsibility for learning shifts the emphasis from MY classroom to OUR classroom. Authoritative teachers appreciate the risks of insisting to adolescents that everything be done "my way." They are more likely to generate a variety of ways that students can meet learning goals and expectations. Finally, authoritative teachers use their power and influence to problem solve rather than punish. Student accountability is linked to students' efforts to develop new skills and strategies that will help them become more capable and responsible.

- **What are your own "no's" and needs?** For example, if you're a neatnik and trash on the floor drives you over the edge, you will want to let students know that this is one of your no's and establish a procedure for kids to tidy up before class is over.

- **What are your discipline goals?** Here are a few ideas:
  - I want to recognize and support positive behaviors so we can establish a set of behavioral norms that are clear to all students.

  - I want to intervene effectively when students are engaged in behaviors that are unsafe or disruptive.

  - I want to promote a sense of mutual respect, courtesy, caring, and empathy in the classroom.

  - I want to understand the sources of problematic behaviors so I can help students meet their underlying needs more effectively.

  - For chronic misbehaviors and procedural infractions I want to apply consistent consequences that feel fair and help students take responsibility for their actions.

  - I want to involve students in developing meaningful consequences for serious problems.

  - I want students to learn and practice self-management, communication, and problem solving skills that will help them become more behaviorally and academically skillful, responsible, and successful.

- **What are your own triggers? What are your reducers? How do you express your anger?** Knowing what sets you off is a good thing. You have the advantage of preparing yourself for what to say and do when your anger button is pushed, and you can let students know where not to go. When you do get upset, frustrated, or angry, what are the reducers? What will help you to stop, defuse the emotional charge that you feel, and get re-centered so that you can think clearly about what to do next? For example, you might experience a situation where you feel so upset that your best response is to stop what you are doing, take a few deep breaths, walk to the other side of the room, and say, "I'm too angry to deal with this right now; we'll make a time later to talk about this when I can hear you and you can hear me." When the class has really blown it behaviorally or academically, how do you want to communicate your negative feelings? Expressing your frustration, anger, and disappointment is a tricky thing. Do it too often and it sounds like a broken record to kids: "Blah, blah, blah... here she goes again." Think about picking your battles carefully. Expressing negative feelings has a different impact if you do it once a month rather than several times a week. If you rehearse what you want to say and know how you want to involve students in addressing the issue, your message will have a greater impact on more students.

- **Know that you have choices for how you manage conflict**
  Each conflict management style has potential uses and potential limitations, but sometimes we get stuck and rely on one style most of the time. There is no one style that's the right way to handle conflict. The art of effective conflict management is using the most appropriate

style given the situation, your goals, and the state of the relationship. Think about: What styles are you most likely to use with different groups of students? What style are you most likely to use when you feel stressed? What style would you like to use more often/less often to be more effective with your students?

Six Conflict Management Styles

1. **Directing/Controlling:** *"My way or the highway" or "This isn't negotiable"*
    We do not, cannot, or will not bargain or give in. We use this response when safety is an issue and/or we must respond immediately. At other times we are standing up for our rights and deeply held beliefs. It can also mean pursuing what we want at the expense of another person. We may also be caught in a power struggle and not see a way to negotiate to get what we want. (This is a version of the FIGHT response.) Although you may achieve your goal by using a directing style, your response can potentially damage the relationship.

2. **Collaborating:** *"Let's work it out"*
    We work with others to find mutually satisfying ways to get important needs met. We are interested in finding solutions and in maintaining or even improving the relationship. Other people involved are seen as partners rather than adversaries, and parties work together to share points of view, identify common interests, and explore alternatives before agreeing on a mutually satisfying solution. Using a collaborative style often gives you the best chance for achieving the goal and maintaining a positive relationship.

3. **Compromising:** *"Split the difference" or "Something is better than nothing"*
    We seek the middle ground. Each party gives up something for a solution that might satisfy our needs only partially.

4. **Accommodating:** *"Give in" or "Let it go" or "It doesn't matter anyway"*
    We yield to another's point of view, meeting the other person's needs while letting go of our own, in this particular situation. We may give in to smooth the relationship or it may be an issue that's just not very important to us. Using this style can help you maintain a shaky relationship, but it will not help you achieve your goals. Sometimes accommodation can be a first step before you are ready to tackle the problem.

5. **Avoiding/Denying:** *"Walk away" or "I don't see a problem"*
    We do not address the conflict or we withdraw from the situation or we behave as though the situation were not happening. We leave it to others to deal with. (This is a version of the FLIGHT response.) Avoidance usually comes back to bite you and will not help you achieve your goal.

6. **Appealing to a Greater Authority or a Third Party:** *"Help me out here"*
    We turn to others whom we perceive as having more power, influence, authority, skills, or wisdom to resolve the conflict. If the parties involved bring intense feelings to the situation, it can be helpful for a neutral third party to mediate the situation.

- **How do you react when you make mistakes or lose control in the classroom?**
Every teacher loses it sometimes with a whole class or an individual student. Think about how you usually respond after an incident when your more sensitive or effective self was missing in action. Whatever you choose to do in the classroom sends a strong message to students. If we say nothing or do nothing, we are conveying a message that mistakes are bad—that it's better to cover them up than deal with them openly. Inadvertently, we are also asking students to pretend that the incident never happened or to believe that somehow, as if by magic, the conflict that created the incident has been resolved and everything's fine. Our silence can also imply that it's not important to take responsibility for things we do that affect others negatively, however unintentional.

On the other hand, when we acknowledge our mistakes, admit when we think we've gone off-track, or apologize when it's appropriate, students get the message from our own modeling that all of us have within us the capacity to recover, self-correct, and right ourselves. Owning up in the classroom is not the same as going to confession. Brevity and a light touch go a long way toward clearing the air and moving on gracefully. You might want to try out a three part message that enables you to 1) revisit the incident; 2) reflect on your behavior and take responsibility for what happened; and 3) commit to what you will try to do differently next time. It might sound like this:

> **To an individual student:** "I thought about what I said to you yesterday. It was thoughtless. I wasn't thinking about how that might make you feel. I want to apologize to you and want you to know that I'm going to be a lot more conscious about the words I choose. I'd like to make a fresh start tomorrow. How about it?"

> **To the whole group:** "You know how I'm always insisting that we need to be accountable for our actions. Well, I need to be accountable for what happened yesterday. I behaved badly and turned into Wanda the Witch for a few minutes. The situation isn't nearly as dreadful as I made it out to be. And I'm sorry I used the word slackers in my diatribe. I've tossed away my broom and I'm ready to work out a realistic timeline of what we need to do to get ready for the conference. Can we get started? Good.

> Here are a few more openers:
> *"I went home and thought about what happened yesterday. I don't feel good about the role I played in making the situation worse."*

> *"I'm not happy with my behavior yesterday. I want you to know why I lost it by the end of the period."*

> *"About yesterday, I know I blew it when I..."*

"Just to set the record straight, I realize that what I said yesterday didn't come out the way I intended. My penchant for bluntness went too far. Let me try saying it again minus the "foot in mouth" disease."

"About our conference yesterday. I know I was impatient with you and shut you off before I really heard the whole story. I'm sorry about that. Can we try it again at lunch today?"

- **What helps you depersonalize adolescents' negative or disrespectful speech and deal with it effectively?** This is the bet noire for every adult who spends more than ten minutes with a teenager. If we take kids' verbal assaults and incivilities personally we're in big trouble. The bad news is that some adolescents will go out of their way to say things that are rude and crude, confrontational or provocative. The good news is that most kids will clean up their act if we give them the opportunity. Here are some guidelines and reminders that can help shift our focus from feeling stung to responding pro-actively to students' use of negative or disrespectful language.

1. Two of the challenges of dealing with negative or disrespectful speech are determining, "What's the goal of my response?" and "How much emotional charge do I want behind my words?" If I react to students' poor choice of language as if it's a personal attack on me or my values, the goal stays fixed on expressing my own upsetness. Anger will drive my response and I'm likely to slam down harshly on the student. I'm likely to use emotionally loaded language to say things like, "You're way out of line. What gives you the right to use that kind of language in here?" Or, "Where do you think you are—in the middle of a street fight?" Or, "You have no respect for yourself when you speak like that." Or, "Don't think you can get away with that kind of trash talk. You're out of here for the rest of the period." The problem with this approach is that students get your anger and displeasure with their behavior, but they don't get a chance to learn and practice more effective, more respectful ways of saying what they want to say.

   If I depersonalize the situation, my interest in helping students to become more skillful and respectful will override my need to express my anger and lash out. In most situations, I want to interrupt negative speech using neutral, less emotionally charged language so I can increase the odds that the students will listen, reflect, and self-correct in a way that's more respectful and constructive. So my responses are going to sound more like this: "When you use language like that I have a hard time listening. Try that one more time." Or, "Wait a second. Try saying that again leaving out the loaded language." Or, "Your words crossed the line of respect. Say that again in another way, please." Or, "Here's another way you could say that to get your point across respectfully. Now try it again in your own words." Or, "For me to make a serious effort to listen to you, I need you to make a serious effort to discuss your concern in a way that feels respectful. Can you do that? Let's rewind the tape and try it again."

2. We can remind ourselves we are the ones with the maturity and skills in this situation, not the student. Intention is not the same as impact. Sometimes students are not fully

aware of the negative impact of their language and posturing. Their intentions may in fact be sincere and well-meaning, but their choice of words and tone has the opposite effect when we hear it. If I see myself as the skillful person, my job is to respond in ways that help students become more aware of the impact of what they say and learn to say things more respectfully and constructively. For example, I might say, "Wow, that sounded pretty [hostile, blameful, rude, offensive]. Is that how you wanted it to sound? Tell me again what you want to say." Or I could say, "Here's what I heard. Is that what you really meant to say to me?" Or, "When the words I hear feel so disrespectful, it's hard to even hear you out. Try saying it another way and I will try to listen."

3. We can remind ourselves that most teenagers do not yet possess a full command of language or the ability to switch their modes and codes of speech easily from one context to another. Add to the mix a popular culture that encourages people to use words as weapons. The media is saturated with wise-cracking kids talking back to adults who don't even flinch at the abusive language hurled in their direction. The harangue of invectives that kids hear on TV, on film, and on the radio sounds perfectly normal to American teens. Every time we stop the conversation and insist that students clean up their language, we are one step further in reclaiming a sense of civility in our schools and our lives.

4. We can also try reframing what students say. When students make negative comments that feel offensive, rude, belittling, or blameful, try reframing their remarks in a way that "hunches out" the concerns behind their remark and replaces negative speech with more neutral words and a more positive tone. When we do this, we are letting students know that we want to keep the conversation going, but not on negative terms; we are modeling more appropriate speech by reframing the student's statement; and we're encouraging students to clarify their thinking by asking them to say more precisely what they mean.

Here are a few examples:

Student comment to teacher: Why do we have to read this stupid book about a bunch of religious crazy people?

Teacher response: So you wouldn't recommend *The Scarlet Letter* to your best friend, huh? Tell me how you think those characters in the book are so different from us?

Student comment in class discussion: "What an ignorant thing to say. Everybody knows that's not true."

Teacher Response: "Let's reframe that shall we? What is it precisely about this statement that you disagree with?"

Student comment: "This school sucks. People get suspended for no reason around here. It's just like a prison."

Teacher Response: "I can tell you're upset about this. What is it exactly about the suspension policy that bothers you the most?"

5. In situations when students' comments are beyond correction—when their words are so ugly, shocking, or hateful that they leave us speechless—this is the time to stop, shore up your convictions, and in a quiet and serious voice say something like, "I don't ever want to hear that again. And here's why. Those words violate the right of all of us to feel safe and respected in this room. They shut down our desire to speak openly and listen to each other. That is unacceptable for me."

What you do next may depend on how unsettled the class feels or whether a particular student or group has been targeted viciously. You might stop what you are doing, post some open-ended questions, and ask students to journal while you speak to the student privately. Or you might escort the student to the office and return to class to talk about what happened and why it was upsetting.

The point is that we can't ignore speech that breeches students' trust in us to keep the classroom a safe place. It means we will need to figure out a way to restore a sense of respect without making the offender a new target. Even though it's uncomfortable, you may want to talk with the offending student about what to say to the group later. And you may need to talk to the rest of the class about how they will respond when the offending student returns to class.

- **What kind of time commitment are you willing to make to implement a discipline plan that works effectively for you and all of your students?** This is probably the biggest question of all. Classroom discipline is an area where the more time you put in, especially in the beginning of the year, the more satisfied you'll be with the results. "Front-loading" mini-sessions about all things disciplinary in the first month of school will ensure that your discipline goals, procedures, and protocols are crystal clear to everyone.

One way to support your own intentional practice of implementing guided discipline is to set aside three to four hours each week of out-of-class time that are expressly devoted to discipline planning, implementation, and follow-up. If this becomes a weekly routine, it's not nearly so daunting to make that parent phone call or meet with a group of students in out-of-class time during planning periods or before or after school. Here's what three and a half hours a week (210 minutes) of out-of-class time can get you:

- 50 minutes – Eight "problem calls" a week to parents—to inform parents of behavior or academic problems; to discuss student conferences, discipline plans, problem solving reports, academic contracts; to discuss follow-up consequences; to update a student's progress; or make arrangements for a parent-student-teacher conference

- 25 minutes – One lunch period to conference with students and work with them on discipline plans, self-management strategies, problem solving reports, and academic contracts

- 60 minutes – One after or before school "Conference Hour" to work with students on discipline plans, self-management strategies, problem solving reports, and academic contracts

- 30 minutes – Five "sunshine calls" a week to parents—the goal is to talk to every parent at some point during the semester sharing something their child has done well and something you appreciate about their child

- 15 minutes – 20 thirty second feedback and appreciation notes to students

- 30 minutes – Two one-on-one sessions with students who really need an extra dose of connection, support, and encouragement

In addition, think about how you can integrate discipline practices and protocols into your weekly class plan. During five days of 50 minute classes, here's what you could do:

- During your "Getting to Work" activity that students do upon entering class, you can do two minute check-in's with ten students, two each day.

- Make sure every student gets a positive ten second comment twice a week (when you meet and greet at the door, when students are engaged in group work or independent work)

- Open or close the week with a 10-15 minute activity that focuses on goal-setting, reflection, and behavioral and academic self-assessment

- Do at least one gathering that ensures that everyone in the class gets an opportunity to respond to a question of the week

- Review discipline policies, procedures, and problem solving protocols as needed

- Infuse the teaching or practice of at least two Life Skills into your regular curriculum

- Facilitate a brief class meeting to discuss a concern that affects the whole class, or negotiate a classroom decision

Know Your Students

Who are your students? Do most of them feel connected to school or alienated from school? Do they see school as simply the place to be during the day, that putting up with the boredom and the grind are just part of being an American teenager? Or do you encounter a lot of kids who would really rather be someplace else? Do your students assume that high school is a stepping-stone to the rest of their lives? Or do you have a lot of students who have so little sense of their own futures that school has little meaning for them? Do most of your students feel that adults are on their side or are they mistrustful of adult authority?

Young people's feelings about education, learning, and adult authority, their level of trust and respectfulness toward adults, and their sense of personal hope or disillusionment will all influence what it will take to develop a disciplinary approach that will work for you in your classroom. For kids who feel less connected, respected, and cared for, the words and tone you choose to communicate your expectations will resonate for the rest of the year. For example, if your message about classroom discipline sounds like it's coming from the commander of the fifth Army division, you risk further alienating those who are already looking for any excuse to shut down or act out. On the other hand, if you come across as a "wuss" without clear and consistent disciplinary goals and practices, these students will look for every opportunity to "get by," "get over," and do you in.

The challenge here is to know your students well enough that you can begin to answer these three critical questions:

- What teacher behaviors will set my students off and result in off-task behaviors, confrontations and power struggles, non-compliance, hostility, or disengagement?

- What kinds of disciplinary strategies work best for the students who experience the most behavioral difficulties?

- What kinds of teacher behaviors (encouragement, instruction, and support) will help my students become more self-disciplined and engage in more skillful behaviors more of the time?

Don't forget to ask your students about their thoughts on discipline, fairness, and consequences.

Know Your School

- Do most of your students assume that rules will be enforced fairly and consistently at school or do they feel that "it all depends" on the student, the adult, and the situation? You might be in a school where compliance, orderliness, and "going with the flow" of the adult authority are unspoken expectations for almost all students. Or you might teach in a high school where there are no behavioral norms at all—where students will be testing and watching you from day one to see if you are up to the challenge of creating a disciplined classroom environment within a normless school culture.

- Make sure you know, and your students know, the in's and out's of school-wide discipline policies. Which school policies and rules affect what happens in your classroom? Which school-wide policies are enforced consistently and which ones are rarely enforced at all? For example, if there is a school-wide tardy policy unevenly enforced with no follow-through, you might want to create your own tardy policy within the classroom. In the long run, implementing your own policy and consequences for tardiness, could pay better dividends than griping about a school policy over which you have no control.

2. Prevention

Prevention is all about setting up structures, building community, developing relationships, and teaching skills so that students have what they need to do what we ask them to do. Most of the prevention strategies identified here are included in the classroom practices described in detail in other places in the book.

- **Establish positive group agreements, norms, goals, and expectations (p. 71)**

- **Clarify the differences between (1) boundary violations, (2) procedural infractions, and intra- and inter-personal conflicts and problems and explain the consequences you will enforce.**

Boundary violations – These violations break the boundaries of safety, respect, and trust that you have worked hard to establish in the classroom. They include student behaviors that have a negative, destructive impact on the entire classroom community or interfere with students' learning. Some specific boundary violations include:

- Verbal disrespect (including profanity and other kinds of abusive or negative language)
- Harassment and intimidation
- Destruction of property
- Emotional outbursts or loss of control that make others feel unsafe
- Chronic non-compliance
- Stealing
- Cheating and lying
- Disruptive behaviors that interfere with other students' learning including continuous talking, interrupting others, excessive noise or movement, or negative participation that sucks the energy out of the room

What consequences you apply will depend on the frequency of incidents and the severity of the violation. What's important for students and parents to know is that graduated consequences will always start with a student-teacher conference, and can include writing up a report form, developing a discipline plan, creating a specific consquence that fits a particular violation, a phone call home, a student-parent-teacher conference, an immediate referral to the discipline dean or counselor, or arrangements to participate in special student support programs. Because boundary violations impact the well-being of the classroom community, you might also consider consequences that promote restorative justice, where students give something back by participating in community service or stewardship activities.

Chronic procedural infractions – Examples of procedures are discussed in this section. When students don't follow procedures that you've taught, the consequences should be as consistent as possible. You don't want to get caught in arguments over who's the best lawyer, you or the student. You might, for example, have a standard consequence that kicks in after students are involved in multiple infractions of the same procedure. The consequence might include a phone call home and required attendance at your Conference Hour after school where students write out a report form and meet with you to discuss strategies that will help them follow procedures more consistently.

Intra- and inter-personal conflicts and problems – These kinds of problems require the most open-ended interventions and your best communication skills. Every student's problem is different so there's no magic formula. When students are getting into conflicts with other peers, sending out personal distress signals, or experiencing academic difficulties, they're also more emotionally vulnerable. The problems they exhibit may also be a reflection of underlying issues that aren't apparent in the immediate situation. Consequently, private conferences offer the best chance to connect with troubled students and explore the roots of the problem.

One to one conferences tell kids you care about them – They let students know you're willing to take the time to listen, find out more information, and problem solve together if that's the appropriate next step. Sometimes, a student will request a conference just because they want a safe place to tell their story to someone who will listen with empathy. In other situations, a personal conference may be a first step toward developing a discipline plan or academic contract. And there are other times when more serious issues emerge in a conversation that may best be handled by a staff person who provides special academic assistance or other student support or crisis intervention services.

Guided Discipline and Problem Solving

What do you do when...

Students experience intra- and inter-personal problems or academic problems.	Students engage in boundary violations and procedural infractions
1. Stop and notice the situation, speak with student privately, or arrange to speak later.	1. Invite students to cooperate and self-correct.
2. Acknowledge and defuse upset feelings. Listen and empathize.	2. Give a warning and clarify choices.
3. Use ABCDE problem solving (Assess the situation and Ask what's the problem; Brainstorm solutions; Consider choices carefully; Decide on your best choice and Do it; Evaluate decision)	3. Apply consequences (report form, conference, phone call home, contract, demerit, detention, etc.)

- **Teach and practice procedures**

  The importance of spelling out classroom procedures is discussed earlier in this chapter and in the sections on The First Day of Class and The First Month of School. Dealing with the management and organizational issues listed below is easier when you create clear Step One, Step Two, and Step Three Procedures. Think about including students in the development of procedures—students are usually pretty quick to suggest the easiest way to do something in the least amount of time with the least amount of hassle. The marked * issues present ideal opportunities for opening up the discussion with students and agreeing on a procedure that works for both you and them.

  ## Issues Requiring Procedures

  - Working with different students and getting into groups
  - Moving furniture to accommodate various activities and seating *
  - Cleaning up the room at the end of the period *
  - Taking care of lab equipment *
  - Signing out resources and books
  - Distributing materials *
  - Handing in papers, journals, notebooks, tests, etc.
  - No pen or pencil, books, or materials *
  - When student/teacher needs to be someplace else instead of class
  - Being an attentive audience for peers, guests, and speakers *
  - Tardiness
  - When you've been absent
  - Preparing and organizing portfolios
  - Assignment notebooks
  - When assignments aren't complete
  - Passes *
  - In-class self-grading *
  - Computer time *
  - When homework is late
  - Gum/food/drink
  - When you don't know the assignment *
  - Activities that require silence
  - Making announcements and presenting information in class

- **Teach problem solving protocols**
  Help students to recognize that they always have choices and have control over their behavior. Review the kinds of invitations and interventions that you will use in the classroom, reminding students that the goal will always be to provide information students can use to make a responsible choice for how to self-correct and redirect their behavior. Take time to teach everyone A, B, C, D, E problem solving. This five step process is used throughout the guide for individual, interpersonal, and group problem solving. Sample problem solving protocols are included at the end of this chapter.

  ASSESS the situation and **ASK**, What's the problem?

  BRAINSTORM at least two solutions

  CONSIDER the pro's and con's of each choice

  DECIDE on the best choice

  EVALUATE your decision after it has been implemented

- **Help students get ready to learn**
  The rush of one class after another, from one end of the building to another, means that high school students are making constant transitions as they let go of where they've been, what they've been doing, who they've been with, and what they've been feeling. Think about how you can help students settle in, leave the past hour behind, reconnect with another group of people, and get ready to focus and learn. Depending on your time constraints, your goals for the day, and the emotional state and energy level of the group, try one idea or a combination of ideas described below:

  Do one thing that helps students to settle in (transitioning from noisy to quiet, from high speed movement to sitting still, from the previous experience to here and now)

  - Post a "Getting to Work" activity in the same place everyday so students know what to do immediately when they arrive in your classroom.

  - Try out different kinds of music at the beginning of class to find out what students like, that also helps them to settle in.

  - Pass out briefcase cards on which students can write something on their minds that is hard to stop thinking about, but that they are willing to put in the briefcase for the this period. Collect the cards in a basket and tell students they can pick up their cards at the end of class.

Do one thing that welcomes and acknowledges the group

- Do a gathering (p. 77).

- Do a feelings check-in:

Feelings Cards

- Place blank 5" x 8" note cards and markers in a central location and invite participants to take a note card and write a word that describes what they are feeling in that moment. Allow two minutes to do this.

- Invite everyone to raise their cards so others can see them. Point out the variety of feelings people are naming and let students know that there are no right or wrong feelings in the room.

- You might have students turn to their neighbor to share why they chose the words they did. You can also use these words to create a class list of feelings to post in a prominent place, continuing to expand the list.

- Close by inviting everyone to empty their minds and take a deep breath, exhale, and focus on the front.

Read the Group 1 to 10
Ask the group, "How are you feeling right now on a scale of one to ten, if ten is 'Everything's cool/copasetic/crusin'/mellow, etc.'?" Ask students to say their numbers out loud or write their numbers on note cards.

Do a FedEx Feeling Check-in
Toss out one of these questions and invite them to answer with a one word response:

- What musical instrument do you feel like today?

- What color describes how you feel at this moment?

- If you could be anywhere, where would you be right now?

- What kind of weather describes how you are feeling today?

Do one thing that cues the group that you are ready to begin class as a group.

- When you are ready to begin class, stand or sit in the same place every day.

- If you are playing music, turn it off.

- Invite students to begin class with a very short reading.

- Say, "Let's begin class by_____."

Keep a set of copies of the Feelings Vocabulary (p. 285) that you can hand out when students are doing exercises that involve naming feelings.

- **Build group cohesion and connectedness in the classroom (Chapter 2)**
- **Develop personal connections with each student**
- **Practice negotiated learning and group problem solving (p. 105)**
- **Model and teach life skills looking particularly at the self-awareness and self-management skills (p. 19)**

3. Invitations

Invitations can be the most challenging and satisfying aspect of guided discipline. Invitations involve the countless teachable moments when we create opportunities for students to self-correct, regain control, redirect their focus, make a different choice, and get back on track. Our role is to pay attention to early warning signals from the group or individual students, so we can defuse a situation or eliminate a problem before it requires a more serious intervention.

Educators have used the term, "with-it-ness" to describe teachers who are acutely sensitive to the environment around them. Their antennae can pick up the first signs of potential problems even as they continue their instruction. When we notice students who look bored, blue, disengaged, or distracted, when we see kids who are already off-task and looking for trouble—the way we approach them will influence their willingness to cooperate. And, cooperation is, after all, the goal here. The words we choose, along with our tone of voice, pacing, and body language, will let students know right away whether we see their behavior as a severe breech of conduct or a little slip-up that's easily remedied.

When we see students veering off-track, if we rush to the scene in a squad car, we risk creating more commotion than the situation warrants. The student is caught in the flashing lights for everyone to see. High drama and negative attention create high anxiety; and when anxiety rises, students are unable to listen, think clearly, and shift gears. When we send in the sirens, kids will probably become more, not less, defensive and resistant. This is not a particularly winning formula for getting students back on track.

Feelings Vocabulary

afraid	affectionate	agitated	aggressive	aggravated
alert	accepted	amazed	ambivalent	amused
angry	annoyed	anxious	apologetic	argumentative
ashamed	awkward	bad	belligerent	bored
brave	calm	cared for	cautious	challenged
cheerful	clear	clumsy	cold	concerned
confused	contemptuous	contented	cranky	curious
defeated	delighted	depressed	despairing	desperate
determined	disconcerted	disappointed	disgusted	disrespected
down	ecstatic	elated	embarrassed	empty
energized	enraged	enthusiastic	envious	exasperated
excited	exhausted	fearful	focused	foolish
friendly	frightened	frustrated	funny	furious
good	grateful	greedy	grief-stricken	guilty
happy	hateful	heartbroken	helpless	hopeful
horrified	hot	humiliated	hurt	hysterical
impatient	independent	indifferent	inferior	intimidated
irritated	jazzed	jealous	jolly	joyful
jumpy	kindly	left out	let down	lonely
loved	loving	mad	malicious	mellow
mischievous	miserable	mixed up	negative	nervous
nice	sorrowful	obstinate	optimistic	pained
paranoid	peaceful	peeved	perplexed	playful
persecuted	pleasant	powerful	powerless	prepared
proud	puzzled	ready	regretful	relieved
remorseful	respected	righteous	sad	safe
satisfied	secure	sedate	smart	supported
self-conscious	self-pitying	shocked	shy	skeptical
silly	spiteful	strange	stuck	surprised
suspicious	sympathetic	tenacious	tense	terrific
ticked off	threatened	thrilled	timid	tired
trusted	uncertain	uncomfortable	uneasy	unsafe
unworthy	up	upset	vengeful	victimized
victorious	vindictive	wary	wonderful	weird
worried				

On the other hand, if we wander over to a student during a casual classroom stroll, we can check out what's going on quietly, almost invisibly. When our approach is friendly, interested, and low-key, we're conveying that this is a check-in, not a catastrophe. For adolescents, the lower the stakes are, the more likely they will give us a listen and respond cooperatively.

Invitations make kids feel respected and cared for because they create a way for us to connect with them rather than criticize them. By sharing observations, providing information, and soliciting a student's take on a situation, we are also communicating our confidence in students' ability to take responsibility for changing their behavior and making different choices. We feel good because these interactions help young people practice effective self-management skills. Students feel good because they (not teachers) are making the final choice about what to do, so students experience the satisfaction of doing something for themselves.

The invitations included here involve interactions that take anywhere from a few seconds to two minutes. You might try out one strategy a week and see how it works for you.

Invite cooperation using verbal, physical, and written prompts
Instead of offering the warning, lecture, mean stare, or cranky sigh, post a written reminder, or give a visual or verbal prompt. Here are some examples:

- Stand in a certain place that everyone knows means to stop and listen up as a whole group.

- Use a timer, chime, or lights off as a cue to switch partners, move to the next problem or question, return to your original group, put away materials, etc.

- Use phrases like, "eyes front please," "that's half your time," "folders out," "trash pick-up," etc.

- Post announcements on the door that students will see as they walk in.

- Give instructions three ways.

- When a student's attention is wandering, point to the agenda or the assignment that's posted and ask, "Where are we right now?" Or "Let's review what we've already done today." Or "What's left on the agenda for today?"

- Write giant notes to class about deadlines and other reminders.

- For students who always have to have the last word or who want to speak ad nauseum, say "That's an interesting point. Let's see what others have to say." Or say "Twenty seconds please." Or "You've spoken twice already. I want to hear what others have to say."

- Ask students to predict how long it will take to do particular task.

- Change your proximity to the student or change the student's location.

- When you notice a student blanking out, say, "So what's next?"

- For students who rarely pay attention to what others are saying, ask them to restate what the previous student said or invite them to ask a question to better understand the previous speaker's perspective.

Use enforceable statements and limits that communicate what you will do instead of demanding what students will do

- Instead of "Open your books to page 24, NOW," try "I'll be working with the problems on page 24."

- Instead of "You can't go to the bathroom when I'm giving directions," try, "Feel free to use the bathroom when I'm not giving directions."

- Instead of "Don't turn in sloppy work," try "I will only read papers that I can easily read and that have no ragged edges."

Give students opportunities to self-correct
- For off-color, inappropriate, or excessively goofy remarks, say:

  - "Can you save that for _____? Thanks."

  - "Are you sure this is a good time to _____?"

  - "Did I hear you right? Tell me again."

  - "Is this the right place for that?"

- Point out a way that students can be helpful. Say, "It would be great if you could help me get all of these review materials to different home groups. Can you help me out with that?" Or, "Before we focus on the presentations, let's put everything away except your feedback cards and move chairs so we can all see."

- Make an offer or "trade-off." Say, "If those of you who need some more review are willing to come in at lunch today, or after school, I'll delay the test for a day. Deal?"

- Make a request. Say, "This is a request, so you can say 'yes' or 'no.' I'd like to request that we delay our field trip for a week so that we can finish completing our projects. Does that work for everyone?"

- Make an observation of what you see and check out students' understanding of the task at hand. "I see you _____. Tell me what you think the task is right now."

- Encourage students to use language they have already learned in class.
  Have these cues posted:

  - "When you think something is unfair, you can say, I'm not sure _____ is fair
    because _____. It would feel more fair if we could _____. Can we talk about that?"

  - "When you think _____, you can say, _____."

  - "When you need _____, you can _____."

  - "When you don't know _____, you can _____."

Use an "I message" when you want a kid to know how her or his behavior is impacting you
or the class. I feel _____ when you _____ because _____. If your request doesn't get the change
you want, you might say, "I've said what I wanted to say now, and I will make a time to talk
about this with you later." Or "I was hoping that telling you how I felt about this would make
a difference in what you choose to do right now."

Offer chances to make a choice
- Give at least two choices that you can live with that are both do-able and will meet
  the immediate goal. Say,

  - "You're welcome to _____ or _____."

  - "Feel free to _____ or _____."

  - "Would you rather _____ or _____?"

  - "What would work best for you right now? _____ or _____?"

  - Tell me two choices you can make right now. Okay, which is your preference?

  - If you continue to_____, what do you know will happen next?

- Encourage students to rethink the choice you see them making. Say: "It looks like you're
  making a choice to _____. Do you really want to do that?"

- "Tell me what you think this choice will get you? What's another choice you could
  make right now?"

- "What choice is going to keep you out of trouble right now?"

- "What choice will help you get back on track?"

- "What do you think? Does this choice feel more like a Win-Lose or a Win-Win?"

For students who are off-task or becoming a distraction to others, offer the options of (A) doing something in the next ten seconds that indicates they are back on task or (B) stopping and writing out an ABCD problem solving form (p. 312) that will be discussed later. For some students, the realization that option (C) to "just sit there doing nothing" doesn't exist makes option (A) pretty attractive.

Help students to redirect their focus

- Give information that can redirect the student's behavior.

    - "Here's the trash can for the gum."

    - "We're on page ____."

    - "Here are the two things your group needs to complete this period."

    - "If we don't complete our review today, you might discover some information gaps when you take the test tomorrow."

- When the group has lost focus or the energy in the room is at a low ebb, do a two minute exercise or warm up that helps students "empty," relax, and refocus.

- When a student is rambling and off-point in a discussion, refocus attention by restating the relevant point, or direct questions to the group that are back on the subject or ask how the off-point topic relates to the main issue in discussion, or ask the student to summarize the main point.

- Name the wish a student is feeling and commiserate to bring the student back to dealing with the situation at hand by saying, "It sounds like you wish you could _____. I get that because sometimes I want to _____. Right now, though, we're here." "Can you get your focus back for the next half hour? Then you're done for the day." Or, "Can you hang in there for the rest of the period? I'd really appreciate that."

- For students who are pokey and have a hard time with completion:
    - Name what the student has already accomplished.

    - Describe what's left to do in a way that shows your confidence in the student to do it.

    - Chunk the task into small steps, so students can name what they have done and what they need to do.

    - Ask students to predict how long it will take to do each step and check in with student at each step.

    - Set a specific amount of time for each step.

Use two minute problem solving strategies

- For students who are stuck, ask them to take two minutes to think through the ABCD problem solving process. Check back with them in two minutes so they can tell you their decision.

> **ASSESS** the situation and **ASK**, What's the problem?
>
> **BRAINSTORM** at least two solutions
>
> **CONSIDER** the pro's and con's of each choice
>
> Make your best **DECISION**

- When two students are involved in a conflict, you can ask them both to take two minutes to write down 1) what's not working and why; 2) what I need to work it out; and 3) two solutions I'm willing to try. Check back with both of them in two minutes to share solutions and ask them to choose one that will work for both of them.

- When it is appropriate, focus on Win-Win solutions rather than consequences. Ask the student to name the problem and suggest a solution to resolve it.

- When students are reluctant to participate in a particular activity or work on a specific assignment, ask them to take a minute and write down an alternative way to complete a task or meet the goal or expectation. If we insist that there is only one way to do the task or that students must do it our way, we risk provoking further resistance.

- When you notice a student who is having trouble getting started, take a minute to say, "I've noticed you're having a hard time getting started. Stop for a minute, and write down in your own words what you think the task is. Then name one thing that's getting in the way of doing it and one thing you can do to feel like you've accomplished something today."

- When you hear a complaint or concern, just say, "And?" to give the student the space to be more specific and make a responsible suggestion.

When the group gets stuck

- When the group is stuck in "glazed over," "surly," or "goofy" mode, and you want to shift the energy or activity, STOP. Name what you see and try one of these options:

  - Invite everyone to get up and stretch and walk around for a minute.

  - Acknowledge that whatever you are currently doing in class is not working. Give the group a couple of options for what to do. Take a quick vote, and do "the people's choice."

- Sometimes you have to just give in to the moment and let the goofiness run its course. It might be a matter of saying, "This is going nowhere productive. I'm going to take a three minute break and then see if we can get our focus back. Deal?

- Sometimes tensions within a group worsen simply because no one will actually say out loud what's bothering them about the behavior within the group. One way to break the logjam is to ask individuals to write down on note cards comments or behaviors that feel hurtful, upsetting, or damaging to individuals or the group.

You might suggest these starters: I don't like it when_____; It feels frustrating when_____; It bothers me when I see/hear_____.

Collect the cards and read some of them out loud in the back of the room. After you've read their comments, give students time to think and talk:

- How did it feel to hear these comments?

- What kind of climate do the actions named in these comments create?

- Given what you've heard, what agreements should we revisit?

- Where do we go from here?

After people talk, you might want to pass out another round of cards asking each person to write down one thing that he or she can do to improve the situation or change the direction. Again, collect the cards and read some or all of them.

Let students know what they can do when they're upset and angry
- Provide ways for individual students to "cool off" or "take five" so they have the time and space to recover and regain control before they reconnect with the group.

- Say, "Take a minute to get a drink, and when you get back to your seat, we'll start again."

- Say, "I can see you're too upset to focus right now. Take a few minutes to stop, take a few breaths, and relax a bit. Let me know when you think you're ready to rejoin us. Does that work?"

- "Hunch out" what's bothering a student, and name and accept the negative feelings. "I can see you're frustrated with this. It's the last thing you want to be doing right now, isn't it?" Wait for a response and agree on one thing the student can do right now.

- For some students, the best response is asking them what they can do for themselves to cool down, saying, "I know you need a little time to chill. What can you do for yourself to feel more relaxed and in control?"

- When a student walks into your classroom already steaming and ready to blow, quickly take the student aside and say, "You look like you're ready to blow. On a 1–10 scale, how upset are you? Take some time to cool down. Give me a signal when you feel like you're down to a five."

- Teach students about anger cues, triggers, and reducers. Cues: How do you know in your body and your voice when you're getting angry? What are the physical signs of anger? Triggers: What are the situations and behaviors that are most likely to make you angry? Reducers: When you're already "angry," what can you do by yourself that can help you cool down? What can a friend do or say that will help you cool down?

- For some students, writing can help them calm down. You might say, "Try writing down what you're feeling and what you can do today to feel more in control."

- Sometimes students are so emotionally flooded that nothing is going to help them to focus back on their class work. A pass to the library can be a good idea when kids need a quiet place to collect themselves. Obviously, if a student needs someone to talk to immediately, providing a note and pass to student support services is a helpful choice.

When invitations don't work, interrupt and de-escalate conflicts and confrontational behavior quickly and calmly

- Keep these questions in mind before you intervene with a student:

  - What are my long-term goals for the student—academically and behaviorally?

  - What do I say and do now to maintain the relationship?

  - What do I say and do now in public? What do I say and do later in private?

  - How do I create the physical and emotional space for the student to save face?

- Try one of these strategies to de-escalate potential power struggles, knowing that no strategy will work for every student. What you say to a boy with whom you have a solid relationship will differ from your strategy with the girl in the corner who's angry all the time and waiting for any excuse to stir things up.

  - "Drop the rope" in power struggles or try not picking up "the rope" at all. Remind yourself that the goal right now is to de-escalate the situation by lowering the decibel level, defusing the emotional intensity, and diminishing the drama. You might say, "I'm not going to argue about this now." Or, "I'm through discussing this for now." Or, "I heard what you said and I need to think about it."

  - Call their bluff. "Which is it going to be? Work with me after school or solve it yourself here in the classroom?"

- Notice the problem and postpone dealing with it until you have the space and time for a private conversation.

- Try "fogging," by saying something unexpected or changing the subject and moving on.

- For students who are argumentative or hostile to what other students say, you might try, "You have the right to your opinion [belief, feelings]. Can you try and summarize both points of view?" Or, "Can you restate that as question?"

- When students who are visibly upset or angry about something said in a discussion, say, "You had a really strong reaction to that comment. Let's hear what others feel about this."

- Accept the feelings even as you stop the unacceptable behavior. "I know you're upset about this and that you know the consequence." Or, "I know you're angry and you know the drill. Right?" Or "I can see how angry you are and I don't want you to have to leave class. Here's the deal. Do you think you can _____or _____for the rest of the period?" Or "I know you think this is unfair, and I want to talk with you about it later. Right now, I need you to _____. Can you do that?"

- When a student is geared up to argue with you, state both viewpoints. "Here's how I see it and here's how you see it. Do I have that about right? For the moment we're going to have to agree to disagree. Can you do that?"

- For students who count on a "push back" response, acknowledge their power, "You're right. I can't make you do this," and move on.

- Refuse to take responsibility for the student's actions by pointing out the choice that they are making and the consequences of that choice.

- Offer an exit statement. "I'm not going to get in a power struggle with you over this now." Or, "I've said what I needed to say. You're the one who's in charge of what happens next."

- Say, "I want to keep your personal business personal. Let's step outside a minute and hear each other out."

- Sometimes humor tells students you heard what they said and you have faith in them to do what they need to do with your support. For example, a student says, "This is stupid. I shouldn't have to_____" and you say, "Nice try_____." Or a student says, "I can't do this," and you respond saying, "I bet you're thrilled that I don't really believe that."

4. Interventions

More formal and intentional interventions (including following through with meaningful consequences) are needed when invitations don't work, when students engage in chronic procedural infractions or serious boundary violations, or when students' academic or behavior problems become more frequent or intense. For interventions to work smoothly, students and parents need to be absolutely clear about why you're intervening and what will happen as part of the intervention. It is helpful to be simple and direct about your goals for interventions. You might say, "When I decide to intervene in a situation and follow through with consequences, it's for three reasons: I want to name the behavior or academic problem I see and talk with you about it; I want you to understand the effects of your behavior on yourself and others; and I want to work with you in a constructive way that will help you get back on track."

When everyone knows that certain protocols and consequences are always going to be applied, students are less likely to put up a fuss and parents are more likely to support your efforts. Some suggestions for implementing effective interventions include the following:

- **Enforce consequences for boundary violations and procedural infractions consistently**

- **Make one-on-one conferencing a daily practice**
  Teacher-student conferencing (from the one minute check-in to longer conferences to address serious issues) serves many purposes. It's the ideal structure for listening when students are upset, for identifying academic and behavioral problems, for problem solving with a student, and for discussing students' completed report forms after they have committed violations and infractions.

  A useful guideline for one-on-one conferences is to listen first, defuse student's upset feelings, and find out more information before you problem solve. Here are some suggestions for getting the most out of a student conferences:

  Begin conferences by inviting students to speak first. You might use any of these openers:

  - "So what's up?" "What's going on?" "What was that about yesterday?" "A lot's been going on. Tell me what you're feeling right now." "You really sounded upset earlier. Is that right?" "So tell me what I should know about what happened."

  - Then stop and wait for a response before you say anything else. The goal is to defuse the emotional charge and let the student know that you're willing to listen.

  A couple of reminders about listening...

  - Listening to a student doesn't mean you agree with what the student is saying.

  - Listening confers respect and indicates your desire to understand the student.

- Listen first and listen attentively—before you assume, judge, correct, or problem solve.

- Don't get defensive and take the student's upset feelings personally—you're the one using your skills to defuse and understand.

- Defuse the student's upset feelings by acknowledging and reflecting the student's feelings and emotional state and restating what the student has said so he or she knows you understood.

- Encourage the person to talk by saying, "Tell me more," "What happened?," "How do you feel about that?," "What do you need right now?," "Is there anything else bothering you?"

When students bring a problem to you:

- Tell them that you appreciate their willingness to talk about it.

- Say little and let the student talk it through.

- Ask student if he or she wants to problem solve. Sometimes just listening to a student's story is enough. If a student does want to problem solve, you might ask, "Where would you like to go from here?" Or, "What would a good solution look like?" or "What might be one step you can take toward resolving this today?"

- Try to identify sources of misbehavior and explore other ways to meet that need. For example, was the misbehavior a way to gain attention, exercise power, protect one's identity and dignity, seek revenge, or convey inadequacy?

- When young people use absolutes or they over-generalize, help them to clarify their thinking and speak more precisely to their own situation. You can respond by saying, "Always? That never happens? Everyone does that? Are you sure that you're the only person who...?"

- With students who are really having a hard time, choose to work on one behavior at a time. Try to eliminate or limit any negative feedback. Ask the student what you as a teacher can do to help. Create a daily check-in with the student. Give encouraging feedback when you see the student engaging in the desired behavior.

- When conferences get bogged down—when you're stuck or a student is stuck or try these responses:

  - It sounds like you're not ready to talk about this, so I will have to decide.

- I'm unwilling to try that because _____. Do you have another idea?

- That's a good idea. What consequence do you think would be fair if you don't do this?

- I want to hear what you have to say and I want you to hear what I have to say. Can we try that?

- I'm not interested in fault finding or blaming. I'm interested in solutions.

- For students who continue to express disinterest, dislike, or boredom with the course, it is hard to help them move out of the land of "not learning" without naming what is making this a bad experience for them. You might say, "It sounds like you're really stuck and can't find a way to make this class okay for you. So let's start where you are. Cover a page with everything you dislike about class. Then we'll talk and see if we can work together to find a way out of this." This strategy can produce three positive results. First, you're catching a student off guard because you're not asking her to pretend that everything's fine when it isn't. You're validating that a student's negative feelings are real. Second, you're telling the student that, "Just because you don't like class, doesn't mean I can't like you." You're communicating that it's worth your time to listen and try and understand what's going on. Third, this kind of quick exercise usually provides a lot of information that can be useful in plumbing underlying resistance, and it gives the two of you a place to begin working on a plan.

- **Make sure that problem solving reports, discipline plans and academic contracts play a central role in follow-up consequences**

    Develop individual behavior plans where you and students agree on the specific actions the student will take, how you will support the student, and the consequences the student agrees to carry out if the behavior expectations are not met.

    Look on page 20 at the list of self-awareness and self-management strategies. You might ask students to pick one that they want to work on and you might pick one that you want them to work on.

    Take a look at the problem solving report forms (p. 306). Included are report forms for various kinds of boundary violations, procedural infractions, intra- and inter-personal conflicts, and academic problems.

- **Have a re-entry conference when a student returns from a disciplinary referral or suspension** If students have committed serious boundary violations that are automatic referrals to the dean of discipline or the student support center (abusive language directed at the teacher, continued defiant behavior, fighting, stealing, etc.), it's critical to have a re-entry conference for several reasons. A re-entry conference creates a marker between what happened in the past and a fresh start. The student needs to communicate to you what will be different upon her return to the classroom. More specifically, students need to identify different choices they will make so the unwanted behaviors are not repeated. A re-entry conference also gives you the opportunity to review your expectations and discuss ways that you will monitor student's behavior, check in to see how things are going, and agree on a warning signal at the first sign of a situation that could spell trouble. Re-entry conferences can also help displace the feeling of being adversaries by communicating your confidence that a student can change while providing support to make it happen.

- **Communicate with parents by phone, e-mail, notes, and conferences**
  Phone calls to parents are never easy. One strategy that can make phone calls more productive is to conference with the student beforehand, so that you can share what the student intends to do to rectify the situation. Having a script sometimes helps.
  Here are some ideas:

1. Introduce yourself and say what course the student is taking with you. Ask the parent if it's a convenient time to talk for a few minutes.

2. Say something that indicates that you know something about the student—a positive quality that she or he brings to the classroom, something he or she does well, something unusual that she or he knows about, etc.

3. Share the reason you are calling by stating the problem simply. For example, you might say, "I'm calling about an incident that happened yesterday. Here's what happened." Or, "We have a procedure in class about _____. I'm calling because your daughter/son has/has not _____." Or, "I'm concerned about ___ _____'s academic progress. Here's what I've observed over the last couple of weeks." Or, "I've been concerned about a couple of behaviors that have become more frequent in the past few weeks. Your son/daughter has been _____."

4. Share why you are concerned about the particular behavior, explaining how you think the behavior is affecting their child, other students, or the classroom learning environment.

5. Ask the parent if they have any other thoughts or questions about the situation. If the parent is upset, acknowledge their feelings and try to find a common concern or hope that you share about their daughter/son.

6. Explain that you have already discussed the issue with the student who has made a commitment to _____. Inform the parent of any other consequences.

7. Share how much you would appreciate it if the parent would talk to their son/daughter about this. Reassure the parent that this is not the end of the world. You're calling now because you have confidence that the student can turn this situation around. Thank them for their support.

"Sunshine calls" (when you share with a parent something their child has done well and/or something you appreciate about their child) can be a powerful connector between you, the parent, and the student. If it's impossible to get around to making a call to every parent, try to make sure you call the parents of students who don't get the spotlight, students who have made a turn-around, students who you are 95% sure have never received a positive call home.

"Sunshine notes" serve the same purpose and take much less time. Try to do a few every week.

You might want parents to sign specific assignments, tests, and projects or you may want students to choose three of their best "pieces" from class to send home and get signed.

You may also want to send home a course news summary every quarter that describes what students have been studying and doing in class and preview what's coming up.

Let parents know a planning period that you make available every week at the same time for phone calls.

• Use class meetings to discuss problems and concerns that affect the whole group (p. 205)

• Refer students to mediation, counseling services, and student assistance programs

Try to become familiar with all of the special academic services and student assistance programs that are available in your school. Keep a folder of all these programs and services so that you can suggest options.

5. Support and Maintenance

An annoying reality of adolescence is that good behavior and a positive peer culture don't sustain themselves without a big dose of what Linda Albert refers to as the five A's: ACCEPTANCE, ATTENTION, APPRECIATION, AFFIRMATION, and AFFECTION. If you were to set aside 15 minutes a week in each class to support and maintain the positive behaviors of individual students and the group, what would you choose to do?

• **Provide immediate feedback when students are trying out new skills and behaviors**
• Give encouraging feedback that describes what students have accomplished and names the personal quality that they used to do it (p. 144).

• Emphasize a specific skill you will observe and students will practice each week. Provide feedback on how the group and individual students are using the skill regularly and successfully.

• When someone has had a bad day, write a note with words of encouragement and a reminder that they can start fresh the next day.

- Be particularly mindful of situations where students have recovered and bounced back from personal setbacks. Encourage students to tell you what they have learn from these experiences.

- Notice when students do something "out of character" that reveals a different image of themselves.

- Write notes that show that you have noticed the effort students have made to keep their academic contract commitments or sustain a significant change in their classroom behavior.

- **Create classroom routines and rituals that involve EVERY STUDENT (p. 95)**

- **Make connections through 10 second "hits" (p. 41)**

- **Recognize and celebrate the group's efforts and accomplishments (p. 97)**

- **Recognize individual accomplishments in and out of the classroom (p. 99)**

- **Provide differentiated support for students who are struggling (p. 137)**
- Create a set of quotes about people who have overcome great challenges and personal difficulties. Give a quote to a student when you want to acknowledge that they are having a rough time of it and share that other people have overcome difficult circumstances and found meaning and success in their lives.

- Invite a student who needs a little boost of encouragement and support to eat lunch with you.

- For students who have a particularly difficult time dealing with managing anger, controlling their impulses, or handling interpersonal conflict, invite them to write themselves a "congratulations" note when they felt they handled a tough situation effectively.

- Read "Thank You Mr. Falker," by Patricia Polacco

- Hook up a struggling student with a former student who can share what she or he did to turn things around in class.

- Set up 30 second daily check-in's with students who need to be on a short leash. These are the kids who need to know you are not going to stop noticing how they are doing.

- **Create opportunities for students to link personal effort to their successes in the classroom (p. 147)**
- Encourage students to keep a checklist of skills they are learning and mastering.

- Ask students to review the list of self-awareness and self-management skills (p. 20) and identify skills they have improved during the past quarter and skills they want to work on during the next quarter.

- Invite students to tell you one thing they have accomplished this week that they didn't think they could have done a month ago.

- At the end of every grading period have students write their parents a note that describes three things they feel they have accomplished or enjoyed learning during the quarter.

Linking Life Skills to Guided Discipline

The following chart illustrates how life skills are linked to major disciplinary practices described in this chapter. Recognizing the relationship between classroom management and life skills is important for two reasons. A critical element of carrying out any discipline plan is a teacher's capacity to model self-management, communication, and problem solving skills effectively with students when behavioral issues arise. For example, a teacher's capacity to depersonalize students' unskillful behaviors is linked to Life Skill 3: Understand the cause of your feelings and the connection between your feelings and behavior.

Secondly, an effective discipline plan ensures that students have many opportunities to develop and strengthen life skills in the process of taking responsibility for their behavior. For example, when teachers let students know what they can do when they're upset and angry, they are helping students to develop their capacity to manage one's feelings effectively. (Life Skill 4) In addition many of the conferencing strategies and problem solving protocols engage students in reflecting on their behavior, identifying how their behavior impacted others, and developing a plan that supports a different behavioral choice in future situations.

Cluster 1: Self-awareness, self-expression, and self-management skills	
Life Skill	**Links to Guided Discipline**
1. Recognize and name your own feelings	Help students get ready to learn Use problem solving protocols
2. Express your feelings accurately; assess the intensity of your feelings (on a MAD scale of 1 to 10, I feel...)	Let students know what they can do when they're upset and angry Make one-on-one conferencing a daily practice
3. Understand the cause of your feelings and the connection between your feelings and behavior	What helps you depersonalize adolescents' negative or disrespectful speech and deal with it effectively Use problem solving protocols and report forms

4. Manage your anger and upset feelings (know your cues, triggers, and reducers)	What are your own triggers and reducers? How do you react when you make mistakes and lose control in the classroom? Let students know what they can do when they're upset and angry
5. Know what you do that bothers others and accept responsibility when you mess up	Use problem solving protocols and report forms Make one-on-one conferencing a daily practice Have a re-entry conference when a student returns from a disciplinary referral or suspension
6. Self-reflect on your behavior; be able to learn from it, self-correct, redirect, and change when you need to	How do you react when you make mistakes or lose control in the classroom? Give students opportunities to self-correct Help students to redirect their focus Make sure that problem solving reports, discipline plans and academic contracts play a central role in follow-up consequences Have a re-entry conference when a student returns from a disciplinary referral or suspension
7. Make responsible choices for yourself by analyzing situations accurately and predicting consequences of different behaviors	Offer chances to make a choice Clarify the differences between (1) boundary violations, (2) procedural infractions, and (3) intra- and inter-personal conflicts and problems
8. Deal with stress and frustration effectively	Make one-on-one conferencing a daily practice Provide differentiated support for students who are struggling
9. Exercise self-discipline and impulse control	Teach and practice procedures Teach problem solving protocols Enforce consequences for boundary violations and procedural infractions consistently

10. Say, "NO", and follow through on your decisions not to engage in unwanted, unsafe, unethical, or unlawful behavior	Give students opportunities to self-correct Use problem solving protocols Help students redirect their focus Make sure that problem solving reports, discipline plans and academic contracts play a central role in follow-up consequences
11. Seek help when you need it	Make one-on-one conferencing a daily practice Communicate with parents by phone, e-mail, notes, and conferences
12. Focus and pay attention	Help students get ready to learn
13. Set big and little goals and make plans	Make sure that problem solving reports, discipline plans and academic contracts play a central role in follow-up consequences
14. Prioritize and "chunk" tasks, predict task completion time, and manage time effectively	Make sure that problem solving reports, discipline plans and academic contracts play a central role in follow-up consequences
15. Activate hope and optimism and motivate yourself positively	Help students get ready to learn Create opportunities to link effort to classroom success
16. Work for high personal performance and cultivate your strengths and positive qualities	Create opportunities to link effort to classroom success Learn and follow classroom procedures
17. Assess your skills, competencies, effort, and quality of work accurately	Make one-on-one conferencing a daily practice

Cluster 2: Interpersonal communication and problem solving skills

Life Skill	Links to Guided Discipline
18. Exercise assertiveness; communicate your thoughts, feelings, and needs effectively to others	Use problem solving protocols and report forms Make one-on-one conferencing a daily practice
19. Listen actively to demonstrate to others that they have been understood	Make one-on-one conferencing a daily practice
20. Give and receive feedback and encouragement	Provide immediate feedback when students are trying out new skills and behaviors
21. "Read" and name others' emotions and non-verbal cues	Use problem solving protocols
22. Empathize; understand and accept another person's feelings, perspectives, point of view	Make one-on-one conferencing a daily practice
23. Analyze the sources and dimensions of conflict and utilize different styles to manage conflict	Know that you have choices for how you manage conflict When invitations don't work, interrupt and de-escalate conflicts and confrontational behavior quickly and calmly
24. Use WIN-WIN problem solving to negotiate satisfactory resolutions to conflicts that meet important goals and interests of people involved	Teach problem solving protocols Use two minute problem solving strategies
25. Develop, manage, and maintain healthy peer relationships	Use problem solving protocols
26. Develop, manage, and maintain healthy relationships with adults	Develop personal connections with each student Make one-on-one conferencing a daily practice Provide differentiated support

Cluster 3: Cooperation, group participation, and leadership skills

Life Skill	Links to Guided Discipline
27. Cooperate, share, and work toward high performance within a group to achieve group goals	Build group cohesion and connectedness in the classroom Provide immediate feedback when students are trying out new skills
28. Respect everyone's right to learn, to speak and be heard	Use class meetings to discuss problems and concerns that affect the whole group
29. Encourage and appreciate the contribution of others	Recognize and celebrate the group's efforts and accomplishments
30. Engage in conscious acts of respect, caring, helpfulness, kindness, courtesy, and consideration	Create classroom routines and rituals that involve EVERY STUDENT
31. Recognize and appreciate similarities and differences in others	Provide differentiated support
32. Counter prejudice, harassment, privilege, and exclusion by becoming a good ally and acting on your ethical convictions	When the group gets stuck
33. Exercise effective leadership skills within a group	Use class meetings to discuss problems and concerns that affect the whole group
34. "Read" dynamics in a group; assess group skills accurately; identify problems; generate, evaluate, and implement informed solutions that meet the needs of the group	Practice negotiated learning and group problem solving When the group gets stuck
35. Use a variety of strategies to make decisions democratically	Use class meetings to discuss problems and concerns that affect the whole group

How to use problem solving report forms:

The first five color coded report forms (blue, green, yellow, orange, and tan) provide quick ways for students to name what happened, take responsibility for how their behaviors affected themselves and others, and make a plan for what to do differently the next time this situation arises. Writing up a report form and discussing it with you can serve as mandatory consequences when students repeatedly engage in an unwanted behavior.

The pink Academic Assessment form can serve as the first step to developing a learning contract by asking students to reflect on what's getting in the way of their academic progress in your class.

The Personal Problem Solving Form is another way to talk through a problem with a student or conference with a student after they have written up their responses.

The Referral Form can provide information to the disciplinary dean or student support staff people who monitor in-school suspension or a Problem Solving Place where students are referred when their behaviors result in their removal from class.

The Problem Solving Conference Form can serve as a conferencing protocol for in-school suspension or referrals to the Problem Solving Place. It can also be used for re-entry conferences when students return from suspensions or referrals.

HANDOUT 1

Blue Form: Inappropriate/Disrespectful Remarks

Name of Student _____

---

1. What did I say that was inappropriate or disrespectful?

---

2. How was this inappropriate or disrespectful? (Identify the impact on students, staff, classroom, or the school environment.)

---

3. Which fits?

❏ It would have been better not to say this at all because...

❏ I could have said it this way:

---

4. Next time I feel this way, I could try:

A.

B.

C.

Staff Person's Name _____ Date_____

Follow-up:

HANDOUT 2

Green Form: Classroom Conflicts

Name of Student _____

1. What happened? **What did I do?**	**2. What was I supposed to be doing?** **How do I feel about what happened?**

3. Two ways I could have handled this situation differently: A. B.	**4. Next time I feel this way, I could try:** A. B. C.

Staff Person's Name _____ Date_____

Follow-up:

HANDOUT 3

Yellow Form: Procedural Problems

Name of Student _____

1. Procedural infraction:

2. Instead of following the procedure, I chose to:

3. We have this procedure because:

4. Two things I can do that will help me follow this procedure in the future:

   A.

   B.

Staff Person's Name _____ Date_____

Follow-up:

HANDOUT 4

Orange Form: Boundary Violations

Name of Student _____

┌─────────────────────────┐
│ 1. Boundary violation: │
│   │
│   │
│   │
│   │
│   │
└─────────────────────────┘

2. What did I do that broke the classroom boundaries of trust, respect, and safety?

3. How did it impact the community negatively or interfere with other students' learning?

4. Two things I can do that will help me follow this procedure in the future:

A.

B.

Staff Person's Name _____ Date_____

Follow-up:

HANDOUT 5

Pink Form: Academic Assessment

Name of Student _____

---

1. What's going on that tells me I'm having academic difficulties?

---

2. How am I feeling about what's been going on?

What's getting in the way of being academically successful?

---

3. Three things I can try to get myself back on track:

A.

B.

C.

---

4. Two things my teacher can do to support my efforts:

A.

B.

Staff Person's Name _____ Date_____

Follow-up:

HANDOUT 6

Tan Form: School Rule Violations

Name of Student _____

1. School rule violation:

2. Instead of following the rule, I chose to:

3. We have this rule because:

4. Two things I can do that will help me follow this rule in the future:

A.

B.

Staff Person's Name _____ Date_____

Follow-up:

HANDOUT 7

Personal Problem Solving Form

Name of Student _____

ASSESS the situation and **ASK**, "What's my problem?"

BRAINSTORM SOLUTIONS Picture what the situation would look like if it were solved. Write down every idea whether you like it or not. Think of solutions your friends or parents might suggest.

CONSIDER the pro's and con's of each **CHOICE** What are benefits? How is it respectful, responsible, and reasonable? Will this choice help me get what I need? What are the negatives and limitations?

	+	−
1.	1.	1.
2.	2.	2.
3.	3.	3.
4.	4.	4.

DECIDE on the best choice. Why is it a better decision than other ideas?

EVALUATE the decision after it's been implemented. How did it work? What did you learn?

Date:_____

Teacher's Name _____

Student's Name _____

HANDOUT 8

Referral Form for the Problem Solving Place

Date _____ Time _____ Class_____

Student's Name _____

Teacher's Name _____

Reason for referral _____

_____

Briefly describe the incident and what triggered the misbehavior. _____

_____

How often has the behavior occurred in the last two weeks? _____

_____

What strategies and interventions have I tried already? _____

_____

What change in behavior would you like to see when the student returns? _____

_____

List any other information that would be helpful to know. _____

_____

HANDOUT 9

Problem Solving Conference Form

Getting the Story Out

• What did you do that got you here?

• What happened?

• How are you feeling about what happened?

Taking Responsibility

• How did your behavior affect others or the learning environment?

• When you got in trouble, what were you supposed to be doing?

• How did your behavior get in the way of your own learning?

Problem Solving

• What could you have done instead that would have been a better choice?

• What can you do the next time you're in this situation?

• What steps can you take to prevent this from happening again?

Getting Support and Keeping on Track

• What can the teacher do to support your change in behavior?

• What else will can you do for yourself to help keep on track?

CHAPTER 6

Becoming Partners in Learning

This chapter compares two hypothetical classrooms to illustrate how a Partners in Learning classroom might look, sound, and feel different from a more traditional high school classroom. The Partners in Learning classroom provides a glimpse of a seasoned teacher on a really good day when everything is clicking. The goal is to show how the practices described throughout this guide can be integrated into the development of a unit of study, implementation of a specific lesson, classroom organization, and daily interactions and interventions with students. Key practices are annotated at the end of the two case studies. The next section of the chapter offers ways to reflect on changes you make and suggests how you might partner with others in your school who are interested in implementing new teaching practices and strategies. The final section moves beyond the classroom to invite teachers to become advocates for the kind of high school experience all students deserve.

A Tale of Two Classrooms

The two teachers I have imagined represent two different approaches to high school teaching. Mr. Green and Mr. Brown are experienced social studies teachers. I am also assuming that there are several features common to both classrooms. Mr. Green and Mr. Brown work in large, fairly conventional high schools. Students are of mixed ability. Although Mr. Brown's school has moved to 100 minute block period for humanities classes and some electives, both teachers are expected to teach a traditionally sequenced US history course. Both teachers love history and ideas, and they both feel strongly that a big part of their job is providing students with opportunities to read critically, think deeply, and write clearly. They both expect students to cite evidence, make informed judgments, and write essays that demonstrate their understanding of people, events, and ideas that shape important forces in US history.

Welcome to Mr. Green's US History Class *(50 minute class period)*

As you walk into Mr. Green's room, you notice his desk in front of the blackboard and six rows of five desks lined up facing the front. There is a bulletin board of student essays and some posters of the US Constitution and Declaration of Independence. There are also several bookcases of resources that students are free to use. Mr. Green approaches the march of US history chapter by chapter. The reading assignment from yesterday is written on the board along with this question: "What events and conditions led the federal government to take a more activist role in regulating business?"

When the first bell rings and students begin charging in, Mr. Green is sitting at his desk, gathering together a stack of papers to be handed back. He looks up as the second bell rings, and students quiet down after flinging themselves in their assigned seats rather noisily. Mr.

Green stands up, chats informally with a few kids near his desk, and asks students to review the chapter while he hands out quizzes from yesterday. As he makes his way up and down rows, he has words of praise for some and stony silence for others. He reminds students who are failing this quarter that they need to come and see him at lunch on Thursday or Friday of this week to work out what they can do to improve their grades.

Then Mr. Green says, "Let's get down to business. Your assignment last night was to read about clashes between American industrialists and American labor at the turn of the century." Mr. Green looks at his seating chart and then says, "Monique, please identify some of the conditions that led to conflicts between factory owners and workers." Monique offers an incomplete response to this query, and Mr. Green calls on several other students to summarize the reading assignment and discuss how and why the federal government stepped in to regulate business. He peppers the question and answer conversation with stories, quotations, and old newspaper headlines showing how the growth of industry and the growth of cities transformed the way people lived and worked at the end of the 19th century.

Mr. Green is a good storyteller and captures the attention of some students who begin asking other questions about the factory system, working conditions, and monopolies. Other students are doodling, finishing other homework, or staring at nothing. Long ago, Mr. Green resigned himself to accepting that some students will be with him all the way, while lots of others will get their act together and tune in right before a major assignment is due or the day before a test.

Mr. Green is committed to improving literacy across the curriculum so most of his assignments and tests involve writing essays. He is dedicated to working with students before and after school on their writing, but he also expects students to make the choice to come to him for help. He hands out a group of essay questions, explaining that the students will each choose one question to write about. He reads several of the questions, each time asking the whole class what issues and evidence they might include if they were choosing this particular question to write about. He points out resources that they might use to complete their essays. A few students pipe in with the usual procedural questions about when the essay is due and how long it has to be. The bell rings and everyone scrambles.

Nine out of twenty-six students have spoken during the 50 minute period. The discussion has emphasized mostly recall questions, with Mr. Green dialoguing with one student at a time while everyone else listens.

Welcome to Mr. Brown's US History Class *(100 minute block period)*
Mr. Brown's approach to the curriculum is to take a large chunk of time and emphasize one or two themes that reflect key questions that students have generated earlier in the course. His desk is in a corner. Student desks and chairs are clustered in groups of four and chairs can be easily arranged in a circle or square. It's hard to identify the front or the back of the room, because every wall has a special function that's different.

Maps hang from one wall, which also contains photographs of working life at the turn of the 19th century and questions about the present learning unit on change and growth in the industrial age. Shelves by the windows contain resource books and file folders of articles and excerpts on various issues, and student projects and essays are clipped to plastic clothes-line rope running from one side of the room to the other.

On another wall, each class has its own space that includes pictures of students, clippings, questions, quotations, and files for assignment instructions, extra handouts, and student papers. Classroom agreements, expectations for the quarter, the big picture plan for the week, and the agenda and goals for today's activities are posted by the blackboard.

When the first bell rings, Mr. Brown is at the door to greet students as they walk in. He says "Hello" to each student by name and hands each student a voting ballot that looks like this:

Referendum on Proposed City Ordinance #132

No employer in the city of _____ may employ 14 to 17 year olds more than 15 hours a week during any time period when they are enrolled as full time students in middle or high schools.

Please circle Yes or No and jot down at least two reasons for your vote.

YES

NO

Mr. Brown pulls aside a couple of students noting, in a casual way, that he has seen a difference in their participation in class, and he describes specific situations where he noticed their contributions. He checks in with a girl who has been dealing with the pressures of a divorce at home and asks another student how the basketball team is feeling about the loss last night. He reminds another student that they need to set up a time to talk about a plan for finishing and doing some incomplete work.

After the second bell rings, Mr. Brown makes sure that all ballots are in the box and invites students to circle up, moving their chairs from behind their desks so that everyone can see everyone else. He reviews the agenda for the day that's been posted, asks for two volunteers to count the ballots, and takes about 5 minutes to do a quick go-around with students encouraging them to speak out, saying, "So what do you think of this proposed city ordinance? Good idea? Bad idea? Not sure?" Some students take a pass, while others eagerly share their opinions. Students announce the vote count and the "No's" win handily.

So he pushes a little further, asking, "Why might a community recommend limiting the hours per week that students can work?" Although one student brings up the problem of competing with adults for the same jobs, most students raise concerns about long work hours having a negative impact on school involvement and homework. Mr. Brown notices that the students doing the talking are kids who don't have jobs, and he knows that over a third of the kids in this class work very long hours.

He calls for a quick tally of the number of hours various students work per week. To non-working students the number of hours that other students work is shocking. "For those of you who work more than 15 hours a week, how would the passage of this ordinance change your life right now?" As one student responds, two students are already having an intense conversation by themselves; Mr. Brown reminds them about the agreements the class has made about talking and listening in the whole group, asks them to focus on the speaker, and assures them that everyone who wants to will get a chance to speak.

The conversation is intense as students reveal how this ordinance would affect them. What stands out are the kids who talk about how dependent their families are on their income. The group is witness to the anger and concern expressed as these students tell their stories.

"So you can see," he says, "that for many of you this would be a very big deal. If this ordinance was going to be voted on in our community three months from now what would you want to do?" Now the students are juiced. Kids call out actions they would take, from public hearings, to protests, to getting lists of all eighteen year olds to encourage them to vote "No," to mounting a letter writing and phone call campaign to parents.

"The kinds of laws and regulations that governments choose to pass or not pass, affect us very personally, even though we might not think about it very much." Mr. Brown closes by saying, "So take a minute and think through your response to this question, 'Should a government have the power to limit the hours that people can work?'" Mr. Brown gives students a minute to think about this and asks students to turn to the person next to them and explain their reasoning. After two minutes he says, "We'll come back to this question later in the week."

"Now let's see what you discovered from your interviews and research."

In the beginning of the year, students brainstormed a huge list of topics and questions that reflected what they thought were truth and lies in the history they had been taught and what they wanted to learn more about in the North American past and the world that they live in today. This unit is organized around student questions related to the world of work and the power of citizens and governments to change what is unjust. Questions ranged from "Why does the government suck up to business?" to "Why don't all workers have health insurance?" to "Why didn't reconstruction change the working status of most Black people?" to "Why should government be able to tell a business what to do?"

Last week Mr. Brown asked students what they knew about the working history of people within their families. For the most part students didn't know very much. Mr. Brown admits that he didn't either. He challenged students to think about how they could collect data that will help them understand how the world of work has changed over the last hundred years.

After ideas were tossed out, he gave students a page of job statistics and an excerpt from Studs Terkel's book *Working*, asking home groups to assess how each source brings to light different dimensions of working history. The class agrees on three methods of data collection, and then small groups develop questions and protocols that will help them gather information consistently for each method.

- In extended interviews, find out about the work histories of four family members from four different generations. (Students generate a list of questions to ask in the interviews.)

- Make a chart or graph that shows your family's work history across four generations (more if possible), getting information on at least 20 people in your family. (Students brainstorm various ways that they can present their data to the rest of the class.)

- Find census data and labor statistics that will show you what kinds of work people did, in what numbers, from 1900 to 1990. (Students divide up decades and agree on the kind of data that they want to collect across decades.)

To provide a model for what to do and to generate a little curiosity, Mr. Brown shared the chart he created that presents his own family's work history. Having grown up in a city, he told the class how surprised he was to discover how many of his relatives were farmers in the first part of the century. Students ask more questions about his "work story," and then Mr. Brown sets aside time to discuss any questions or problems related to their research assignment.

Today, the students who collected statistical data make their presentation to the whole class, and the class has a chance to react to the group's findings, looking for trends and changes from one decade to another. Then Mr. Brown divides the class into groups of six that include students who used each different method for collecting data. "As you listen to personal interviews and family work histories, use your journals to note how the world of work seems to change across time and generations and write down other questions that emerge from the presentations you hear."

Mr. Brown asks for a volunteer to be the timekeeper in each group; each student will have about five minutes to present what they have learned. One group seems to have trouble getting started and Mr. Brown goes over, observes what he sees, asks them what's going on, and discovers that two students don't have their data. He asks the group what feels like the best way to move forward right now and what feels like a fair solution to the missing data problem. The two students agree to pool their data together and make a presentation later in the week. In the meantime, a couple of students volunteer to switch groups so that the number of presentations per group balances out.

He continues to roam from group to group, listening and jotting down bits of conversation that can provide bridges to their historical study. He winks and gives a "thumbs up" to a couple of students after they finish speaking. When time's up, Mr. Brown asks students to close their group conversation by each naming something new that they learned or something that they appreciated about a particular presentation.

Then Mr. Brown asks students to go back to their own home groups saying, "Considering what you've heard from all the presentations this morning, discuss what you learned with your home group partners and agree as a group on what you think are the biggest changes in the world of work over the last century. Here are some starters that might help frame your speculations:"

The Changing World of Work in the US

From...	To...
More people who...	More people who...
More jobs that...	More jobs that...
Less opportunity for...	Greater opportunity for...

What conditions, kinds of work, or opportunities did not seem to change over time? Why do you think that is?

"Take about 15 minutes to do this and post your charts on this board, initialing your chart paper." After their newsprint sheets are posted, students note the most common responses from chart to chart, and Mr. Brown circles the ones that students identify. He asks students to share what they discovered that really got their attention. Finally, Mr. Brown asks the group to speculate on forces and factors that brought about the changes they have described. Students mention unions, the growth of technology, changes in the global economy, more people living in cities, more government regulation, civil rights laws, more educational opportunities.

"So now," Mr. Brown begins, "we have some sense of how work and working conditions have changed. We're going to examine a turbulent period in the last century before these changes kicked in." He points to and reads a couple of the questions written on large strips on the bulletin board:

- What brought about the shift to a more activist role of government? Should governments be able to regulate the places we work, the things we buy, and the services we use? Why or why not?

- How do labor unions help change working conditions for employees? How influential are unions today?

- Should governments have the right to ban products that are harmful to its citizens? Do governments have a responsibility to make sure that businesses operate in ways that are safe, decent, and fair?

- If you put up the money and take the risk, shouldn't you be able to run your business any way you want? After all, you're creating wealth and more jobs!

"These questions emerged from your brainstorm at the beginning of the year. We're going to live with them for awhile. In your exhibition you'll be investigating how government laws and regulations affect a particular job or business that interests you. It could be a sports franchise, the sale of guns, the production of Nike shoes, the Internet—you name it. Or you might want to explore how laws and regulations have changed a job that's been part of your family's work history. But first we need to find out more about the conditions that stimulated greater government involvement and citizen activism in labor and business."

Mr. Brown asks students to pick up reading packets, so each home group receives a set of four packets that are blue (urban workers and their families), yellow (industrialists and businessmen and their families), green (organizers, reformers, and activists), and beige (agricultural workers and their families). Some students groan and Mr. Brown says, "I know, I know. Some of you are not exactly thrilled to see a reading packet. But it's hard to judge whether governments and citizens meddle too much or too little in other people's business unless we know what all the fuss was about a 100 years ago."

Students take a few minutes to decide which students will read about which groups. In preparation for work in their home groups later in the week, students review instructions that require students to highlight interesting details, quotations, and images that will help their home group partners get a good picture of their particular group. Each student is to choose one passage to read to their home groups that they think best captures the hopes, fears, and concerns that characterize their group. Mr. Brown encourages students "to keep writing questions and notes in the margins as you read. What do you agree or disagree with? What makes you mad? What makes you say, 'Now that person's speaking the truth!'" This reading packet will go in their portfolios as an example of how students respond critically to other people's words and stories.

Mr. Brown takes a minute to see if anyone has any questions before they begin reading. One student calls out, "I'd rather read my packet with someone else who's reading about the same group of people." This sounds fine to Mr. Brown, who invites others to partner up if that works for them. The reading time gives Mr. Brown a chance to do some personal check-in's with students, especially with those who struggle with reading. When time is called, Mr. Brown asks students to turn to their journals and complete this sentence, "After today's class, I'm left wondering..." He reminds students that they are welcome to come in tomorrow morning if they want to review their readings before class. "I'm counting on all home groups being prepared. On my 1 to 10 scale, this is probably a 9.5."

In closing, Mr. Brown points to the agenda and invites students to say what they liked best or what they would change about class today. As the bell rings, he congratulates the class on persevering through another 100 minute marathon of US history. He talks privately with a few kids, sharing what he noticed about their participation today. To one boy who rarely speaks, Mr. Brown says, "I really appreciated your willingness to talk about your job and your family. It gave other kids a chance to see what it's like to live in your shoes. Thanks."

Every student has spoken in the whole group and every student has shared their research, conclusions, and questions in small groups. Equally important, every student has listened to each other as they contributed new knowledge and perspectives to the issues raised in class today.

So What's the Difference?

Mr. Green is not a bad guy, but he's worn down, having acquiesced to the "game of school" as Robert Fried so aptly describes the deal teachers make: "I'll pretend to teach all of you while most of you pretend to learn." He's willing to settle for quiet compliance and learning that emphasizes memorization. ("I will be reasonable. You don't mess with me, and I won't mess with you. Do your work and I will work with you. It's your choice and your initiative whether you do well or not.") These tacit agreements prop up a system driven by relentless grading (otherwise kids will do even less work) and content coverage (if it's the third week of January, we must be studying _____). (Fried, 1996) Mr. Green still delights in those moments of genuine engagement with a few students; yet, the group comes to life so rarely, that these encounters will make Mr. Green's semester, not his day.

Every good teacher knows that you will never engage every student's attention, interest, and seriousness all the time. But a big difference in these two classrooms is Mr. Brown's intentional commitment to construct a learning environment where more of these moments are possible every day for every kid.

An Annotated Description of Key Classroom Practices

I'd like to offer an annotated explanation of key practices that make Mr. Brown's classroom a place where he and his students have created a learning community where they have become partners.

Practices	Examples
Develop personal connections among and between students and teachers	Mr. Brown meets and greets students at the door. Students sit in a circle at the beginning of class as a way to acknowledge that they are a group of learners who are in this together, not just individuals, rushing in, doing their time, and scrambling when the bell rings. Mr. Brown makes personal connections with kids throughout the class period. He also shares something about his own life with students, inviting students to consider this room as a place where people can feel safe to be real instead of going through the motions of faking it. Mr. Brown knows these kids pretty well. In journals, they've written about themselves, their goals and hopes, what they need for the classroom to be a good place to learn, and what gets in the way.

Emphasize student-centered learning that is personally meaningful

Students routinely make choices about what they are learning and how they go about doing their work and accomplishing their goals in the classroom.

More importantly, students are responsible for constructing major projects around something that's important to them. In addition, Mr. Brown tries to create opportunities for students to connect what they are learning to the world outside. Each year students work on an action research project that links local community history to current political, cultural, social, or economic issues.

Mr. Brown is only too aware of how boring history is to most students. Although he is required to teach a sequential history course, he chunks larger periods of time into a unit that addresses key questions and themes that students generated in the beginning of the year. He has chosen to make the world of work a linchpin for this unit so that students can bring their own issues and questions around work and careers to their investigation.

He also wants students to have a better understanding of how citizens' efforts, past and present, can spur government to redress injustices and temper the harsher aspects of market capitalism. At the same time, he wants students to struggle with what you get and what you give up in attempting to make laws and regulations that provide the greatest good for the most citizens. So Mr. Brown begins by sparking curiosity about work in their own families and grabbing students' attention with the ballot on limiting student work hours. The controversy over limiting work hours creates a bridge to historical controversies around the length of work week and the age and hours for child laborers.

The exhibition that each student designs creates a way to explore present business and labor practices in the global marketplace and speculate about the future role that governments might play in regulating multinational corporations.

Establish clear norms, boundaries, procedures, and consequences

Students and Mr. Brown have negotiated their agreements for classroom norms of behavior, which serve as a daily reminder and tool for group assessment

Build a cohesive community of learners

The class sinks or swims as a team. Students know that they can't be invisible and that opting out is not an option.

Students have had a voice in choosing their home group partners; they are aware that they are responsible to and for each other, especially when they each have responsibility for contributing specific knowledge that will be applied to a task that involves all four of them.

Students participate in generating ideas and questions that form the basis for important tasks and projects.

HH

Set high academic and behavioral expectations and provide high caring and high support to meet them

Mr. Brown has not sorted his class into those who get it and those who don't. There are important tasks and exhibitions that everyone is expected to complete meeting minimum standards of mastery.

From the first day of class, students know they won't receive F's but "incompletes" on important tasks. They are responsible for making a plan to complete or re-do major tasks, tests, or projects within three weeks.

On the other hand, Mr. Brown is aware that students come to class with different sets of skills and resistances, and need different kinds of support, especially regarding reading. So he has negotiated with the reading teacher to be available to work with students in study periods, at lunch, and before school.

Mr. Brown also talks privately with some kids about how they can translate qualities and skills that make them successful "outside" so they can utilize these same qualities and skills to become more successful at "doing" school.

Mr. Brown models the interview assignment before the due date, so students who need a clearer picture of the task have it.

The pacing of the class respects the shifting energy of adolescents; they get to talk, observe, listen, read, discuss, write, and move around.

Students know they can tell Mr. Brown when an activity is a dud, when explanations aren't clear, or when they have a better idea for how to do an activity. They also know that if they mess up, it's not the end of the world. Their grades are determined more by their accumulated efforts toward improvement and mastery and the quality of their performance on projects that they design themselves.

There are a few kids Mr. Brown checks in with every day; noticing what they do, discussing goals they've set, and asking them about their lives. This is a kind of attention that's feels different for these kids who are slowly shifting away from their acquired hostility and indifference about school and learning.

Affirm diversity in your classroom

Students share personal stories about their lives that provide an opportunity for students to appreciate the differences in their experiences and discover what they share in common.

He is aware that most of his students are descended from families of enslaved Africans who migrated from rural southern communities or families of Europeans who immigrated here 3 or 4 generations ago. Mr. Brown has consciously selected readings that explore the lives of northern urban workers and southern agricultural workers between 1880 and 1920. He realizes there will be some discomfort when students confront the racial, ethnic and class prejudice that influences the treatment of workers and their families. This awareness informs his choice to include writings of important organizers and reformers of the time and also prompts Mr. Brown to search for readings that provide a far more mixed portrait of industrialists and businessmen so students will be less likely to categorize this group as having one monolithic point of view.

Integrate multiple ways of knowing and learning

Differentiated learning is the norm in Mr. Brown's classroom. Students speak and listen as much as they read and write. Students are used to working individually, as a whole group, and in small groups. There is always more than one way to complete an important project or assignment.

Mr. Brown is also aware that some students are more effective learners when big tasks are "chunked," while others are ready to run with an idea and want to make their own way. Thus, all instructions for major assignments are written with optional space for students to make a plan for how they will complete the assignment.

Model, teach, and practice self-awareness self-expression, and self-management skills

By bringing in the controversy over work hours, Mr. Brown created an opportunity for students to express their feelings and direct their emotional intensity toward constructive problem solving.

Students are cued to respond to the readings critically, and the readings are intended to stir up emotions by describing the lived experience of very different groups.

Model, teach, and practice interpersonal communication and problem solving skills

Throughout the class, Mr. Brown models attentive listening, serving as witness rather than judge when student share their opinions and stories in a circle.

Students are also used to giving feedback to each other about the work that they do.

Model, teach, and practice cooperation, group participation, and leadership skills

In home groups, each student has shared observations, defended their thinking, and worked to reach consensus. Student have practiced explaining, summarizing, and responding to questions in their interview groups.

When a group has problems working together, Mr. Brown checks out the situation and expects students to stay with the problem and work it out.

Some Thoughts About Implementing New Practices in the Classroom

As you try out new practices, change your routines, and toss out some of the old parts of yourself, here are some other thoughts to keep in mind:

• Map out the first week of school introducing one or two practices each day.

• Make sure you've got a good reason for doing what you want to do. What needs does it meet? How does it benefit you, the group, or individual students? How might it help improve student performance?

• As you introduce more practices over the next month, identify three or four that you would like to incorporate into your weekly routines.

• Note the icons that are associated with each practice so that your choice of activities reflects variety and balance.

• Think about practices and strategies that you want to include as part of your closure activities at the end of each grading period.

• Keep checking in with the whole group and individual students who are your "climate barometers" to get feedback about how specific practices and strategies are working for different kids; whether your pacing and timing is about right; and how comfortable and competent students feel about using new skills and doing things in a new way.

Tracking What You're Trying Out

The goal here is to devise an easy system to document what you've done, when you did it, how it worked, and how you might do it in the future. You don't want to forget the words or the hook you used that got kids' attention and cooperation. You want to note why a strategy worked well for one group and was a dud for others. Most importantly, you want to remember how you took ideas in this book and reworked them given your students, your school, and your personal way of doing things. This guide is just a starting point—it's your creative adaptations that you want to save—so write them down!

Whatever system you create, try to keep all your notes in one place in a notebook or on a computer file. This provides a visual record of where you started and how your teaching practices continue to evolve. For the obsessively organized, a file box of note cards can do the trick, too. You can "tab" sections by practices, activity types, or time of the year. You can track different classes by using different colored cards to record what you did in each class and write additional notes on cards at a later time.

And then there are those of us who never have much time to reflect on what we're doing and even less time to write about it. For the organizationally impaired or time deprived, use this book as your journal. Write in it, attach Post-it Notes to pages you are using, and clip other stuff to the cover.

As you jot down reflections, you may want to ask yourself these questions:

• Describe what practice, skill, strategy, or activity you did, why you did it, and when you did it.

• How did students experience what you did?

• What benefits did you see from doing this? For yourself? The group? individual students?

• Any differences in how different classes experienced this?

• Any changes you already made or would make the next time you try this?

• Other opportunities when you would like to use this practice, skill, strategy, or activity again?

Going Solo or Working Together?

When it comes to changing habits and practices or starting something new, everyone needs something different to make it work and make it last. Some folks need a big window of time to chew on the idea for awhile and try things out slowly, carefully staging and planning along the way. Others just jump right in, do something once, and it becomes part of their repertoire for life. Some of you may prefer experimenting by yourself first, while others get energized by the collaborative dialogue that emerges from working together.

School situations can also influence how you go about implementing changes in classroom practice. For some of you "going solo" is the path of least resistance, especially if you are in an environment where many of these practices might be viewed as "fluff and frills." On the other hand, your school or your department may have decided to develop a set of common practices and guiding principles that create a more personalized learning environment. In that case, you've got the green light to work with others to get something going that has enormous potential to institutionalize new practices. However you go about starting up, think about how you can build collegial interest in trying on some different ways to think about what students need, and trying out new ways to meet those needs in the classroom.

Ten Strategies for Changing Classroom Practices in Your School

1. **Find an Ally, Then Have a Chat with a School Power Broker** If you're "on your own," consider sharing what you are doing with at least one other colleague. Talking through what you are experiencing really helps to clarify your own thinking and sustain your motivation to keep going. Then make a time to talk with the most approachable power broker you know who influences decisions about curriculum and instruction. (It might be the principal, but it could be the head of the professional development committee,

a department or division chair, the director of curriculum, or the union president.) Discuss your ideas, invite her to share her thoughts, and look for mutual concern and shared interests. Then hatch a plan that moves you toward implementing other strategies on this list.

2. **Buddy Up** Share this guide with a friend and work out a way to meet and check in once a month. You each might want to try out different practices so you can swap ideas or both try out the same practice to see how it works for each of you.

3. **By Department or Course** As a department, you and your colleagues might decide to implement three or four practices across all courses in your department. For example, a math department might establish new instructional guidelines that include weekly collaborative problem solving and oral or written reflections about the course and how it's going; they might also be brave enough to dump final exams in favor of developing a set of final, but fabulous and fun, math challenges from which each student can choose three.

Or your department might determine that some courses are particularly suited to a specific set of practices. I know a group of physics teachers who designed a whole series of individual and group assessment tools that focused on the quality of collaboration on labs and projects. And you can usually find a fair amount of zaniness in chemistry departments. The chem teachers at one school decided to brainstorm all kinds of crazy ways to meet and greet their students when they walked into class. On a more serious note, they also decided to encourage students to express themselves more openly and discuss issues around self-management to lower the levels of anxiety and hostility when kids were experiencing frustration.

4. **In Lower Tracked Courses, in "De-tracked" Courses, and Courses that Support Struggling Students in Higher Tracks** Universal tracking (where kids stay in the same "ability track" for the duration of their academic course work) is unjust and debilitating. But it's not going away anytime soon. I think we're morally obligated, then, to make efforts to make lower track classes less dehumanizing and hurtful, and more engaging and purposeful for the kids who are stuck in them. It's all too obvious that most high schools run into serious trouble trying to teach kids well who are already labeled low ability. The practices in this guide can be particularly helpful in bringing demoralized teachers and kids back to the "land of the living and learning" in lower tracked classes.

There is, at least, some good news on the tracking front. There are some passionate parents and teachers who are pushing the boundaries of traditional tracking by demanding that some courses be "de-tracked." For example, at many schools, some whole grade levels or required courses in Social Studies and English are now grouped heterogeneously, or special sections are open to any student in the school. These "de-tracked" classes are often intentionally designed to be more learner-centered, student-friendly, and community-minded without sacrificing rigorous academic work and high expectations.

In one school, for example, teachers agreed that every student in every American Studies course would complete and present an action research project linking an historical issue they studied to a current issue in their community or the nation at large. Because teachers made a choice that no one could fail, the entire approach to teaching and learning changed. Practices that offered a wider array of learning strategies, a stronger sense of connectedness, and more personalized support for individual students were crucial to helping every student get to the finish line successfully.

Some schools also offer special classes for struggling, but hungry, students who want to keep up and succeed in their College Prep or AP classes. These teachers have introduced practices that encourage students to support and teach each other. They also make a habit of beginning Monday's class with a gathering where students identify their goals and challenges for the week, and ending Friday's class with a closing, assessing their efforts and accomplishments.

5. **By Grade Level** At another school the English department agreed to set aside the first two weeks of all English 10 sections for the teacher and students to establish a real learning community. Since the literature theme for 10th grade was "People and Communities in Conflict," they also introduced communication skills that they would practice throughout the year. Ninth grade students are often overwhelmed by the transition to high school, making a mess of deadlines for big assignments and preparations for big tests or assessments. So 9th grade teachers at one school decided to hold class meetings with all 9th graders to get their input about the problem and to generate solutions that would improve completion rates and performance. A group of teachers and 9th grade students then met to negotiate a set of guidelines, supports, and consequences that greatly reduced students' academic problems.

6. **With a Team or Cluster of Teachers** If you and three to five other colleagues work with the same group of students for one or two years in a house, special academy, or cluster, you have the advantage of deciding on common practices, boundaries, and expectations for students across your classes. You can identify social skills that you want all students to develop and then discuss how each teacher will integrate specific practice of those skills into their respective courses. Teams also have the advantage of developing common disciplinary practices, support structures, and rituals and celebrations that recognize the efforts and accomplishments of groups and individuals.

7. **As a Homebase Teacher or Advisor** Many of these practices and strategies are easily adaptable to advisories and home base groups.

8. **With Other SPED or Title I Teachers** If you are a SPED or Title I teacher, chances are you are already familiar with both the rationale for these practices and many of the practices themselves. This guide can augment the affective and social skill development you already do with young people, and it may be a stimulus for developing some common practices in all SPED and Title I classrooms.

9. **With a Study Group** Find some stipend money and some time to establish a study group, whose membership crosses staff roles and departments, to explore, in depth, current issues around teaching, learning, and adolescents. (See the Bibliography for selected books.) This group might choose to read and reflect together, interview teachers and students, and gather and analyze data about current practices in your school. If you have the administration's blessing, the group could also write a case statement that gives you a platform to present and discuss your analysis and recommendations with other groups in the school community.

10. **As Part of a Summer, Year Long, or Multi-Year Staff Development Strand** Work with others to hold a Partners in Learning summer institute open to all staff, or create a professional development strand where the same group of staff can meet four or five times throughout the year. As part of its work in high schools, Educators for Social Responsibility helps schools to develop these opportunities. One goal of ESR's Partners in Learning institutes and courses is to train practicing teachers to become mentors, coaches, and advocates who can work with their own faculties to spread the word and support their colleagues in changing the norms of teaching and learning in their classrooms. Another approach that some schools take is to require all new, incoming staff to participate in a series of workshops and dialogues that center on the issues raised in this book.

Becoming an Advocate for the Schools Students Deserve

Unfortunately, changing norms that define quality teaching and learning will never happen one teacher at a time. Too often the teachers I meet who are the most gifted at reaching a diversity of kids feel the most isolated. Even though their classrooms reveal exemplary efforts to balance intellectual rigor, relevance, and relationships, these teachers worry about provoking sneers and jeers from "old school" faculty and administrators. The self-contained nature of classroom life (one teacher and a group of students behind a closed door) often leads to exceptionalizing teaching excellence. It's commonplace to hear teachers brush off innovative practices by saying, "Well, she can teach that way, but that's just her. I could never do what she does."

Therefore, good practice often goes underground and unrecognized, while teaching norms that have outlived their usefulness go unchallenged among the whole faculty or school leadership team. Teachers are more likely to continue experimenting and pushing the boundaries of their practice when there is time to reflect on their work with other like-minded colleagues. In addition, it is easier to feel committed and hopeful when your efforts in the classroom are supported by systemic reforms within the larger school culture.

You can go it alone and close your classroom door, or you can join like-minded colleagues in becoming advocates for changes that will make your high school a better place to learn and teach. Being prepared to defend your teaching practices is a big deal. Know why you believe what you believe and do what you do. Think about how to frame your arguments in ways that support the goals of more traditional teachers. Share personal stories that show how changes you made helped you to turn around a class or turn around a student.

When I hear about school change initiatives that bomb, I ask around to get a sense of what happened. One dynamic that contributes to the defeat of good ideas is almost always the same. The staff who are the most committed to implementing changes are likely to be either too quiet or too zealous in faculty association meetings where new initiatives need to be discussed and approved.

Great ideas aren't enough when large faculties hesitate to vote yes on anything that shakes up the status quo. Silence or fuzzy explanations don't make converts out of fence-sitters. Knowing in your gut what should be done is one thing, but making a convincing case to skeptics and fence-sitters is something else. (It's important to separate the "negaholics" from the skeptics and fence-sitters. "Negaholics" maintain a "just say no" position to any new idea. This stance shouldn't be confused with a skeptic's interest in critical inquiry).

High school faculty are often uncomfortable taking on an advocacy position. Most secondary teachers pride themselves in playing the role of the informed skeptic, a role honed by training in the liberal arts and sciences that encourages sorting for differences, looking for what's missing or what's wrong, and doubting any idea that promises too much. After all, these are the same higher order thinking skills we want our students to use. So letting go of our practiced ambivalence is hard. But if we don't let go, we risk being unable to act. Serious change will never happen if schools insist on resolving every last "yes, but" before taking the first step.

William Perry, an ethical theorist, gives us a way out of paralysis without sacrificing the roles of critical friend and friendly critic. He suggests that given the available evidence and an awareness of one's own values, people can choose to make a commitment that emerges from a new understanding and many sides of truth. "I will be whole-hearted while tentative, fight for my values yet respect others, believe my deepest values are right yet be ready to learn." (Dacey and Kenny, 1997, p. 153) One would be hard pressed to find better advice for negotiating the change process in schools.

Mustering up the courage to claim your public voice is hard to do by yourself. Form a group with people who share your vision. Savvy teachers utilize well-worn democratic practices— dialogue, collaboration, compromise, and "back door politicking"—to get what they want. Time spent rehearsing and preparing presentations; listening carefully to concerns and responding to them honestly; finding key allies who will speak up (especially AP teachers, coaches, pushy parents, and board members); and schmoozing one-on-one with the undecided—all of these activities will help to galvanize the support, trust, and good will necessary to implement changes that really stick.

So talk to other teachers and parents. Write a grant that supports you and your colleagues in efforts to tackle issues you care about. Ask students what they think, and involve them in the process. The good news is that a cadre of powerful teachers can make things happen, particularly in pilot programs that only involve volunteers in beginning phases. In time, these kinds of efforts can set the stage for more ambitious systemic reform.

Some Final Thoughts

As you think about getting started, I'd like to pass on a couple of last thoughts. When you are trying something new, try taking on the perspectives of observer and learner. Forgive your imperfections before you even start and while you're at it, forgive your students, too. Nobody has it all together the first time. Instead, love the moment when everything clicks because it won't last nearly long enough. Love your capacity to take in what is happening so you can stop to check things out before bulldozing your way to silence or anarchy. Love that you really can learn from your mistakes and love that you've got two more sections to try it out again, and see if it works any better. Love the safe climate you've created so kids will be straight with you and show you who they really are. And the next time you try something that works for nineteen kids, but bombed out for six, say to yourself, "The lesson wasn't perfect and it was still successful!" Good luck.

BIBLIOGRAPHY

Abdal-Haqq, I. (1994). Culturally responsive curriculum. *ERIC Digest.* Washington, DC: Department of Education.

Adelman, H. and Taylor, L. (2001). *Enhancing classroom approaches for addressing barriers to learning: classroom-focused enabling.* UCLA Center for Mental Health in Schools. Washington, DC: Center for Mental Health Services, U.S. Department of Health and Human Services.

Anderson, L. and Krathwohl, D. (2000). *A Taxonomy for Learning, Teaching, and Assessing: A Revision of Bloom's Taxonomy of Educational Objectives.* New York: Longman.

Aronson, E. (2000). *Nobody Left to Hate: Teaching Compassion After Columbine.* New York: Worth Publishers.

Bandler, R. (1989). *Reframing: Neuro-linguistic Programming and the Transformation of Meaning.* Moab, UT: Real People Press.

Bandler, R., Van Nagel, C., Siudzinski, R. (1993). *Mega-teaching and Learning: Neurolinguistic Programming Applied to Education.* Portland, OR: Metamorphous Press.

Bandura, A. (1997). *Self-efficacy: the Exercise of Control.* New York: Freeman.

Baron, J. and Sternberg, R. (1986). *Teaching Thinking Skills: Theory and Practice.* New York: W H Freeman & Co.

Benard, B. and Marshall, K. (1997). A framework for practice: tapping innate resilience. *Research/Practice 5* (1) Minneapolis, MN: Center for Applied Research and Educational Improvement.

Brooks, D. (2001). The organization kid. *The Atlantic Monthly* (April, 2001).

Canfield, J., Hansen, M., Kirberger, K. (1997). *Chicken Soup for the Teenage Soul.* Deerfield Beach, FL: Health Communications.

CASEL (2002). *Social and emotional competencies.* Chicago, IL: CASEL. University of Illinois.

Catalano, Richard F. and Hawkins, David. (1992). *Communities that Care.* San Francisco: Jossey-Bass.

Claremont Graduate School (1992). *Voices from the inside: A report on schooling from inside the classroom.* Claremont, CA: Institute for Education in Transformation.

Costa, A. (2001) *Developing Minds: A Resource Book for Teaching Thinking. 3rd Edition.* Alexandria, VA: Association of Supervision and Curriculum Development.

Csikszentmihalyi, M. and Schneider, B. (2000). *Becoming Adult: How Teenagers Prepare for the World of Work.* New York: Basic Books.

Dacey, J. and Kenny, M. (1997). *Adolescent Development.* Boston: McGraw-Hill.

Darling-Hammond, L. (1997). *The Right to Learn: a Blueprint for Creating Schools that Work.* San Francisco: Jossey-Bass.

Finnegan, W. (1999). *Cold New World: Growing Up in a Harder Country.* New York: Modern Library Paperbacks.

Fried, R. (1995). *The Passionate Teacher.* Boston: Beacon Press.

Gardner, H. (2000). *Intelligence Reframed.* New York: Basic Books.

Goleman, D. (1998). *Working with Emotionall Intelligence.* New York: Bantam Books.

Henderson, Nan, Benard, Bonnie, and Sharp-Light, Nancy. (2000). *School Wide Approaches for Fostering Resiliency,* Thousand Oaks, CA: Corwin Press.

High Schools of the Millennium, American Youth Policy Forum (2000). 1836 Jefferson Place, NW, Washington, DC 20036 (www.aypf.org).

Jobs for the Future, 88 Broad St., 8th Floor, Boston, MA 02110 (www.jff.org).

Johnson, D., Johnson, R., and Holubec, E. (1994). *Cooperative Learning in the Classroom.* Alexandria, VA: Association for Supervision and Curriculum Development.

Kohl, H. (1994). *"I won't learn from you" and Other Thoughts on Creative Maladjustment.* New York: The New Press.

Marzano, R., Pickering, D., Arredondo, D., Blackburn, Guy J., Brandt, Ronald S., Moffett, Cerylle A., Paynter, Diane E., Pollock, Jane E., Whisler, Jo Sue. (1997). *Dimensions of learning teachers manual, 2nd edition.* Alexandria, VA: Association for Supervision and Curriculum Development.

McCarthy, B. (2000). *4Mat About Teaching; Format in the Classroom.* Barrington, IL: Excel Press.

NASSP (National Association of Secondary School Principals) (1995). Summary of normed climate survey data. Reston, VA.

Nieto, S. (2000). *Affirming Diversity: the Sociopolitical Context of Multicultural Education.* New York: Addison Wesley Longman, Inc.

Ohanian, S. (1999). *One Size Fits Few: the Folly of Educational Standards.* Portsmouth, NH: Heinemann.

Palmer, P. (1998). *The Courage to Teach: Exploring the Inner Landscape of a Teacher's Life.* San Francisco: Jossey-Bass.

Payton, J., Wardlaw,, D., Graczyk, P., Bloodworth, M., Tampsett, C., Weissberg, R. (2000). Social and emotional learning: a framework for promoting mental health and reducing risk behaviors in children and youth. *Journal of School Health.* 70 (5).

Phelan, P., Davidson, A., and Yu, H. (1998). *Adolescent Worlds: Negotiating Family, Peers, and School.* New York: Teachers College Press.

Poliner, Rachel and Benson, Jeffrey. (1997). *Dialogue: Turning Controversy into Community.* Cambridge, MA: Educators for Social Responsibility.

Powell A., Farrar, E., and Cohen, D. (1985). *The Shopping Mall High School: Winners and Losers in the Educational Marketplace.* Boston: Houghton Mifflin

Pruitt, David (Ed.). (2000). *Your Adolescent.* American Academy of Child and Adolescent Psychiatry. New York: Harper Resource.

Public Agenda Foundation (2002). Reality Check on Education 2001 (www.publicagenda.org).

Rasool, J. and Curtis, C. (2000). *Multicultural Education in Middle and Secondary Classrooms: Meeting the Challenge of Diversity and Change.* Belmont, CA: Wadsworth/Thomson Learning.

Renyi, J. (1993). *Going Public: Schooling for a Diverse Democracy.* New York: The New Press.

Schneider, B. and Stevenson, D. (1999). *The Ambitious Generation: America's Teenagers Motivated but Directionless.* New Haven: Yale University.

Sarason, S. (1990). *The Predictable Failure of Educational Reform:* San Francisco: Jossey-Bass.

SCANS Report (1991). Secretary's Commission on Achieving Necessary Skills, US Department of Labor. *What work requires of schools: a SCANS report for America 2000.* Washington, DC: US Department of Labor.

Senge, P. (2000). *Schools That Learn: a Fifth Discipline Field Book for Educators, Parents, and Everyone Who Cares About Education.* New York: Currency Doubleday.

Sergiovanni, T. (1994). *Building Community in Schools.* San Francisco: Jossey-Bass.

Silverman, S. and Casazza, M. (2000). *Learning and Development: Making Connections to Enhance Teaching.* San Francisco: Jossey-Bass.

Steinberg, A., Cushman, K., Riordan, R. (1999). *Schooling for the Real World: the Essential Guide to Rigorous and Relevant Learning.* San Francisco: Jossey-Bass.

Sylwester, R. (1995). *A Celebration of Neurons: an Educator's Guide to the Human Brain.* Alexandria, VA: Association for Supervision and Curriculum Development.

Walberg, H. and Haertel, G. (Eds.). (1997). *Psychology and Educational Practice.* Berkeley, CA: McCutchen Publishing Corporation.

Werner, E. and Smith, R. (1992). *Overcoming the Odds: High-risk Children from Birth to Adulthood.* New York: Cornell University Press.

WestEd. Healthy Kids Survey (2002) Los Alamitos, CA: WestEd.

Wlodkowski, R. and Ginsberg, M. (1995). *Diversity and Motivation.* San Francisco: Jossey-Bass.

Zins, J., Elias, M., Weissberg, R., Greenberg, M., Haynes, N., Frey, K., Kessler, R., Schwab-Stone, M., and Shriver, T. (2000). Educating the Mind and Heart. *CASEL Collections.* Chicago, IL: CASEL, University of Illinois.

RECOMMENDED RESOURCES

In addition to the books and articles referred to in the bibliography, these resources offer additional perspectives on adolescence and teaching and learning in high schools.

Adolescent Development

Adams, G. (2000). *Adolescent Development: Essential Readings.* Oxford, UK: Blackwell Publishers.

Csikszentmihali, M. and Larson, R. (1984). *Being Adolescent: Conflict and Growth in the Teenage Years.* New York: Basic Books.

Gauvain, M. (2001). *The Social Context of Cognitive Development.* New York: Guildford Press.

Levy-Warren, M. (1996). *The Adolescent Journey: Development, Identity Formation, and Psychotherapy.* Northvale, NJ: Jason Aronson Inc.

Scales, P. and Leffert, N. (1999). *Developmental Assets: A Synthesis of the Scientific Research on Adolescent Development.* Minneapolis, MN: The Search Institute.

Case Studies and Portraits of Adolescents

Corwin, M. (2001). *And Still We Rise: The Trials and Triumphs of Twelve Gifted Inner-City Students.* New York: Perrenial Press.

Hersch, P. (1998). *A Tribe Apart: A Journey in the Heart of American Adolescence.* New York: Ballantine Books.

Olsen, L. (1997). *Made in America: Immigrant Students in Our Public Schools.* New York: The New Press.

Suskind, R. (1998). *A Hope in the Unseen: An American Odyssey from the Inner City to the Ivy League.* New York: Broadway Books.

Community Building and Reflection in the Classroom

Butler, S. (1995). *Quicksilver: Adventure Games, Initiative Problems, Trust Activities, and a Guide to Effective Leadership.* Project Adventure. Dubuque, Iowa: Kendall/Hunt Publishing.

Chappelle, S. and Bigman, L. (1998). *Diversity in Action.* Beverly, MA: Project Adventure.

Jones, A. (1999). *Teambuilding Activities for Every Group*. Richland, WA: Rec Room Publishing.

MacGregor, M. (1997). *Leadership 101: Developing Leadership Skills for Resilient Youth – Facilitator's Guide*. (youthleadership.org).

McFarlane, E. and Saywell, J. (1995). *If (Questions for the Game of Life)*. New York: Villard Books.

Project Adventure (1995). *Youth Leadership in Action: A Guide to Cooperative Games and Group Activities*. Dubuque, Iowa: Kendall/Hunt Publishing.

Rohnke, K. (1984). *Silver Bullets: A Guide to Initiative Problems, Adventure Games, and Trust Activities*. Project Adventure. Dubuque, Iowa: Kendall/Hunt Publishing.

Sakofs, M. and Armstrong, G. (1996). *Into the Classroom: Outward Bound Resources for Teachers*. Dubuque, Iowa: Kendall/Hunt Publishing.

Van Linden, J. and Fertman, C. (1998). *Youth Leadership: A Guide to Understanding Leadership Development in Adolescents*. San Francisco: Jossey-Bass.

High School Teaching and Learning

Baloche, L. (1998). *The Cooperative Classroom: Empowering Learning*. New York: Prentiss-Hall.

Brookfield, S. and Preskill, S. (1999). *Discussion as a Way of Teaching: Tools and Techniques for Democratic Classrooms*. San Francisco: Jossey-Bass.

Brown, J., Benard, B., and D'Emidio-Caston, M. (2000). *Resilience Education*. Thousand Oaks, CA: Corwin Press.

Daniels, H., Bizar, M., Zemelman, S. (2001). *Rethinking High School: Best Practice in Teaching, Learning, and Leadership*. Portsmouth, NH: Heinemann.

Kohn, A. (1996). *Beyond Discipline: From Compliance to Community*. Alexandria, VA: Association of Supervision and Curriculum Development.

Krovetz, M. (1999). *Fostering Resiliency: Expecting All Students to Use Their Minds and Hearts Well*. Thousand Oaks, CA: Corwin Press.

Muse, D. (Ed.) (1995). *Prejudice: A Story Collection*. New York: Hyperion Books.

Newman, J. (1998). *Tensions of Teaching: Beyond Tips to Critical Reflection.* New York: Teachers' College Press.

Tomlinson, C. (1999). *The Differentiated Classroom: Responding to the Needs of All Learners.* Alexandria, VA: Association of Supervision and Curriculum Development.

Schmuck and Schmuck. (1988). *Group Processes in the Classroom.* Dubuque, Iowa: Wm. C. Brown.

Zemelman, S., Daniels, H., Hyde, A. (1998). *Best Practice: New Standards for Teaching and Learning in America's Schools.* Portsmouth, NH: Heinemann Press.

School and Classroom Culture

Deal, T. (1999). *Shaping School Culture.* San Francisco: Jossey-Bass.

Delpit, L. (1996). *Other People's Children: Cutlural Conflict in the Classroom.* New York: The New Press.

Maran, M. (2000). *Class Dismissed: A Year in the Life of an American High School, A Glimpse into the Heart of a Nation.* New York: St. Martin's Press.

Meier, D. (1996). *The Power of Their Ideas: Lessons for America from a Small School in Harlem.* Boston: Beacon Press.

Murphy, J., Beck, L., Crawford, M., Hodges, A., and McGaughy, C. Thousand (2001). *The Productive High School: Creating Personalized Academic Communities.* Oaks, CA: Corwin Press.

Perrotti, J. and Westheimer, K. (2001). *When the Drama Club Is Not Enough: Lessons from the Safe Schools Program for Gay and Lesbian Students.* Boston: Beacon Press.

Sizer, T. (1984).*Horace's Compromise: The Dilemma of the American High School.* New York: Houghton Mifflin.

Sizer, T. (1997). *Horace's Hope: What Works for the American High School.* New York: Houghton Mifflin.

Sizer, T. (1992). *Horace's School: Redesigning the American High School.* New York: Houghton Mifflin.

Sizer, T. and N. (1999). *The Students are Watching: Schools and the Moral Contract.* Boston: Beacon Press.

Tatum, B. (1997). *Why Are All the Black Kids Sitting Together in the Cafeteria? And Other Conversations About Race.* New York: Basic Books.

Social and Emotional Learning

Cohen, J. (Ed.) (1999). *Educating Minds and Hearts: Social Emotional Learning and the Passage into Adolescence.* New York: Teachers' College Press.

Lieber, C. (1998). *Conflict Resolution in the High School.* Cambridge, MA: Educators for Social Responsibility.

Love, P. and Love, Anne (1995). *Enhancing Student Learning: Intellectual, Social, and Emotional Integration.* ASHE-ERIC High Education Report #4. Washington, DC: The George Washington Graduate School of Education and Human Development.

Salovey, P. and Sluyter, D. (Eds.) (1997). *Emotional Development and Emotional Intelligence: Educational Implications.* New York: Basic Books.

Vorrath, H. and Brendtro, L. (1985). *Positive Peer Culture.* Hawthorne, NY: Aldine De Gruyter.

ABOUT THE AUTHOR

Carol Miller Lieber, ESR's secondary program specialist, is a national leader in integrating principles of prevention, equity, and social and emotional learning into everyday practices and structures for middle and high schools. In her thirty-five years as an educator, Lieber has taught students at all grade levels, co-founded an urban secondary school, and served as a faculty member at Washington University, University of Missouri, and Lesley University in Cambridge, Massachusetts. Through ESR, she has developed Partners in Learning, a program that helps secondary educators create safe, caring, and respectful cultures and classroom learning environments with the goal of facilitating healthy development and academic success for all students. She is the author of many publications including *Conflict Resolution in the High School* and *Conflict in Context: Understanding Local to Global Security*.

ABOUT ESR

The mission of Educators for Social Responsibility is to make teaching for social responsibility a core practice in education so that young people develop the convictions and skills to shape a safe, sustainable, democratic, and just world. ESR is a national leader in social and emotional learning, conflict resolution, violence prevention, and diversity education. ESR offers comprehensive programs, staff development, and resources for adults who teach children and young people at every developmental level, preschool through high school, in a range of settings: K-12 schools, early childhood centers, and after-school programs.

ESR's work fosters children's social, emotional, and ethical development by helping them learn to: commit to the well-being of themselves and others; manage feelings positively and resolve conflicts nonviolently; solve problems cooperatively; value diversity, understand cultural differences, counter bias, and confront prejudice; think critically and creatively; and make responsible decisions and take meaningful actions.

For more information about ESR:

esr

EDUCATORS *for* SOCIAL RESPONSIBILITY
23 Garden Street
Cambridge, MA 02138
617.492.1764
www.esrnational.org

ABOUT THE PARTNERS
IN LEARNING PROGRAM

Partners in Learning provides training, resources, and technical assistance to help middle and high schools develop a safer, more welcoming and respectful school climate, personalize the learning environment, and improve the quality of communication and relationships among staff and students.

The aim of Partners in Learning is to assist educators in building healthy secondary school communities that facilitate school success for all students and reduce aggressive and other high risk behaviors among students. ESR's research-based approach is informed by principles of prevention and resiliency and promotes developmentally appropriate practice to meet the intellectual, cultural, and social/emotional needs of diverse learners.

Core components of Partners in Learning include:
- A school envisioning retreat, establishment of a steering committee, and an annual review and planning process
- 24-hours of training for staff and ongoing consultation and coaching
- Peer mediation and student leadership programs
- Self-management and interpersonal skill development for students
- School-wide prevention and anti-harassment initiatives

Optional components include:
- Needs assessment including focus groups and baseline data analysis
- Student advisory and orientation programs
- Review and revision of school discipline policies and programs
- Administrator consultation, training, and coaching
- Assistance in developing small learning communities

We customize all of our programs to meet each school's specific needs and entry points.

For more information about Partners in Learning or our programs and resources, call **1 . 800 . 370 . 2515** or go to **www.esrnational.org**

TOOLS FOR PARTNERING

To order these resources, call **1 . 800 . 370 . 2515** or go to **www.esrnational.org**

Grades 9-12

Conflict in Context: Understanding Local to Global Security

Gayle Mertz and Carol Miller Lieber

Current and timely, this new curriculum introduces high school students to the key concepts and skills needed to be responsible citizens. Aided by numerous case studies based on actual international issues, students will learn that a complex consideration of security must go beyond military issues to include economics, human rights, and more. Over 40 carefully developed lessons stress skills such as researching, mapping, dialogue, critical thinking, and informed analysis. (ESR 2001)

Grades 9-12

Conflict Resolution in the High School: 36 Lessons

Carol Miller Lieber with Linda Lantieri and Tom Roderick

This comprehensive, sequenced curriculum will help secondary educators address conflict resolution and problem solving; diversity and intergroup relations; social and emotional development; and building community and creating a Peaceable Classroom. Includes sections on implementation, assessment, and infusion of conflict resolution throughout a standard curriculum. (ESR 1998)

Grades 7-12

Dialogue: Turning Controversy into Community

Jeffrey Benson and Rachel A. Poliner

Through ten skill-focused chapters, this unique curriculum paints a portrait of nonadversarial dialogue through the story of Centerville, a fictional town caught in a controversy over whether or not to mandate school uniforms. Teachers learn techniques and structures for helping students build skills such as listening, researching issues, understanding and appreciating different perspectives, and creating solutions. Well-suited for social studies or English teachers, as well as student-government and debate-team advisors. (ESR 1997)